DEREK PERCY: AUSTRALIAN PSYCHO

DEREK PERCY: AUSTRALIAN PSYCHO

Alan J. Whiticker

First published in 2008 by New Holland Publishers
This edition Published in 2021 by New Holland Publishers
Sydney • Auckland

Level 1, 178 Fox Valley Road, Wahroonga 2076, Australia
5/39 Woodside Ave, Northcote, Auckland 0627, New Zealand
newhollandpublishers.com

www.newhollandpublishers.com

A record of this book is held at the National Library of Australia.

Whiticker, Alan.

Australian psycho : the crimes of Derek Percy / Alan J. Whiticker.

ISBN: 9781760793401 (pbk.)

Percy, Derek.
Serial murderers--Australia--Biography.
Murder--Investigation--Australia--Case studies.
Infanticide--Australia--Case studies.

364.15230994

Managing Director: Fiona Schultz
Editor: Simona Hill
Designer: Yolanda La Gorcé
Production Director: Arlene Gippert

Printed in China

10 9 8 7 6 5 4 3 2 1

Keep up with New Holland Publishers:

 NewHollandPublishers

 @newhollandpublishers

'Every human being is like every other human being, like some other human beings, and like no other human being.'

Clyde Kluckhohn, American anthropologist and social theorist

Acknowledgments

I would like to thank Fiona Schultz, Lliane Clarke, Martin Ford, Diane Jardine and all the team at New Holland Publishers for their faith and support in this project. This book would not have been possible without the cooperation of the relevant police agencies currently involved in the multi-agency investigation of Derek Percy. Special thanks go to Wayne Newman and David Rae (Victoria Police), Adam Barwick, Mark Winterflood and Russell Oxford (NSW Police), Chris Sheehan (AFP), Brian Swan (SAPOL), Steve Gambetta (Film and TV Office, Victoria Police) and to Gary Tippet (*The Age*). Sincere thanks are due to the people who consented to be interviewed for this book, especially Dr Donald Brook, Bill Hutton, Kim White, Wayne Gordes and Ron Anderson.

Disclaimer: The AFP, Victoria and NSW Police do not officially endorse the publication of this book.

Contents

Introduction

I have to confess that I have no time for those 'cold case' detective programs that have proliferated on television during the last decade or so—*CSI*, *CSI Miami*, *CSI New York* and *Cold Case*. Far-fetched plots neatly packaged into a 46-minute programme with all the loose ends neatly wrapped up by the end of the show; complex scientific procedures compressed into unrealistic timeframes; along with fast-paced editing and enhanced computer graphics set against an MTV soundtrack... the reality, obviously, is quite different.

Consider then, a series of unsolved crimes stretching back more than 40 years across four Australian states and territories; with key witnesses—those at least who have not died in the ensuing years and many who were children at the time—having to recall events from four decades ago; where physical evidence is likely to have been destroyed or gone missing because detectives from only a generation past could not have envisaged the impact of DNA technology; and lastly, there is a chief suspect who has never been found guilty of a crime and steadfastly maintains that he 'cannot remember' if he has committed any others. These are just some of the problems facing 'cold case' detectives investigating sadistic paedophile Derek Ernest Percy.

In September 2004 I was contacted by Victorian detectives who were launching a fresh inquiry into Derek Percy's movements in the late 1960s. Percy, who remains Victoria's longest-serving prisoner, was detained in 1970 after being found not guilty by reason of insanity to the abduction and murder of 12-year-old Yvonne Tuohy the previous year. A group of Victorian homicide detectives had started reviewing a number of unsolved crimes including the 1968 disappearance of 7-year-old Linda Stilwell from St Kilda—a case in which Percy had remained a prime suspect. But a peculiar development had occurred. The detectives could not eliminate the now 56-year-old prisoner as a suspect in a number of other unsolved crimes involving children that were committed in Sydney, Canberra and Adelaide while he was still a teenager.

I had recently published my book, *Wanda: The Untold Story of the Wanda Beach Murders* (New Holland Publishers, Sydney) and I had nominated Derek Percy as one of the three main suspects in the unsolved murders of Sydney teenagers Christine Sharrock and Marianne Schmidt in January 1965. Detectives had been given a photo of Percy as a 17-year-old high school student at Mt Beauty in northeastern Victoria in 1965. As my book was based on police transcripts of the Wanda case, had featured interviews with many of the witnesses and was a factual recount of the initial investigation, Victoria Police wanted to know if I could help them with contact numbers of witnesses who may be able to identify Percy at Wanda Beach that day.

I have to admit Derek Percy was still something of a mystery to me; and he had continued to fly under the public radar for several decades because he had been in prison for so long. I was astounded that these detectives now believed that Percy was in western Sydney that summer almost 40 years ago when the two West Ryde schoolgirls went to the beach and tragically lost their lives. The implication was earth-shattering—whether the then-16-year-old Derek Percy followed Christine Sharrock and Marianne Schmidt and her four siblings to Wanda Beach that day, possibly befriending the girls on the train and then murdered them after arranging to meet in the sandhills later that afternoon; or alternatively lay in wait for them in the dunes to commit a frenzied, random attack.

This, of course, is only conjecture; made even more difficult to prove and build a case that will stand up in a court of law. This was the major hurdle that faced Victoria Police as they launched a multi-agency investigation into Derek Percy's movements in the four years before his capture in July 1969. Now in a new century, they were determined to investigate Derek Percy's involvement in the following crimes:

- the murder of Christine Sharrock and Marianne Schmidt at Sydney's Wanda Beach on 11 January 1965
- the abduction of the three Beaumont children from Glenelg Beach in South Australia on 26 January 1966
- the strangulation murder of 6-year-old Canberra schoolboy Allen Redston on 27 September 1966
- the abduction and mutilation murder of 3-year-old Simon Brook on 18 May 1968 in the inner city Sydney suburb of Glebe
- the disappearance and murder of 7-year-old Linda Stilwell from the Melbourne beachside suburb of St Kilda on 10 August 1968.

Several of these crimes, especially the disappearance of the Beaumont children in 1966, had become defining, almost culturally iconic events in Australian criminal history—could Derek Percy have been responsible for some or all of them? Interestingly, Percy had been questioned about many of these unsolved crimes when he was arrested in Victoria in 1969 but instead of denying his involvement he feebly told police, 'I could have done it but I can't remember'.[1] The crime for which he was caught—the abduction and sadistic murder of 12-year-old Yvonne Tuohy and the attempted abduction of 11-year-old Shane Spiller—gives a clear indication, however, of just what Derek Percy was capable.

Derek Ernest Percy is a monster—'our Hannibal Lecter'[2] as one prison official later described him.

Traditionally, the custodial sentence for a 'governor's pleasure' detainee was for a nominal period of 25 years, but Derek Percy would not so easily gain his freedom. Percy had never entered into a rehabilitation program for sex offenders or expressed remorse for his crimes and the Adult Parole Board continually refused to grant him parole during the 1990s. Changes to the Victorian Crimes (Mental Impairment and Unfitness to be Tried) Act in 1997, however, raised fears that Percy would finally be released. Percy was immediately placed under a custodial supervision order and became the focus of a major case review by Justice Geoffrey Eames in 1998.

Percy's first custodial review sparked a media storm of interest and he was publicly linked for the first time to other unsolved cases involving the disappearance, murder and abduction of children. Police in both Victoria and NSW had always suspected that Percy had committed other crimes but because he was safely detained at the 'governor's pleasure' for the murder of Yvonne Tuohy, his potential involvement in these other crimes was never fully investigated. A psychiatrist who assessed him after his arrest in 1969 concluded that he had 'many psycho-sexual abnormalities and was highly likely to have killed other children'.[3]

Dick Knight, one of the original detectives who worked on the Tuohy case and later became Assistant Commissioner of Police believed, as do detectives currently investigating Percy, that he had 'killed before he had attacked Yvonne Tuohy'. No one, they argued, could have committed that murder 'cold' and the prisoner was highly likely to have committed earlier crimes.

But there was the real fear that, at age 50, Derek Percy may be released. Many mental health professionals were concerned that the man he had become after three decades in prison was more of a danger to the community than the shy 20-year-old naval rating who was captured in 1969 after committing one of the worst crimes imaginable.[4] Incredibly, consulting psychiatrist Professor Paul Mullen stated during Percy's review that 'in common with other psychiatrists who have examined Mr Percy subsequent to his trial in 1970, I could find no evidence suggestive of psychiatric illness'.[5]

Had Derek Percy feigned his mental illness in order to get a reduced and more comfortable custodial sentence with the likelihood of a release? Why was he still being detained at the 'governor's pleasure' if he was not mentally ill?

Justice Geoffrey Eames was satisfied on the evidence available to him that 'the safety of members of the public would be seriously endangered if [Percy] was released on a non-custodial supervision order'[6] and confined Percy to prison until his next custodial review in five years' time. Eames declined to set a minimum term to serve because Percy had never sought or received treatment for his unique paedophilic condition. Percy initiated another custodial review in 2003 and he remains the only Victorian offender found mentally unfit to plead who is still in prison.

Psychiatrists agreed that Derek Percy's unique psychological condition, which is described as 'sadistic paedophilia', existed for at least four years leading up to the abduction and murder for which he was confined. The years 1965 to 1969 remain something of a mystery to investigators in regard to Percy's movements, but the period corresponds with the time when five unsolved crimes involving children—the infamous and the not so well-known—were committed.

Detectives believe that Percy was in Sydney in 1965 at the time of the Wanda Beach murders and know that he was stationed there with the navy in May 1968 when Simon Brook was murdered. Percy then returned to HMAS *Cerberus* in Melbourne when Linda Stilwell went missing in August 1968 and was still stationed there the following year when he murdered Yvonne Tuohy. They have had great difficulty, however, placing Percy in Adelaide in January 1966 when the Beaumont children disappeared and in Canberra in September of that year when Allen Redston died. But they continue to probe.

In 2006, I wrote the first definitive account of the disappearance of the three Beaumont children from Glenelg Beach in 1966 (*Searching for the Beaumont Children*, John Wiley & Sons, Brisbane). I knew that Derek Percy was on the periphery of that decades-long investigation but I began to ask myself the same question that detectives in three states were now contemplating—was Derek Percy the 'missing link' between the Wanda and the Beaumont cases? And what other crimes was he involved in?

Police believe that Percy's diaries—written both before and after his capture—provide a clear indication of his possible involvement in other crimes. His writings, which described ways of abducting, murdering and mutilating children, were originally found in his locker at HMAS *Cerberus* and in a search of his cell after he was sentenced. Percy had repeatedly maintained that he hasn't had any violent fantasies since the early 1970s and is fit to be released. The sensational discovery, in August 2007, of boxes of newspaper clippings, diary entries and reams of fantasies Percy had secreted in a Melbourne storage house may finally provide the key to five unsolved crimes committed between 1965 and 1969.

During the past two years I researched the available written material concerning the capture, trial and incarceration of Derek Ernest Percy—newspaper articles, custodial reviews and psychological reports—and also talked to school friends and neighbours who knew him as a teenager and others who had contact with him as an adult. I also applied to the relevant agencies to interview detectives in Sydney, Melbourne, and with the Australian Federal Police. The AFP took the refreshing position that writing about the unsolved Redston case may assist their investigation; that the dissemination of certain forensic elements in the public domain may actually prompt witnesses to come forward. I was afforded access to original case files and investigative reviews and, in a search of the Melbourne Records Department of the Victorian Supreme Court, located a copy of the original court transcript of Percy's trial in 1970.

Australian Psycho is not only the story of Derek Percy. This book details how Australia's law enforcement agencies have worked together to produce a profile of Percy's movements leading up to his arrest in 1969 and investigated his possible involvement in a number of infamous unsolved crimes. Is he the 'bogey-man' we all feared during our childhood—the stranger who preyed on the innocent and the vulnerable—or is he just a phantom, someone who casts a dark shadow over the unsolved and the unknown? If Derek Percy is responsible for any or all of these other unsolved murders, then he may be regarded as the worst child killer in Australian criminal history.

But then, he already is.

Timeline of Events

1948 Derek Ernest Percy, eldest son of Ernest and Elaine Percy, is born in Strathfield, New South Wales.

1956 The Percy family move to Melbourne, first living at Chelsea and then Warrnambool.

1961 Ernest Percy is employed at the West Kiewa Power Station at Mt Beauty in Victoria's north-west and moves his family to Mt Beauty. Derek Percy starts high school at Mt Beauty Elementary High School.

1964–65 Derek Percy is seen by classmates Kim White and Bill Hutton wearing a petticoat, slashing women's underwear with a knife and defecating in the water at 'the gorge' near Mt Beauty. Botany Bay Yacht Club, 6 kilometres from Wanda Beach, conducts the annual moth class national sailing titles.

1965 Christine Sharrock and Marianne Schmidt, 15-year-old neighbours from the Sydney suburb of West Ryde, are separated from Marianne's four younger siblings while walking in the sandhills north of Wanda Beach on 11 January. Their bodies are found buried in the dunes the following day, stabbed to death. The Percy family move to Khancoban, in south-west New South Wales. Derek Percy remains behind in Mt Beauty to finish school but fails his Leaving Certificate.

1966 The three Beaumont children—Jane, aged 9, Arnna, 7, and Grant, 4—disappear from Adelaide's Glenelg Beach on 26 January. Derek Percy starts school at Corryong High School, on the other side of the New South Wales–Victoria border. Six year-old Allen Redston is found hog-tied and strangled to death in a creek bed in the south Canberra suburb of Curtin on 27 September.

1967 The Percy family move to The Entrance and then Newcastle in New South Wales, where Ernie Percy operates a service station. Nineteen-year-old Derek Percy joins the Royal Australian Navy on 25 November. He trains at HMAS *Cerberus* at Flinders Naval Depot, Crib Point in Victoria.

1968 Derek Percy is stationed in Sydney at HMAS *Kuttabul*, Kings Cross on 9 March. Three-year-old Simon Brook is reported missing from the front yard of the family home in the Sydney suburb of Glebe on 18 May. His body is found the following day in a vacant block 400 metres away. In July, Percy is attached to HMAS *Sydney*, which is based in

Melbourne. He goes on leave from 5 August to 22 August. Seven-year-old Linda Stilwell disappears from the St Kilda foreshore on 10 August and, despite a wide search, no trace of her is ever found.

1969 Yvonne Tuohy, aged 12, is abducted at knifepoint from Warneet, Western Port Bay in Victoria by Derek Percy on 20 July. Her friend, 11-year-old Shane Spiller, escapes and alerts the authorities. Percy is apprehended later that evening washing the blood from his clothes at HMAS *Cerberus*. The next day Percy leads detectives to the body of Yvonne Tuohy, hidden in a paddock at Devon Meadows, 10 kilometres from where he abducted her. He is charged with murder.

1970 The trial of Derek Ernest Percy begins on 2 April in the Supreme Court of Victoria. After a 6-day trial, he is found not guilty of murder by reason of insanity. He is detained at Pentridge Gaol in G Division psychiatric wing.

1971 On 28 September, Percy is found to have secreted in his cell various written articles describing the torture, murder and mutilation of children.

1998 Justice Geoffrey Eames declines to release Derek Percy after his first custodial review on 2 October under the *Crimes (Mental Impairment and Unfitness to be Tried) Act* 1997. Three psychiatrists agree that Percy is not suffering from a mental illness but still remains a danger to society.

2004 Operation Heats—a multi-agency investigation by Victorian, New South Wales, South Australian and Australian Federal Police—is formed to investigate Derek Percy's possible involvement in five other unsolved crimes involving children. Justice Murray Kellam declines to release Percy after his second custodial review which concludes early in the year. Kellam also declines to transfer Percy from prison to a minimum security psychiatric hospital.

2005 On 20 November, Derek Percy is subpoenaed to appear at the New South Wales coronial inquest into the 1968 murder of 3-year-old Simon Brook in Sydney. Coroner John Abernathy concludes the inquest on 13 December and refers the matter to the Department of Public Prosecutions. Abernathy believes there is a 'reasonable prospect ... that a jury would convict a known person in relation to the offence'.

2006 The Australian Federal Police invites Professor Peter Barclay to review the 40-year investigation into the murder of Allen Redston and make a number of operational recommendations code-named Operation Kobold.

2007	In June, the Director of the New South Wales Department of Public Prosecutions declines to lay charges against Derek Percy. That same month, police discover 35 cardboard boxes of Percy's belongings in a South Melbourne storage unit. They hope that his volumes of written material may implicate him in some of the unsolved crimes being investigated.
2008	The inquest into the disappearance of Linda Stilwell was held in Melbourne; and Derek Percy underwent his third custodial review.
2013	Derek Percy dies of lung cancer, aged 65.
2014	A Victorian court determines Derek Percy abducted and killed 7-year-old Linda Stillwell from St Kilda Beach in 1968.

CHAPTER 1: Cold Case

The year 2000 drew an historical line through all unsolved criminal cases in Australia. In Victoria alone there were more than 200 homicide 'cold cases', many stretching back decades, which remained unresolved. Victoria Police though, had already identified that there was the lack of a coordinated approach in dealing with historical missing person cases—cases in which a homicide was suspected but not proved—and the dawn of a new millennium saw a renewed effort to prioritise and reinvestigate many of the state's most baffling cases.

Detective Senior Sergeant Ron Iddles of the Melbourne Homicide Squad CIB, was the driving force behind this new approach and established unsolved, missing persons 'cold case' units in several regions of the state. Regional detectives were seconded to these units with Detective Senior Sergeant Steve Waddell becoming team leader of the Melbourne Unit, which is based in the Victoria Police offices in St Kilda Road, South Melbourne. Detective Wayne Newman recalls:

> *The unit was to be a breeding ground for detectives who wanted to come to the homicide squad… we would come in with a lot of enthusiasm and fresh ideas under the guidance of experienced detectives. Each region has a number of missing person cases that were believed to be 'suspicious'… not just runaways or someone missing of their own volition and who did not want to be found by their families. Melbourne was no different.*[1]

The brief of the new unit was to reinvestigate 'unsolved missing persons cases' and to prepare a brief for inquest. Detective Senior

Sergeant Iddles stated at the time that '20 to 30 suspicious disappearances'[2] had been identified by police for investigation, with most requiring coronial inquests. Iddles explained that prior to 1985 when the state law changed, there was no legal requirement to hold an inquest in a missing person's case. He believed now, however, that such public hearings of all the known evidence helped families with their unresolved grief.

'If we believe a death has occurred, we have two hats to wear—as the coroner's agent and secondly, as Victoria Police investigators,' says Wayne Newman. Two earlier cases brought to coronial inquest were the disappearance of 12-year-old Terry Floyd from the Victorian gold town of Maryborough in 1975, which resulted in an inquest in 2001, and 7-year-old Eloise Worledge from suburban Beaumaris in 1976, for whom an inquest was held in 2006. One of the unsolved missing persons cases that took top priority was the disappearance of Linda Jane Stilwell from St Kilda in 1968. The renewed investigation was originally thought to take a matter of weeks. It is still ongoing.

Detectives David Rae and Wayne Newman were not even born when Linda Stilwell went missing from the esplanade at St Kilda in August 1968. The Stilwell case was not known to them and they had never heard the name 'Derek Percy'. Reviewing the Stilwell case files in January 2004, the detectives came across a media report of Percy's capture in July 1969 for the murder of Yvonne Tuohy. This in itself was strange because Percy was not mentioned in any other file in the Stilwell investigation. The detectives immediately familiarised themselves with Percy's background to determine what the connection was, if any, with the disappearance of young Linda. 'It was a case of "let's not put the blinkers on and focus in on him alone,"' Newman says. 'There were a lot of other suspects interviewed and exonerated... but as a result we started to take a closer look at Percy with the view of excluding him from the [Stilwell] investigation.'

Rather than trying to 'include' a suspect in a particular

investigation—to find reasons why the suspect committed the crime and look for opportunities to place him at the crime scene—police investigators often work from the opposite angle—to exclude suspects or 'persons of interest' from a particular investigation. Either way, if Percy was involved in the disappearance of Linda Stilwell, the case was going to be particularly difficult to solve—there was no body, no weapon, no independent witnesses to the abduction or murder, no identifiable crime scene and no forensic evidence.

The detectives read over all the case files for the attempted abduction of 11-year-old Shane Spiller and the abduction-murder of his friend, 12-year-old Yvonne Tuohy, from Warneet on Melbourne's Westernport Bay in July 1969. The events of that Sunday afternoon show the depths of depravity that Derek Percy plumbed. Percy grabbed the little girl and held a knife to her throat but Spiller, who was carrying a small tomahawk to chop wood, waved it at their abductor and was able to escape. Percy bundled the little girl into his car and drove off while Spiller hid in the bush and then ran to a nearby road and flagged down a passing motorist. The little boy was able to give police a detailed description of the man and his car—even identifying a naval badge on the car window—and the 20-year-old naval rating was apprehended at HMAS *Cerberus*, the naval base at Crib Point, washing the blood from his clothes.

Taken to Frankston Police Station, Percy claimed that he had 'no memory'[3] of the girl or her murder. Fearing that Percy had committed the crime 'in a frenzy' and had shut it out of his memory, Detective Sergeant Dick Knight 'took Percy through the process [of remembering] in reverse'[4] so that the accused could reveal where he had hidden Yvonne Tuohy's body. Her bound and gagged body was found in bushland at Devon Meadows, 10 kilometres from where she had been abducted. Her wrists had been tied around her back, her throat was cut and she had been disembowelled.

One of the items in the archived Tuohy case files recorded that a naval colleague of Percy had phoned the Homicide Squad after his arrest in 1969 and volunteered: 'Regarding Linda Stilwell, have a look at Derek Percy'.[5] There were also records of interview showing that Percy had been questioned by New South Wales detectives about the murder of Sydney toddler Simon Brook in May 1968—three months before the disappearance of Linda Stilwell and 14 months before his eventual capture for the murder of Yvonne Tuohy. 'Cold case' detectives were amazed—Percy had been a suspect in two other unsolved crimes involving children but investigations had suddenly come to a halt when Percy was detained at the governor's pleasure in April 1970.

Reviewing the Tuohy case files, detectives noted a reference to a police registration number belonging to a probationary constable who knew Derek Percy as a teenager in Mt Beauty, in northeast Victoria. The young constable spoke to Percy at Melbourne's Russell Street headquarters on the day after he was apprehended in 1969—perhaps he knew something of these other 'matters' Percy was originally asked about. The registration number belonged to Ronald Anderson, who left the force in 1988 and had since returned to live in Mt Beauty. What he told Rae and Newman changed the course of their 'cold case' investigation.

Anderson told detectives that when he asked Percy about three other crimes—Linda Stilwell and Simon Brook in 1968, and the disappearance of the three Beaumont children from Glenelg Beach in 1966—incredibly, Percy placed himself at each crime scene.[6] Anderson gave his handwritten notes to the police but because Percy had confessed to the Tuohy murder, there was only minimal follow-up with the other unsolved cases. There was no physical evidence linking Percy to the disappearance of Linda Stilwell and there was also the issue of jurisdiction—Victoria Police were not in a position in 1969 to investigate unsolved crimes committed interstate.

But in 2004, the situation was different. 'Our responsibility was to investigate the Linda Stilwell matter,' Wayne Newman says, 'and to determine where Percy was on or about 10 August 1968 but we realised there was a bigger picture ... Here was a bloke who killed in 1969, investigators believed he had killed before, he was a suspect in the Linda Stilwell disappearance—how many others?' Ron Anderson provided a statement to the detectives. The recounted conversation with Derek Percy was not 'word for word' but was very close to the content and meaning of his original discussion. But would it be enough in a court of law?

There was already a lot of speculation in the media, dating back to Percy's first custodial review in 1998, that he was involved in other unsolved crimes against children. But how could a teenager have been in three different states—New South Wales, Victoria and South Australia—when these crimes were committed? This was an issue that had never been explained. Detectives Rae and Newman researched all the unsolved crimes involving the abduction, murder and mutilation of children in south-east Australia in the years from 1965—when Derek Percy was only sixteen and first started showing 'deviant behaviour'—to 1969 when he was captured. The young detectives identified five key 'cold cases' in which Percy could have been involved.

The Wanda Beach Murders (1965)

On 12 January 1965 the bodies of two 15-year-old school girls were found mutilated, raped and partially buried in sandhills at Wanda Beach north of Cronulla. The previous day, Christine Sharrock and Marianne Schmidt, next-door neighbours from the Sydney suburb of West Ryde, had taken Marianne's four younger siblings to the beach by train. Cronulla Beach was closed because of inclement weather and after having something to eat the older girls took the younger children on a long, winding walk into the dunes north of Wanda Beach. Why the teenagers went into the dunes—whether it was a spur of the moment decision or because they had arranged to meet someone there—has been the focus of much conjecture for over 40 years.

At about 2.00pm on that Monday afternoon, approximately 400 metres past the Wanda Beach Surf Lifesaving Club, the younger

Schmidt children—Peter, aged 11, Trixie, 9, Wolfgang, 8 and 5-year-old Norbert—complained that the wind was whipping sand against their legs. Christine and Marianne left the children huddled between two dunes on the pretext that they would head back to Cronulla, collect the belongings they had left on the rocks and catch the train home. Instead, the two girls headed off over the dunes in a northerly direction toward Botany Bay. Wolfgang Schmidt later told detectives that when he went looking for the girls he saw them walking with a 16-year-old 'surfie' boy. In a further interview he told detectives that the boy was seen earlier that day hunting for crabs and had a knife in a sheath on his hip. When Wolfgang went looking for the girls a second time, the boy was walking southward along the beach. The knife was missing from its sheath and the boy wouldn't say where the girls were.

The younger Schmidt children waited until 5.00pm before walking back to Cronulla, gathering their untouched belongings and returning home on the train to West Ryde. When the girls' bodies were discovered by teenager Peter Smith and his three nephews the following afternoon—partially buried, head to foot having given the illusion that only one body lay under the sand—detectives were appalled by the callousness and viciousness of their deaths. Marianne Schmidt had been stabbed multiple times and had her throat cut with a large serrated knife; Christine Sharrock, who had made a run for her life but had her skull fractured with a blunt object, was dragged 35 metres back to where her friend lay dead or dying and was also stabbed multiple times.

The murder of two young girls on a public beach shocked Sydney and led to a record £10,000 reward being posted by the New South Wales government. Despite an extensive police investigation involving 10,000 witnesses and more than 80,000 typed pages of information, no one was ever charged with the murders.[7]

The Disappearance of the Beaumont Children (1965)

On the morning of Wednesday 26 January 1966, the three young children of Jim and Nancy Beaumont caught a bus to Glenelg

Beach from their home in the Adelaide suburb of Somerton Park. Their father Jim was working that day as a linen goods salesman and their mother allowed the children to go to the beach unattended—a decision not unusual for the children, despite their ages or the times. The children were told to return on the midday bus and to bring 'pies and pasties' from the local cake shop home for lunch. Nancy Beaumont gave the children eight shillings and sixpence (about 85 cents) for their lunch and fare.

When the children did not return on the midday bus Mrs Beaumont was not immediately worried. They probably missed it, she presumed, and would be home on the next bus at 2.00pm. Some friends called in that afternoon and when the children did not arrive home, she wanted to look for them but they could be walking home any number of ways and she wanted to be there when they returned. Jim Beaumont came home early from work at 3.30pm and immediately went to the beach and searched for the children. With no trace of them found, the panic-stricken parents contacted the police.

An elderly eyewitness came forward and said that she had seen the three children 'frolicking' on a grass area known as Colley Reserve beside the beach with a tall blond man aged 35 to 40. The children were running through sprinklers with the man and flicking him with their towels; they then put their belongings with his on a seat and waited for him to get dressed. A worker in a nearby cake shop told police that she remembered the children buying their lunch with a £1 note—which was a lot of money for a child in those days. The children disappeared without a trace and there was no reported sighting of them after midday.

The ensuing search and extensive police investigation resulted in one of the most baffling mysteries in Australian criminal history. A Dutch clairvoyant, Gerard Croiset, was even flown to Australia by concerned citizens and he identified a local warehouse where, he maintained, the children had accidentally been buried. For the next 40 years, until the warehouse was eventually demolished, this was thought to be the resting place of the children's bodies. Hoaxes, vilification of the children's parents, and countless sightings and random theories fuelled public fascination about the fate of the three Beaumont children.

The abduction of two young girls from Adelaide Oval in 1973, 9-year-old Joanne Ratcliffe and Kirste Gordon, aged just 4, was later linked to the disappearance of the Beaumont children seven years before. The crimes were eerily similar—multiple abductions from a public place with no trace of the children found—as was the identikit image of the man seen walking with the girls out of Adelaide Oval to the description of the suspect in the Beaumont disappearances.[8]

The Murder of Allen Redston (1966)

In the 1960s the Redston family lived in the Canberra suburb of Curtain. Brian Redston was a professional soldier and he and his wife had four children—their eldest son and second eldest child was 6-year-old Allen. On the afternoon of Tuesday 27 September 1966, Allen Redston returned home from school eating an iceblock. Mrs Redston told Allen to take his 4-year-old brother Peter to the shop and buy him an iceblock as well. Minutes later Peter Redston returned by himself and told his mother that Allen was playing with his next-door neighbour. In fact, Allen had not even gone to the shop with his brother.

Allen and Peter Redston had gone in separate directions when they left the house—Peter to the shop and Allen to play with another local boy named Phillip Keenan. The older boys walked into another street, separated and Allen ventured down to a local creek area to play. His family did not see him alive again.

When Brian Redston arrived home he did not realise that his son was missing. Allen often remained outside playing with neighbourhood kids for long stretches and when he did not come home in time for dinner at 5.30pm the Redstons started without him. After finishing dinner Brian Redston sent his daughter Anne and son Peter to neighbouring houses to see if Allen was there.

When it became dark, Mr Redston went with volunteers and searched for his son down by a local creek, which was a popular haunt for children, but called police at 7.00pm when there was no sign of the boy.

The following morning the body of Allen Redston was found hidden among reeds in a creek bed by a neighbour, George Sadewater, who had joined the search party with his German Shepherd dog. The little boy's body was wrapped inside a trench coat, rolled in a piece of carpet and placed inside a large polythene bag. The boy's hands had been tied around his back and he had been strangled to death with a hog tie. A length of rope, connecting to the child's legs, had been wrapped tightly around his neck. Drag marks indicated that the creek bed was not the primary crime scene; the trench coat, carpet and bag had been taken from a nearby rubbish tip used by local builders. The victim had not been sexually assaulted and a person of medium build could have dragged the bundle into the creek bed. At the time police speculated that Allen's death may have been an accident; the result of a game or a trick played on him by another boy. The chief suspect at the time was an older boy seen in the area riding a red bike but the identity of that teenager was never fully determined.[9]

The Murder of Simon Brock (1968)

On Saturday 18 May 1968, 3-year-old Simon Brook was playing in the front yard of his home in the inner Sydney suburb of Glebe when family friends called in to visit his parents. When his father, university lecturer Donald Brook, called for him about 30 minutes later, Simon was not there—the boy had crawled through a hole in the fence at the bottom of the garden and gone into Jubilee Park which adjoined the Brooks' home. Dr Brook and some friends walked to the park to look for the boy but found no trace of him. Local police were contacted at 1.30 pm by the boy's concerned parents.

Police, volunteers and locals looked for the boy for the remainder of that cold afternoon but no trace of him was found. Truck driver, Eric Barnier, saw the boy walking 'hand in hand' with a man on Federal Road, on the opposite side of the park, at about 12.35pm on the day he disappeared. The man was about 20 years old with wavy hair and a thin face. Barbara Lrbec, a local woman who was returning from work in the city, arrived at her home in Alexandra Road at about 1.30pm and saw Simon standing by himself. Police believed the man had sent the boy ahead on foot and was following some distance behind.

The following day at 7.20am, labourer Felici Lampasona was working on a block of units being built at 268 Glebe Point Road when he went into bushes adjoining the block to relieve himself. There he saw what looked like a 'big doll', but on closer inspection it was the body of the boy lying on his back, his face covered by his pair of long orange trousers. He was naked from the waist down and though he had been suffocated or strangled, his throat also had been slashed and his genitals had been mutilated post mortem with a razor blade. The blade, which police later discovered belonged to a batch of government 'L4' issue stainless steel blades, was lying beside the body. Government Medical Officers later discovered that the little boy had been strangled with two wads of newspaper rammed down his throat.

The murder of Simon Brook launched an intense police investigation that targeted known sexual perverts in the Glebe area and attempted to track down the source of the one piece of evidence they had—the razor blade. Several other details regarding the murder were never revealed but Dr William Rowe, a leading psychiatrist who gave evidence at the inquest, described the murderer as someone who had a 'sexually disordered urge'.[10]

The Disappearance of Linda Stilwell (1968)

Seven-year-old Linda Stilwell disappeared from an amusement park named Little Luna Park near the esplanade at St Kilda Beach on 10 August 1968. She had gone there that afternoon with her elder siblings—Karen, 11, and Gary, 10—from their newly-occupied,

South Melbourne apartment in Middle Park. The Stilwells were an English family who had immigrated to Australia aboard the *Fairsky* in 1965. The marriage between the parents, Brian and Jean Stilwell, floundered and the father took the youngest member of the family—2-year-old Laura—to live in New Zealand. Linda was the 'tomboy' of the family—confident and outgoing—and made friends easily.

When the three Stilwell children decided to explore St Kilda pier that Saturday afternoon they befriended some boys carrying fishing rods and sat in boats tied to the pier, fishing and playing in the water. A man came and yelled at the children for being in the boat and confiscated the fishing rods of the boys, saying they could pick them up at St Kilda Police Station. Karen, the eldest of the three children, immediately returned home and told their mother that they had got into trouble. Gary and Linda remained with the boys as they argued whether to go and get their rods back. Gary got tired of the arguing and also returned home but Linda was determined to stay. Although she was only seven, she assured her brother that she would find her own way home or ask someone the way.

But Linda did not return home. Apparently, she played with the boys along the St Kilda esplanade until 5.00pm when they left her as it started to become dark. Karen and Gary looked for their sister before their mother went searching and contacted the police at 6.30pm.

Police originally believed that Linda may have run away because she missed her father but eye witness accounts by several people on the esplanade that afternoon raised their worst fear. A woman from the suburb of Kew who was walking along the esplanade at 5.15pm saw a little girl answering Linda's description rolling down a hill while a 'dark man' sitting on a bench watched her play. Two middle-aged men sitting in cars also spotted the little girl, who was later seen running after the man at about 6.00pm. The witness said the little girl was struggling to keep up with the man but was laughing and appeared happy. Linda's mother told the press that her daughter was 'very trusting and would have believed any story that an adult told her'.

The disappearance of Linda Stilwell from a seaside suburb echoed the disappearance of the three Beaumont children from Glenelg Beach in 1966. The description of the man—5 feet 11 inches, slim with curly hair, dark complexion—was too sketchy to be of any use. A wide search of Port Phillip Bay, a thorough police investigation and the involvement of clairvoyants found no trace of the little girl.[11]

⊗⊗⊗

The best hope for a conviction in one of these unsolved crimes is for detectives to build a profile of Derek Percy's *modus operandi* in the one case he was known to have committed and to look for comparative points of coincidence and opportunity in these five other crimes. 'We formed the opinion that these cases were all inter-connected,' Detective David Rae says, 'and formed "a course of conduct" regarding Percy's behaviour from an early age leading up to the Yvonne Tuohy matter in 1969. After we discovered these developments, which were quite significant and we thought were a definite line of enquiry, we approached our Senior Sergeant… once and for all let's investigate, albeit decades later, if Percy is involved in one or all of these.'[12]

In 2004 a multi-jurisdictional agreement, code-named Operation Heats[13] was signed by deputy police commissioners in three states (New South Wales, Victoria and South Australia) as well as the Australian Federal Police to investigate Derek Percy's possible involvement in a number of unsolved crimes in the late 1960s. Multi-agency police investigations had been undertaken before in this country,[14] but the scope and size of this investigation was different. Although the respective police agencies of each state and territory had access to the original case files, the one, undeniable element continuously working against detectives was the passage of time. If any one of the five 'cold cases' was solved, it would be a record in Australian law enforcement history.

Detective Wayne Newman located the original documents relating to Percy's arrest for the murder of Yvonne Tuohy 35 years before. Contained in these files were the original handwritten 'articles' confiscated from Percy on the night he was captured, the original statements concerning the murder as well as a number of Shell touring maps that were found in the glovebox of Percy's car. On one of the maps of Sydney's inner-western suburbs, a pink texta pen mark highlighted a route from Birchgrove (near Cockatoo Island Navy Dock) to Parramatta Road at Leichhardt. Jubilee Park in Glebe, where Simon Brook was lured away from his home, is only a short distance away.

Dave Rae contacted Detective Senior Sergeant Adam Barwick of the Sydney Homicide Squad, who was then in charge of reviewing and prioritising more than 500 'cold case' murder and missing person investigations in New South Wales dating back 50 years. Victoria Police were reinvestigating the disappearance of Linda Stilwell from St Kilda in 1968, Rae told Barwick, and were launching a fresh investigation into the movements of Derek Ernest Percy. Barwick had never heard of Percy's name being mentioned in any unsolved crime in Sydney. He knew of the Brook case but quickly familiarised himself with the original investigation records, a copy of the inquest material and photographs from the crime scene.

For Sydney 'cold case' detectives, the revelations that Percy was a suspect in the murder of a little boy 36 years ago provided them with the first real opportunity in years to bring a suspect to justice. 'Over the years the Brook case had remained unsolved for a number of reasons,' Detective Barwick says. 'There was not enough evidence; the case was old and witnesses had died. If Percy was responsible for the murder of Simon Brook, this was the best chance to try him in Sydney and make him answer for it.'[15]

South Australian Police, perhaps protective of the unfair reputation Adelaide's 'City of Churches' has garnered for bizarre, predatory murders over the past 40 years, refuses to comment publicly on any ongoing investigation other than confirming in an official press release that Derek Percy remains 'a person of interest' in the disappearance of the Beaumont children.[16] Wayne Newman says, 'Brian Swan [the detective who has been in charge of the Beaumont case since 1988] who is a very experienced investigator—he doesn't go off on tangents and chase wild theories—has been extremely cooperative to our investigation. The sort of cross-agency dialogue had been very helpful.'

Australian Federal Police Detective Chris Sheehan recalls, 'Derek Percy did not come to my notice until I became the case officer of the Redston case and was contacted by Victorian Police. I am always wary when people start talking about Wanda Beach and the Beaumont children because everyone wants to solve these crimes... the alarm bells didn't start ringing but I thought I better have a look at it. I made some initial inquiries to see what Percy was in gaol for.'[17]

What he read about Percy disturbed Sheehan but there were some aspects of the Tuohy murder that did not fit the Redston case. 'You look at the crime scene in regard to the other murder [Tuohy] and ask yourself whether the person who committed that murder committed this one by conducting a behavioural analysis of the crime scene,' Sheehan says. 'Whether Percy committed the Redston murder or not, we need to be able to eliminate or include him in the inquiry.'

'In our society child murder outside the domestic situation is, thankfully, an extremely rare occurrence,' Sheehan explains. 'Because of that fact alone you have to include Percy in any investigation because he was (is) a child murderer. It may just be a terrible coincidence that Percy was active around the same time of Allen's death. But it would have been neglectful of the police agencies not to include the Redston case in their investigation.'

And yet there is another victim from Derek Percy's unknown past. In August 2002 Shane Spiller, the child witness whose testimony helped capture Derek Percy in 1969, disappeared from the New South Wales south coast town of Wyndham. Spiller had lived there for many years but had only recently received a crimes compensation payout for his 'decades of trauma'.[18] In 2000 Spiller was awarded $5000 in compensation but on appeal the amount was increased to the maximum $50,000. Spiller told locals that he was still scared that Derek Percy may be released and that he 'might just take off' one day, but when local police found his four-wheel-drive parked in front of his shack, they feared Spiller had somehow met with foul play.

'As far as Percy is concerned,' Detective Wayne Newman reflects, 'we first wanted to learn more about his background... what sort person he was from an early age, in particular his teenage years, leading up to his arrest. We were given an opportunity I don't think we'll ever get again... to reinvestigate these other outstanding matters and to find out just what sort of individual we're dealing with.'

Detectives found that there was a pattern of deviant behaviour from very early on in Derek Percy's childhood. There were a number of incidents that should have alerted Percy's parents, if in fact they didn't, that he was a dangerous individual. It is now known that when he was growing up in Mt Beauty (Victoria), Khancoban (southern New South Wales) and Jesmond (central New South Wales) during the 1960s, Percy, a budding paedophile, was identifying local children—some of them the siblings of his friends, the sons and daughters of neighbours or the children of complete strangers he saw playing on beaches—as potential victims for his sadistic fantasies.

The emergence of DNA technology in the last 20 years has revolutionised 'cold case' investigations but unlike the world of film and television, science is not necessarily the 'golden key' that unlocks every unsolved case. There is no DNA material available from the Beaumont and Stilwell investigations, for example, because there are no identifiable crime scenes and the victims' remains were never found. The problematic status of crime scene exhibits from the other three cases is explored in chapters of this book devoted to those crimes. Will DNA technology finally provide detectives working on Operation Heats with the opportunity to link Derek Percy to one or more of these unsolved crimes?

Somewhere, in the volumes of original paperwork, countless interviews and ongoing forensic investigations, detectives have attempted to answer the following question—who is Derek Ernest Percy?

CHAPTER 2: Who is Derek Percy?

Mrs Casarotto didn't like the boy staying with the Hosking family next door to her.[1] Call it a mother's inkling or just gut instinct, but there was something strange about the skinny teenager that she just couldn't put her finger on. The 17-year-old was staying with the eldest son of the Hosking family because his own family had moved to Khancoban in southern New South Wales and he needed to finish his leaving certificate at Mt Beauty High.

The Casarotto family didn't know the Percys—Mrs Hosking said that they were a quiet, hard-working family and she knew nothing of rumours that their oldest boy had been responsible for a series of petty thefts and burglaries that had broken out in the little Victorian township. Somebody was stealing women's clothing from the washing lines of Mt Beauty—'snow dropping' the locals called it.

One Saturday, however, Mrs Casarotto had taken her two young daughters to visit a cousin who was sick in hospital. When the family returned, several of her daughters' dresses had been taken from inside her house. The worried mother suspected the teenager next door—the fence that divided the two properties was certainly low enough for him to gain entry into her yard and the Hoskings knew that she kept a spare key to her house in a tin can behind the gate. But how could she prove it? The boy was leaving Mt Beauty soon to rejoin his family and Mrs Casarotto didn't want to cause any trouble for her next-door neighbours.

Some time after the teenager had left Mt Beauty, a neighbour found a bundle of clothing hidden under a blackberry bush. Several dresses were wrapped up in a bundle of items, which included dolls and some newspaper clippings. The most disturbing aspect of the find was that the eyes of the women pictured in non-descript newspaper advertisements had been pencilled in to make them look strangely sinister and the breasts and genitals were cut out with a razor blade. The neighbour showed the items to Mrs Casarotto and she quickly identified the dresses as those missing from her household. Her daughters, however, were too old to play with dolls. When she called to her next-door neighbour, Mrs

Hosking recognised the dolls as belonging to her daughter. The implication was clear—the person who took the items had been inside both households. Mrs Hosking was not so sure, but the realisation hit Mrs Casarotto like a Melbourne tram—'It's Derek!'

⁂

Derek Ernest Percy was born in Strathfield, New South Wales on 15 September 1948, the eldest son of Ernest and Elaine Percy. Ernie Percy was a New South Wales railway electrician, a job that was deemed an 'essential service' during World War II and kept him out of active duty. Mr Percy stayed with New South Wales Railways for nearly 25 years before taking a job with the State Electricity Commission in Victoria. In 1956, the year Melbourne hosted the Olympics, the Percy family, which had grown to include three young boys, moved to Chelsea, a suburb southwest of Melbourne on Port Phillip Bay. The following year, the Percys' youngest son died of diphtheria at the age of just ten months. In postwar Australia, which was experiencing a migrant boom mainly from European countries, this highly contagious upper respiratory tract illness was responsible for more deaths than any other disease.[2]

In 1958, the Percys relocated to Warrnambool, on the other side of the state on the southeast coast facing the open sea, when Ernest Percy was employed by the local power station. The preference for seaside living allowed Ernie to indulge in his life's passion—sailing. At a time when 18-foot boats were taking all the glory in national competition, Mr Percy liked to compete in 12-foot restricted and unrestricted class yachting—one-man 'moth class' sailing. Percy also built his own boats and experimented with twin hull boats—catamarans—which were still a novelty in the late 1950s. Percy's boat, a catamaran named 'Kittycat,' was ahead of its time and was banned from certain competitions because it was just too fast.

In 1961, Ernest Percy was promoted to Kiewa Valley's hydro-electric plant and the family moved to Mt Beauty, near Bright, in the state's northeast.[3] Their eldest son Derek started at Mt Beauty Higher Elementary School that year and stayed until the end of Fifth Form in 1965. Elaine Percy, who had recently given birth to another son, rarely let her eldest boys out of her sight, which was understandable given that she had lost one son in infancy and both boys suffered from chronic lung infections. As part of the boys' physical therapy the Percys regularly took turns at night 'pummelling' them on the back to break the build-up of phlegm in their lungs before they went to sleep. Mrs Percy forbade her eldest sons from playing Aussie Rules but the brothers would borrow gear from friends for the occasional football game. Even so, Derek Percy enjoyed solitary activities. He collected stamps, loved to read and draw, especially sailing boats, and like many teenagers, he kept a diary.

The Percy family also shared Ernie's love of sailing to some degree. Elaine Percy would crew for her husband while her two boys would take turns sailing with their dad in between heats of competition or recreationally while on family holidays. Perhaps it was because the family was landlocked in Mt Beauty that the Percys planned regular caravan holidays. They often travelled to moth class yachting competitions in their V8 Studebaker, to places such as Yarrawonga, Port Phillip Bay and on the east coast of Victoria. The family was also known to visit Sydney and The Entrance, on the New South Wales Central Coast, where the parents of Mr and Mrs Percy still lived, and even as far as Adelaide on at least one occasion.

One Melbourne newspaper later tried to explain these family holidays as comprising a 'murder map'[4] of unsolved crimes involving children, but more than 40 years after the events, dates and destinations proved almost impossible for detectives to verify. In the summer of 1964–65 the Australian moth class championships were being held in Sydney for the first time in years, given that each state took turns hosting the event. The Botany Bay Yacht Club hosted the 1964–65 championships—several kilometres from where two teenage girls were murdered at Wanda Beach on 11 January 1965. Was Derek Percy also there?

According to unsubstantiated reports Derek Percy allegedly 'travelled to Adelaide' by himself one Christmas and visited 'an aunt' in Canberra but this is disputed by the family. The Percys were not financially well-off and Ernie Percy and his wife were particularly frugal with money. The mother of one of Derek Percy's friends told police: 'I can also recall that Derek travelled to Adelaide on holidays by plane on one occasion.'[5] The Percys, however, do not appear to be the type of people to send their teenage son alone on a plane to Adelaide. For what purpose? The Percys had no relatives in Canberra and actually sailed to Adelaide together in 1965, stopping off at the Barossa Valley. But this was when the family was living at Mt Beauty and not in January 1966 when three children went missing from Glenelg Beach.

Former school friends have provided detectives with snippets of information from Percy's past. 'I would talk to Derek on a regular basis but I wouldn't call him one of my mates,' Mt Beauty classmate Kim White recalled.[6] 'My best mate was a bloke named Bill Hutton while Derek was mates with Ron Anderson, Peter Crouch and Ken Hosking… from my dealings with Derek, I thought that he was a bit different and I found him to be a loner and hard to get to know. I am a friendly, affable type of person but Derek pretty much kept to himself and didn't say much. I was keen on playing sport back then and I captained the school cricket side and football team. Derek played both football and cricket but he was better at cricket. He was a fair batsman.'

The school uniform at Mt Beauty consisted of black shoes, grey trousers, light grey shirt, grey v-neck jumper with green and gold pattern on the 'v' and green and gold pattern around the cuffs, and a green tie with gold diagonal stripes. To save money Elaine Percy made her son's school ties in a coarse fabric which was not a perfect match for the school pattern. Money was always an issue; while most boys rode brand new bicycles, the Percy brothers brought second-hand bikes after saving pocket money earned from local jobs. Derek worked in the tobacco fields with different friends, while his younger brother got a job with a local butcher. Derek brought a dark maroon second-hand bike with racing 'ram's horn' handlebars while his brother paid £4 for his bike—a considerable sum for the time—but the boys were made to earn every cent.

Derek Percy was a familiar sight in Mt Beauty riding around town on his distinctive, dark maroon bike. One Mt Beauty local later told police that while Mrs Percy allowed her middle son a modicum of freedom, her eldest son was kept on a much tighter rein. 'Derek had to get permission to go anywhere with us outside of school hours and she would question his intentions,' she recalled.[7]

Bill Hutton, another former classmate, recalls, 'Derek did well at school generally; he was not overly studious but he was naturally good at what he did'.[8] But Percy was also an intense loner with some unsettling personal habits. He had a nervous tick that didn't endear him to the seniors—a disturbing habit of hawking and spitting phlegm—and he showed signs of a sadistic streak even back then. Bill Hutton recalls Percy flicking students with a long key chain that he kept on a leather strap on his belt. 'Whenever we would complain about it and tell him to nick off, he had the girly, high-pitched laugh of his... it was eerie.'

※※※

In 1964, a small crime wave hit Mt Beauty when women's underwear began to disappear from clothes lines. There are few secrets in a small country town and soon Derek Percy's name was being mentioned in hushed tones around town and at his father's workplace as being the phantom 'panty' thief. According to some locals[9] Ernie Percy threatened to sack any worker who suggested that his son was the person responsible for the thefts, but an incident witnessed by two school mates at a local gorge not only proved that Derek Percy was the culprit, but gave possibly the first indication that his life was in inner turmoil and that the teenager was dangerously disturbed.

On a warm Sunday afternoon toward the end of the year, Kim White and Bill Hutton walked to a local swimming hole known to Mt Beauty locals as 'the gorge'.[10] The gorge was a bush area about 5 kilometres outside town along the West Kiewa River. Steep embankments located on each side of the river are littered with caves, large water rocks and broken electricity company equipment and although it took over an hour to walk to the remote area, the gorge was an attraction for local teenagers to explore. A dirt road cut into the south side embankment above the gorge and because the road was considerably higher than the river, someone walking along the road could look down from a height of over 15 metres into the gorge.

The day Kim White and Bill Hutton walked to the gorge, they saw what appeared to be a young girl in a petticoat walking in the bush below them about 100 metres away. 'Perhaps there are some girls skinny-dipping,' Bill Hutton remarked to his friend, but as they crept closer they realised that it was in fact Derek Percy, their Mt Beauty schoolmate, wearing a silky, see-through pink-coloured women's negligee.

'That's Percy!' White blurted out. He recalls the events of that day as if it happened yesterday. 'Bill then picked up a rock and I thought that he was going to throw it into the river near Derek to scare him. I then said to Bill, "No, this is not normal, let's see what he does."' The teenagers lay down on the grading side of the road to conceal themselves and to see what Percy was up to.

'The next thing I saw was that Derek had a knife in one of his hands,' White recalls. Like many local boys, Percy often carried a sharp knife in a cowskin sheath around his waist. 'Derek then began to wave the knife around like he was acting something out. At the same time he was making funny noises but you couldn't hear anything clear. I then saw that there were two bundles of clothes on the rock near Percy. One bundle appeared to be women's clothing and the other bundle appeared to be Percy's clothes.'

Percy was staring transfixed into the water but suddenly began to slash at a bundle of clothing in a violent and aggressive manner and cut and stabbed at the crotch of a pair of knickers and the humour quickly drained from the situation. Bill Hutton was about 15 metres away from him but he was close enough to see Percy's face. 'I would describe Derek's eyes as being full of excitement, a glazed look, but I recall there was something very cold and sinister in the look,' he later told police.

Percy then took off the petticoat and standing naked at the water's edge, he did a most peculiar thing—he defecated into the water. White later recalled, 'He then got up, dressed in his own clothes, rolled up the women's clothing and put the women's clothing under his arm. I couldn't see the knife at this stage and I thought that it must have been among the clothing.'

Percy then began to rock-hop down the river while Kim and Bill, still sticking to the road, followed him from a distance. They saw Percy hide the women's clothing under a rock near an old broken bridge before walking up to the road, getting on his bicycle and riding off toward town. The boys walked down to the area and turned over the rock covering the items. They didn't touch any of the clothing and couldn't see a knife so they put the rock back in place.

Percy's school mates looked at each other in amazement; they were shocked at what they had seen and couldn't comprehend the enormity of what had happened. White's mind was racing ahead of itself. 'I thought that Derek might have killed someone in the area where he was doing the act with the knife and both Bill and I walked upstream… but I didn't see anything.' He went to the water's edge and had a drink from a rock pool just as human faeces floated past him. Bill Hutton couldn't help himself. 'Whitey, that's Percy's!' White was too shocked to laugh.

The pair then walked back to Mt Beauty and met some school

friends at the local swimming pool. They told two girls about what they had seen but they weren't believed—it was the middle of the conservative 1960s, and such things just didn't happen in a small country town of 2000 people. 'I decided not to tell my parents,' White explains, 'but we couldn't wait to confront Derek about it the following day at school in front of our mates.' The boys could not have imagined the significance of the situation, or the potential impact of a public humiliation of their school mate, but they were determined to see Percy squirm in front of his peers.

'We were on the oval at the first break,' White continues. Derek Percy was there along with about 12 other classmates. 'In front of the others I then asked Derek in a loud voice what he was doing at the gorge the day before dressed in women's clothing. Derek had this nervous habit of spitting and he began to spit on the ground. Derek said he wasn't at the gorge the day before and I told him that Bill and I had seen him there... [he] kept on saying that he wasn't there.'

Most of the other students thought that the two teenagers were merely making the story up 'to create some mischief', and finally Ken Hosking and Peter Crouch intervened and told them to 'lay off' Derek and to leave him alone. White and Hutton told Max Davies, the Vice Principal of the school, what they had seen but were advised not to spread rumours about Percy. 'Don't go bringing those sorts of things up,' White remembers his teacher advising them, 'it'll only cause you trouble.' Both boys were larrikins and were in regular trouble at school and so the incident was easily dismissed. But Peter Crouch, whose family was friends with the Percys, told his mother that Derek had been seen in the bush by two friends wearing women's clothing and news of 'the gorge incident' churned the local rumour mill.

The 'gorge incident' was a significant event in the life of Derek Percy. It revealed Percy's private preoccupation with faeces, his fascination with the stabbing or cutting of underpants and the wearing of female clothing. The incident also provides an early echo of the crime for which he would be held accountable almost five years later—the murder of Yvonne Tuohy—and possibly, five other unsolved crimes.

Derek Percy was a regular contributor to Mt Beauty's High School magazine *Yurnga*. After a visit by members of Corryong High School, which is about two hours away to the north of Mt Beauty, Percy wrote, 'The Corryong High School visit was on the whole a great success. It would be a good idea to arrange other school visits… these trips would give people a chance to make friends, and perhaps pen-friends in other districts.' Percy found it difficult to make friends, especially of the opposite sex. His profile in the school's 1965 yearbook reads:

Favourite saying: 'It depends.'
Ambition: Playboy.
Probable fate: Bachelor.
Perpetual occupation: Isolating himself.
Pet aversion: Girls.

Percy even contributed a poem, entitled 'The World of a Tornado'—a typically puerile piece of teenage poetry with one telling line: 'the tornado has struck, the damage is done'.[11] Derek Percy's inner world was indeed like a tornado and the 17-year-old was spinning out of control.

A former headmaster at Mt Beauty, Mr John Hehir, states that Percy was 'a good student who obtained good marks until 1965 when his grades deteriorated'.[12] There are many theories to explain why Percy failed his exams at the end of 1965—from the allegation that he had already committed his first murder the previous January while on holiday in Sydney, to the fact that his parents had moved to Khancoban in New South Wales and Derek had been left behind in Mt Beauty to stay with the Hosking family. The truth lies somewhere in between, or a simpler explanation may be that, according to the Victorian education system at the time, a student had to pass a minimum of four subjects, one of which was English, to obtain 'the Leaving'. All Derek Percy would have had to have done was fail English and he would have had to repeat Fifth Form. Although former classmates think it unlikely Percy would have failed this subject it is apparent, with the onset of puberty, that Percy was dealing with a number of personal and psychological issues.

As early as 1965—the year his grades collapsed and he failed his leaving certificate—Percy began writing down bizarre and violent sexual fantasies and he would continue the habit for much of his adult life. His father first discovered some of his son's disturbing sexual 'jottings' while the family lived at Mt Beauty—writings filled with coarse sexual references involving children and a fascination with defecating and urinating—and immediately burnt them.

Mr Percy later told detectives that he spoke to his son about the writings but did not confront him about the theft of underwear in the town or ever speak to him about the 'gorge incident'.[13] Mrs Percy had not heard any rumours of the 'gorge incident' but on several occasions she had to publicly and vehemently defend her son when the subject of the 'snow dropper' was raised in her presence. But what can't be denied is that the 'snow dropping' incidents suddenly stopped when Derek Percy left Mt Beauty and joined his family at Khancoban, only to begin again in his new home town. There were also reports of a 'peeping tom' prowling the area, and soon Percy moved to the 'next level' of his troubled psychosis and physically involved younger children in acting out his fantasies.

Sometime in 1966, when the Percys were living at Khancoban, Derek was accused of an indecent assault on two young sisters in a caravan at the rear of a neighbouring property. The Percys were friends with the neighbouring family and 17-year-old Derek had little difficulty luring the girls into the caravan. Once inside, he either pulled down the underwear of one of the girls or encouraged her to take off her panties and touched her vagina. The assault only ended when the girls' mother called out for her daughters to come inside and one of them, who was aged about six at the time, told her what happened. The girls' father spoke directly to Ernie Percy about the incident and Mr Percy promised him that he would deal with the issue and that it wouldn't happen again. The Percys talked to their son about the incident but after a visit to the family doctor, no further professional help was sought. Ernie and Elaine Percy later said that despite these alarming signals—the 'snow dropping' allegations, this sexual assault and the discovery of Derek's writings—they thought their eldest son was 'shy but normal'.[14]

In 1966, Derek Percy repeated Fifth Form at Corryong High School, which was 30 minutes southeast of Khancoban across the New South Wales–Victoria border. This allowed the older Percy brothers, who were now in the same school grade, to complete their leaving certificate under the Victorian syllabus. The second of the Percy brothers—a shorter and stockier version of Derek but more athletic and gregarious—formed a new circle of friends at his new school but Derek Percy struggled to relate to his peers. Derek's younger brother later told detectives that he had very little to do with his brother during their final year of school together.

Ron Anderson caught up with his former school friend when Mt Beauty and Corryong High Schools went to the Snowy Mountains for an inter-school skiing competition. 'There was some talk of an incident involving Derek and two girls in a caravan,' Anderson recalls. 'Derek was under a bit of pressure at school. I think he was going to be expelled at one stage but nothing happened.'

However, at the end of that year, Ernie Percy promptly retired and invested his superannuation in a Shell service station in suburban Wallsend in Newcastle, New South Wales. The Percys lived at The Entrance with Mrs Percy's mother while Ernie Percy trained at the Shell Depot in Carrington Street, Sydney, for about six weeks. As part of his preparation for his new career Mr Percy also had to complete a practical course at a Shell training station situated on Victoria Road, near the Iron Cove Bridge, in the inner-city suburb of Pyrmont. Derek allegedly visited his father there in

1967. The Shell training garage, which has since been demolished and replaced by high-rise apartments, had an uninterrupted view southwest across Rozelle Bay of sporting fields known as Jubilee Park in suburban Glebe. In 1968 it was the scene of the shocking abduction and murder of a 3-year-old boy.

***

As far as detectives are concerned, 1967 was Derek Percy's 'lost year'. Having finally gained his leaving certificate, Percy wanted to continue his schooling and enrolled at Gosford High School but the differences in the New South Wales curriculum led him to drop out of school altogether. His tried to get a job in a drafting office, but was under-qualified. After the Percys relocated to Jesmond, a suburb of Newcastle, Derek and his younger brother worked at their father's petrol station for most of that year. Derek Percy is believed to have spent recreational time visiting local beaches and sailing on Lake Macquarie. Having once dreamed of being a sail-maker, he decided to join the Royal Australian Navy (RAN) at the end of the year after he turned 19.

Perhaps it was yet another family upheaval, perhaps his intense sexual fantasies were all-consuming, but Derek Percy became increasingly withdrawn from those who should have known him the best—his family. But then something was not quite right with the network of family relationships—a distant, authoritarian father; a protective, overbearing mother; a sibling rivalry with his younger brother and a non-relationship with his infant brother. Mrs Percy's mother also moved in with the family, and having three generations under the same roof was another potential source of conflict within the family. Tellingly, in the 20 months Percy was in the navy (late 1967 to mid-1969) he visited his uncle in Sydney and family friends back in Mt Beauty but returned to the family home in Jesmond on only one occasion—Christmas 1967—while he was on leave.

Most importantly, his family did not realise that he was

continuing with his 'lewd' writings that documented increasingly violent sexual fantasies. During 1967, while Derek was living in the family home at Jesmond, his grandmother found some of the articles in a rubbish bin. When confronted by his parents Derek told them that another boy had given them to him during his final year at high school. Once again the Percys dismissed the matter, at grave peril as it transpired, for if they had a closer look at their son's writings they may have finally sought the professional help he so desperately needed. 'Kidnap two girls at Barnsley,' Percy later wrote in one chilling scenario. 'Then take them to a secluded place. When I get there blindfold them and have a good look and feel.' Barnsley is a seaside suburb of Newcastle.

Before he joined the navy in 1967 Derek Percy made a concerted effort to obtain his driver's licence. His younger brother had already gained his licence as soon as he turned 17, as was the law in the 1960s, and Derek, now aged 19, needed a car to travel around Melbourne and Sydney while he completed his naval training. Derek learned to drive in his mother's Datsun sedan and he later purchased a similar model grey-coloured station wagon with the licence plate EUU 786 for which Mr and Mrs Percy went 'guarantor' and registered in their name. Derek's father even gave his son a 'Go Well! Go Shell!' sticker for the side window.

Derek Percy joined the navy on 25 November 1967, and trained at HMAS *Cerberus* at Flinders Naval Depot on Melbourne's Westernport Bay. Percy already knew the area because he had lived in Chelsea, an hour away to the north, as a boy in the 1950s. Shane Watt, who also joined the navy that year and was later a chief petty officer and Vietnam veteran, spent 11 weeks in a naval dormitory with the shy teenager and two other trainee naval personnel. Watt remembers Percy as being intelligent but a social recluse. 'Percy was [training] in electrical and I was doing gunnery,' Watt recalled. 'He was very quiet, he never went out, and didn't seem to want to go out with us guys from the dormitory… from what I can recall he used to read a fair bit.'[15]

Percy already had an affinity with the sea and sailing but he also liked the structure and order of navy life—it occupied his time and his mind. Senior navy officials considered him as a candidate for officer training because of his high level of intelligence. Percy was assessed as having an IQ of 122 which is in the top 15 per cent of the population. But Shane Watt's impression of the quiet young man was at odds with what was happening inside Percy's mind. 'He was very quiet and wasn't violent, and he didn't get into fights,' Watt recalled. 'It seems amazing to me that the [navy] psychological tests didn't pick up his problems.' But then no one had picked up on Percy's 'problems'. When his mind wasn't occupied, Percy was engulfed by sadistic fantasies involving children.

Derek Percy was on leave from the navy between 23 December 1967 and 7 January 1968, when he returned home to Newcastle for Christmas, before returning to HMAS *Cerberus* where he remained until 8 March. The following day Percy joined HMAS *Melbourne*, which was stationed in Sydney at that time. Percy lived at HMAS *Kuttabul*, the naval base at Kings Cross, and travelled to the *Melbourne* which was docked at Garden Island each day.

Sometime in 1968 Bill Hutton, who was on leave from the air force, returned home and was surprised to see his former classmate at the home of Peter Crouch. Percy also visited his uncle who lived in the Sydney suburb of Canley Vale, on at least three occasions between 9 March and 1 July while he was attached to HMAS *Melbourne* in Sydney. Percy's relatives later told detectives that they could not remember the exact dates of these visits. This at least proved to detectives that Derek Percy had a workable knowledge of how to get around Sydney, either by car or rail.

The Taylor family of Yagoona were friends with the Percys and had known Derek since he was a baby. Derek visited them on 31 March 1968 and stayed overnight before catching the train to HMAS *Kuttabul* the next morning. Several days after his visit, Derek contacted the Taylors' teenage daughter and invited her to the Moscow Circus, which was performing at Wentworth Park.

Three-year-old Simon Brook was abducted from the front yard of his home alongside Jubilee Park in Glebe—which is just one kilometre west of Wentworth Park—and murdered on Saturday 18 May 1968.

On 1 July 1968, Derek Percy was attached to HMAS *Sydney*, which was based in Melbourne. He served there until 5 August, when he went on leave until 22 August. Eight-year-old Linda Stilwell was taken from St Kilda pier on Saturday 10 August—her body was never found. On 23 August 1968, Percy returned to HMAS *Sydney* for one day and was then transferred to HMAS *Queensborough*, which was also based in Melbourne. He served on that ship from 24 August 1968 until 7 March 1969. He then took leave from 8 March to 29 March. Percy returned to the *Queensborough* on 30 March 1969 and was stationed there until 1 April.[16]

After this, Percy returned to HMAS *Cerberus* where he remained for the next four months. About this time a young girl riding her bike on the Mornington Peninsula was approached by a young man in a 'creamy' coloured station wagon with a sticker that said 'Go ...!' on the window. The little girl escaped.[17]

Late on Sunday night 20 July 1969, Newcastle police visited the home of Ernest and Elaine Percy and broke the news—their eldest son, Derek Ernest Percy, had been arrested in Melbourne for the abduction and murder of a little girl.

CHAPTER 3:
The Abduction and Murder of Yvonne Tuohy

In 1969, Bill Hutton was in the Royal Australian Air Force while his best friend and former Mt Beauty classmate Kim White was training as an electrician for the State Electrical Commission in Melbourne. The friends had kept in regular contact in the more than three years since they had left high school, along with several other boys from the close-knit Mt Beauty community now scattered throughout the state. But on Monday 21 July 1969, a ghost from their past was plastered over the front page of *The Age* newspaper. A 20-year-old naval rating from HMAS *Cerberus* had been apprehended and charged with abducting and murdering a 12-year-old girl at Warneet. Hutton couldn't believe what he was reading; neither could Kim White, and he phoned his friend at work that morning. When Hutton answered the phone, the friends said the same words at the same time—'Derek Percy!'

The pair quickly recounted the summer afternoon at the West Kiewa River almost five years before when they had witnessed Percy's bizarre behaviour at the gorge. 'No one believed us,' White recalls, 'but they believed us now.' Later that evening White received another call from another former classmate at Mt Beauty. Ron Anderson, one of their team-mates in the school cricket team and a close friend of Percy's at school, who was now a probationary constable at the homicide squad's Russell Street headquarters. Anderson asked White and Hutton to come to the city watchhouse and tell the police what they knew about Percy. And there was more. Detectives wanted Anderson to talk to Percy 'as a friend'—to get him to open up to him. Ron Anderson was going to ask him about his possible involvement in a number of other unsolved crimes involving children.[1]

✻✻✻

On Sunday 20 July 1969, Australian newspapers were filled with coverage of Apollo 11's historic journey to the moon. Within 24 hours Neil Armstrong would become the first man to walk on the lunar surface, symbolising the heights of human endeavour and achievement up to that moment in time. But literally another world away, at a secluded Victorian beach on a winter's afternoon, 20-year-old Derek Percy was about to demonstrate the depths of depravity few human beings could imagine existed. Increasingly isolated from friends and family and consumed by his violent sexual fantasies, the young man's sadistic world collided with the lives of two innocent children.

That Sunday, Frank Spiller was painting the side of the family's weatherboard weekender at Warneet, a small hamlet to the north of French and Phillip Islands on the edge of Westernport Bay. Mr Spiller, who was a well-known motorcycle racer on the Darley 'Short Circuit' at Bacchus Marsh, brought his young family down from Armadale in South Melbourne for weekends and holidays. Shane Spiller, aged 11, asked his father if he and a friend, Yvonne Tuohy, the daughter of a local shopkeeper, could walk to the water for 'a hike'. It was a fine but crisp winter's day and Mr Spiller later remarked that 'he thought it was a good idea for the kids to get some fresh air'.[2]

The family of Yvonne Tuohy, who was the youngest of three sisters and in her first year at the local high school, had only moved to Warneet the previous summer. The 12-year-old school girl had befriended Shane Spiller during school holidays at the Westernport Bay hamlet. Shane took a small tomahawk to chop some wood and build a fire when the pair got to a secluded area named Ski Beach. The little boy tucked the tomahawk into his belt, as he had seen Indians do on countless cowboy movies. It was a decision that was to save his life, only to have it lost again decades later.

The children walked down the road away from Warneet and went off on a side track that led to the beach. The track divided around a grassy clump and a small car park was situated on the left side. As he passed the car park Shane noticed two cars—a green Ford Falcon station wagon and a light-coloured Datsun station wagon. The Datsun was facing the water and had 'navy' stickers on the window—they had an anchor and a chain on them, he later recalled. Shane also noticed the young man sitting in the driver's seat as he and Yvonne walked past.

In a frantic stream of consciousness, Shane later recounted what happened when they got further down the track: 'I wanted to go to the right and Yvonne wanted to go to the left; so I went to the right, well away, and I turned back to see if she was coming and I started walking towards her but when I had taken a few steps, or a little way, towards her, a man came out—from I don't know where, just from anywhere I would say—just jumped out and came out and he put one of his arms around Yvonne's shoulders, and grabbed her shoulders or her hands or something, and he had a knife in his hand.' The man was holding a red-handled knife at the little girl's neck but Shane also noted a leather sheath the man was wearing around his waist.

Shane instinctively drew his tomahawk and held it up in the air in a threatening motion. The man called out to him, 'Put it down and come here or else I'll hurt the girl.' The scared little boy thought for a few seconds before running into the bush. As he ran away Shane could hear Yvonne calling out to him, 'Shane, Shane, help me, Shane. He's going to cut my neck.' Crawling through the bush so the man could not see him, Shane heard a car start and was sure that the man had driven off. Shane crawled through the bush to the main highway and waited for a car to drive past so that he could get help for his friend; hoping against hope that the man who had abducted Yvonne didn't drive past. When a car came about 15 minutes later, Shane still had the tomahawk in his hand.

The Payden family, who were driving from Tooradin to Warneet that day, stopped to see if the little boy waiting on the side of the road was lost. Shane told them that a stranger had abducted his friend—a car matching the description Shane gave them had passed their vehicle on Warneet Road at about 12.30 pm going 'pretty fast'. There was only one person in that car, Mr Payden remembered, but the man was sitting very high in the seat. Another car stopped, and a second family gave the frightened boy a warm cup of tea. The families took Shane to where Yvonne had been abducted and had 'a good look around' but there was no sign of her, the man or his car. They took Shane to Yvonne's house and he told her parents what had happened to their daughter. Shane was then taken to his home, shaken and undoubtedly traumatised.

The Little family were also out driving that afternoon and were travelling to Cranbourne along Fisheries Road at Devon Meadows, about 10 kilometres north of Warneet. At about 2.45 pm, they stopped 400 metres north from the Baxter-Tooradin Road intersection and pulled off onto a track where Bill Little saw a clearing where they could make a cuppa. Mr Little nosed his car into the clearing and backed his car up on to the edge of the track and built a fire while his children searched for cans to prop up their billy. While gathering twigs, Little heard voices at the end of the track which finished off into thick scrub.

'There were two distinct voices,' Bill Little later recalled, but he could not tell if they were male and female. He could see the corner of a car around the bend of the track and called his children back just in case it was a couple who wanted to be alone. He went back to start the fire and ten minutes later, heard the engine of the car start up. Looking up he saw the rear of the car as it backed along the track and noted that it was a small, light-coloured Datsun station wagon. The car passed within a metre of the family and Mr Little saw that the back seat was covered by an eiderdown quilt and there was something 'lumpy' underneath it—it was an irregular shape, not flat. Little did not get a good look at the man driving the car, 'just a fleeting glance', because the driver's head was turned away as he backed the car out onto the roadway.

It struck Bill Little as strange that there was only one person in the car. He later remarked, 'I was looking for another occupant.' He did not see where the car went when it got back onto Fisheries Road but it headed north. The Littles finished their cup of tea and arrived home at about 5.00 pm. It was only then that they heard the news broadcasts of a missing girl and the search for a Datsun station wagon and immediately contacted the police. By that time the search for 12-year-old Yvonne Tuohy was in full swing.

※※※

Senior Constable Alan Hyde, who was attached to the 'wireless control' police at Brunswick, was in Area Car 2 with two other crew members, Detective Coates and Constable White, when he received a radio call at 3.40pm to go to Warneet and assist in the search for an abducted girl. Arriving at 4.30pm, Constable Hyde had a discussion with a number of adults, including a distressed Mr Tuohy and 11-year-old Shane Spiller. But events were already rapidly unfolding. Before they could mount a search for the missing girl they were instructed to go to Flinders Naval Base at Crib Point and report to the naval police office—police had already found the suspect's car. Homicide Squad Detectives Ken Robertson and Bernie Delaney were travelling to the area from Melbourne's Russell Street headquarters to take up the search for the missing girl and would be joined by detectives from Dandenong CIB.

Des Stephens was an electrical mechanical weapons engineer attached to HMAS *Cerberus* at Flinders Naval Depot and shared cabin CM-13 with three other men, one of whom was Derek Ernest Percy. On Saturday afternoon all four had 'gone ashore' on weekend leave, with Stephens returning to his bunk later that night. Derek Percy did not return to his cabin until Sunday. 'He was always a reasonably, pretty quiet type of chap,' Stephens later said. When Percy returned to base on Sunday afternoon, he appeared calm and in control. 'He just seemed all right,' Stephens remarked.

Stephens was sitting in bed watching the TV show *Hunter*—a

naive Australian spy series of the era filmed in Melbourne, when Derek Percy came in at about 4.30pm. 'What sort of weekend did you have?' Percy asked innocently before adding, unsolicited. 'I have just been playing football this morning.' Percy then said that he would do his 'dobbying'[3]—his laundry—and took the hose the men used to funnel the hot water from a tap into the washing machine and went to the laundry room shared by other cabins in C Block. Stephens saw that Percy had a travelling bag with him and assumed that it was his weekend washing. He then added nonchalantly, 'That's the last I seen [*sic*] of him until when I came back from having tea and the police were with him.'

The police, in fact, were already on base. Percy was no master criminal, for when Shane Spiller escaped he gave the police a clear description of the type of car the man drove, right down to the navy sticker on the window. Flinders Naval Depot at Crib Point, just 34 kilometres to the southwest of Warneet, was the logical place to start looking for the car. Constable Malcolm Grant, who was stationed at Mornington that weekend, received a phone call from Melbourne D24 at 4.30pm to go to Flinders Naval Depot and search for a Datsun station wagon with a navy sticker on the window. Constable Grant arrived there at about 5.00pm, just as Derek Percy was doing his washing.

In the company of naval security staff, Constable Grant searched the navy car parks which held about 200 cars. Percy had made it easy for them—he had parked his car illegally behind C Block and the car was identified within ten minutes. Grant noted that the engine of the Datsun station wagon was still warm and the vehicle appeared to have recently been washed. The car had NSW number plates—EUU 786—and there was a navy sticker on the window along with a 'Go Well! Go Shell!' sticker. The car was locked but Grant could see an eiderdown laid out flat on a mattress in the back.

Senior Constable Grant returned to the police room of naval security, and leading patrolman Max Irving inspected the registration records for the owner of the car—Derek Percy. Irving used the internal piping address system to request that Percy come to the police office but he did not respond. By this time—about 5.40pm—Area Car 2 of the wireless police reached the base and together with patrolman Irving, made their way to Percy's cabin. It couldn't have been any easier for them. They found Percy in the laundry room washing blood from his clothes and listening to a news broadcast of the girl's abduction on a transistor radio.

'Are you Derek Percy?' Senior Constable Hyde asked.

'Yes,' the 20-year old answered as one of the policemen switched off the washing machine.

'What are you washing?' Hyde asked again.

'Dobbies,' Percy answered. Hyde did not know what he meant but he assumed that it was a naval term for washing clothes.

'Where have you been today?' Hyde asked.

'To Cowes [on Melbourne's famous Phillip Island] and then back here,' Percy replied. The young man was calm, Hyde observed. He asked Percy what he had been wearing that day and he pointed to a wet pair of newly-washed jeans on top of the washing basket. Hyde then said to the young naval rating that they wanted to search his locker. Percy made no reply and one of the constables took possession of the washing in the laundry basket and the half-washed items from the machine.

Percy was taken back to his cabin where the police were joined by Lieutenant Commander Riley, the highest ranking officer on duty that night. After informing Percy that they had the Commander's permission to search his belongings, police found a blue navy bag on top of his locker and took possession of a number of items including two magazines and a green, loose-leaf binder with handwritten notes and drawings on sheets of a writing pad. Hyde asked Percy if he had made the drawings and the young man nodded but avoided eye contact and looked only at the floor. Hyde told Lieutenant Commander Riley that he wanted to caution Percy in his presence and though he wasn't arresting the naval rating yet, the young man was not free to leave the base.

Hyde turned to Percy and informed him that they were investigating the abduction of a 12-year-old girl from Warneet at about 12.30pm earlier that day and warned him that there was a strong possibility that he may be implicated in the crime. When asked if there was anything he wanted to say, Percy answered 'no'. The police took Percy outside to where his car was parked and asked him to unlock it. Percy was meekly compliant—leading patrolman Irving rode with Percy as the suspect drove his own car over to the police room on the naval base. Irving later complained of the 'strong odour about the car… as a matter of fact, it nearly drove me ill. I can't be sure what it was.'

Police made a quick search of the car for any sign of the missing girl. A red sheathed knife was found under the driver's seat with congealed blood under the hilt. Two other knives were taken from the glovebox of the car, each in a sheath. One of them appeared as though the blade had been filed down and reshaped. These were shown to Percy and he admitted that they were his but he didn't know why blood was on one of them.

'What do you use them for?' Detective Coates asked.

'Cutting ropes when I am sailing,' Percy replied. Coates looked inside Percy's car; there was carpet on the floor and sand in the pile. He also noted a pungent odour—the smell of human excreta.

Constable Hyde tried to draw a definite response from Percy. 'You can be identified as being in the Warneet area and also the car you were driving. You have been told that a girl has been abducted from there and that you are the owner of the car containing a blood-stained knife that you say is yours. Do you want to tell me the whereabouts of the girl now?'

Percy then gave the first inkling that something wasn't quite right with him. 'I am sorry but I do things that I can't remember after.' Hyde asked him if he remembered being in the Warneet area earlier that day and Percy replied, 'No. I don't remember anything about Warneet.' Hyde was frustrated—Percy didn't smell of liquor, didn't appear to be under the influence of drugs and was 'quite logical' in his conversations and actions. And he was so cold. Percy was placed in a naval cell until Melbourne homicide detectives arrived. Hyde and his crew then left the Flinders Naval Base and went to Fisheries Road at Devon Meadows where Bill Little had seen Percy's car that afternoon and helped search for the missing girl until midnight.

Detectives Robertson and Delaney arrived at HMAS *Cerberus* at about 7.45 pm and after a brief conversation with Percy instructed the young man to change his clothes before they took him to Frankston police station. Before they left, Ken Robertson asked Percy again, 'Do you know anything about the missing girl?'

Percy said, 'No, the other police asked me. I don't know a thing. I would tell you if I knew anything. I have been sitting here just thinking and thinking.'

Robertson pressed him. 'Have you been to Warneet today?'

'I remember seeing a sign that said something about the Warneet Yacht Club,' Percy said, 'and I remember turning towards Warneet to have a look at the club.'

'What time were you in Warneet?'

'I can't remember being in Warneet.'

Robertson tried again. 'About what time did you turn off to Warneet?'

'I don't know. I am not sure. Somewhere about lunch-time.'

'Where had you been before you turned off to Warneet?'

'I left Flinders this morning and drove to Cowes just for a drive.' That was a mistake, or at worst, a lie. Percy had not returned to Flinders the previous night.

'Are you telling us that you can remember what you did before you went to Warneet and immediately after, but you can't remember actually being in Warneet?'

Percy confirmed: 'Yes sir, that's the truth.'

During the night Shane Spiller and Bill Little came to the Flinders Naval Depot and independently identified Percy's car (which was parked in a row of cars so as not to be so easily identifiable) as the one they saw at Warneet earlier that day. At about 10.45 pm Constable

Henry Huggins of Melbourne's Forensic Science Laboratory examined Percy's car. In the ashtray he found a screwed up piece of paper listing certain articles of clothing. He also noted a list of articles found in the car, including a mattress and an eiderdown quilt, a covered foam pillow and a 2-gallon petrol container. There was also a green plastic water bottle, an open packet of Clix biscuits, a packet of Swallows ginger-nut biscuits and assorted bottle tops. The contents of the glovebox had been emptied onto the passenger side front seat and there were a number of road maps, with some routes marked in texta (marker pen). Huggins also noted the type of tyres on the car—Guardian 600 L12 tyres. The following day he would go to an area on Fisheries Road near the South Gippsland Highway and match them to tyre tracks in an open paddock at Devon Meadows.

The detectives left Flinders Naval Depot at 11.15pm and took Derek Percy to Frankston CIB. After giving the accused man a meal, Detectives Dick Knight and Bernie Delaney interviewed him at 12.30am. Although he was given legal advice by a navy lawyer, Percy spoke to the detectives and admitted that he didn't sleep at Flinders the previous night but had gone to Frankston Drive-In by himself and had slept in his car at the side of the road. The following morning he bought some biscuits from a roadhouse café and drove down to Phillip Island. On the way back to Flinders he turned off the road to Warneet but he could not recall anything that happened there.

'The little girl was abducted from the beach at 12.30pm,' Knight said. 'If you drove to Warneet, you must have driven past the beach from which she was taken; what do you say to that?'

'I can't remember.'

'If you were on the road to Warneet at lunchtime and did not return to Cerberus till 4.30pm, how do you account for the time in between?'

'I can't. I can't remember', was all Percy could offer.

Knight told Percy that the little boy who had been with the

abducted girl had identified his car at Flinders Naval Depot earlier that night; another witness had seen Percy on the track at Devon Meadows later that afternoon and had also identified his car. What did he say to that?

'I can't remember,' Percy continued, 'I can't say, if I can't remember.'

Knight then left the room and returned with the red-handled knife found in Percy's car. He placed it on the table in front of Percy and then left the room again without saying a word. Detective Inspector Ford came into the room for the 'soften up'. 'How are you,' he asked Percy. 'Are you being treated alright?'

Knight returned and asked Percy about the bloodstains on the knife. Percy shook his head and looked at the floor. Knight then placed the articles confiscated from Percy's locker on the table. They included detailed drawings of nude women and children, obviously traced from ads in magazines, but with lewd, sadistic additions. 'Did you draw these? Why?' Percy said that he didn't know why. Knight then recounted the evidence mounting against the young man—two witnesses saw his car at Warneet, a bloodstained knife was found in his car and lewd drawings of children were in his possession.

Knight tried again, 'You may know something about the little girl and again I will ask you to help us find her. If she is alive she may need help.'

Percy looked at the floor for a long time and then said, 'I don't know what to do.' The detectives could sense that he wanted to talk; but was Percy merely stalling and thinking about just how much to tell them? When pressed again by Knight, Percy said, 'I can see it now ... I can remember being at the beach and I can see the two children... I was sitting in the car and then I got out and chased the girl.' He then told the detectives that the boy 'pulled out his axe and lifted it over his head.' Percy actually looked frightened at the memory of the tomahawk being waved at him. 'Not a toy one, sir,' he later exclaimed, 'a real one.' It was as if he was the victim.

❋❋❋

It was almost 2.00am and the detectives were determined to get Percy to reveal what had happened. 'Where did you take the girl?' Knight asked. After a short break Ken Robertson returned with a glass of water for the suspect and Percy finally cracked.

'I have been trying to remember,' Percy began. 'I've been trying to think what to do. I know she is dead.'

'Why do you say that?' Knight asked.

'I killed her,' he finally admitted.

Knight warned Percy that he was about to be charged with a serious offence and that he didn't have to say anything but if he did, it would be taken down as evidence. 'I know. I'm trying,' Percy stuttered. 'I will take you there. I think I remember where it is… it is not far from the beach… I can remember now.' There was a track and a clearing off Fisheries Road, Percy told the detectives, but another family was there so he told the little girl to hide under the eiderdown and took her to another spot. 'I will show you. She is there.' The detectives then made arrangements to take Percy to the area. 'I won't be cold, will I?' he asked. Knight just stared at him… there was no thought or concern by him for the missing girl.

At 3.00am three cars of detectives took Percy to a track off the Baxter-Tooradin Road at Devon Meadows. The area is known to locals as 'Fiveways' because five roads intersect the South-Gippsland Highway. Percy told the detectives to drive slowly and tyre tracks could be seen on the edge of one of the dirt roads leading off to an open paddock. Being careful not to disturb the tracks, detectives found Yvonne Tuohy's body hidden under a clump of trees just short of 40 metres away. Percy was taken back to a police vehicle so the detectives could examine the crime scene.

The body of the little girl was lying on its side, the hands tied behind the back with a length of rope. She was still wearing her two-piece gymnasium tracksuit, the top of which was rolled down around her shoulders. The victim was shoeless but was still wearing socks. A singlet, fastened by another length of rope, had been used as a gag but it was later discovered during the post-mortem examination that a face washer had been forced into her windpipe. Her throat had been cut jaggedly from left to right. A sticky substance was smeared on her chest and clumps of grass were stuck to it, indicating that at some time during the attack the victim had been naked. There was a gaping 15-inch about (38 cm) wound from the centre of the chest to the vagina, exposing most of the internal organs. The side of her face and her legs were smeared with a green-mustard coloured substance and mixed with congealed blood.

At 4.00am the detectives took Percy back to the police station at Frankston before transporting him to Melbourne's Russell Street headquarters at 5.05am. Percy ate two hamburgers for breakfast before being questioned again in one of the homicide squad offices. Now Percy took his time answering questions put to him; sometimes he shook his head and stared at the floor; on other occasions he looked at the officers but didn't speak. But the detectives waited patiently for the answers to come and when they did the accused man breathed heavily, focused on the floor with his eyes half-closed and punctuated his short sentences with long periods of silence.

Percy told detectives that he grabbed his victim 'on impulse', threatened her with a knife and forced her into the car. He also admitted that his intention was to abduct the boy as well. Once in his car he gagged his victim and tied her hands because she was panicking and kicking about. When the Payden family drove past Percy's car and observed the driver sitting high in the seat, Percy was actually sitting on top of the little girl as she lay straddled across the driver and passenger seats. Percy was not so forthcoming about details of the sexual aspects of the little girl's murder—he had obviously forced his victim to undress at some stage and had tried to manually strangle her, but he maintained that he couldn't recall any more details or the sequence of events.

Detectives became increasingly less sure that the young man was suffering from genuine forgetfulness—a form of 'hysterical amnesia' psychiatrists would later say—than deliberately feigning that he couldn't remember so as not to further incriminate himself.

Percy was becoming more confident in not answering—'Well,' he considered carefully after one question was put to him, 'I just don't remember'—before fading away into nothingness again. And they were convinced he was lying about his true motives on the day of the murder. Percy was obviously well-prepared for this abduction—he had knives and ropes to abduct his victims and bought biscuits to feed them. He even wrote down a list of clothing to bring with him overnight. Rather than acting on impulse, as he maintained, this suggested that the 20-year-old was actually 'hunting' for victims that weekend.

Later that morning, at 10.10am, Derek Ernest Percy was charged with murder. During the afternoon he re-enacted the abduction and murder of Yvonne Tuohy on film under the direction of the police. But Percy was supremely cunning; he only re-enacted aspects of the crime that he had already told detectives. He volunteered no additional information. When asked why the victim was wearing only socks, Percy indicated where he had thrown the little girl's sandshoes against a nearby fence. They were still there.

Percy, however, made no mention of one important aspect to his murder scenario. Three weeks later, detectives searching along Fisheries Road found five pairs of soiled underpants—each inside the other, as if someone had been wearing all five pairs at once—and two small sheets of plastic with a 'brown, pasty malodorous substance of human origin' on it. The underpants matched a pair found in Derek Percy's washing; detectives did not know what to make of it.

On Wednesday 23 July, Shane Spiller and his father went to Russell Street police headquarters. Taken to a room where a line-up of men had been organised, Shane was asked to identify the person who had abducted Yvonne Tuohy. 'I can see him already,' was his innocent response. As was the practice of the day, Spiller was in the same room as the man who murdered his friend—there were no two-way glass panels or video links in those days—and had to physically go up to the man, look him in the eye and point to him. Having completed the formal identification process detectives gave

Shane a show bag of gifts for his trouble and a police sketch artist drew his picture for him.[4] Bill Little was able to identify the car the accused had driven but could not identify Percy as the man he saw backing out on the track at Devon Meadows because he had not seen his face.

The murder of Yvonne Tuohy and the acts perpetrated upon her body were the worst that hardened Melbourne detectives had seen. Denise Tuohy, Yvonne's older sister, has only recently revealed that Mr Tuohy did not allow any other member of the family to attend the funeral and that Yvonne's name was not mentioned in the family home for the next 20 years—such was the family's grief.[5]

When detectives read the handwritten notes found in Percy's locker and in his car, the accused man had specifically written about abducting a male and female child, just as he had acted out at Warneet. The scenario was disturbing: 'When I get there, blindfold and strip them, tie them to tree with ropes going from behind under armpits, around behind neck and under their arms and then around a tree. Nail a stick to the tree and tape their heads to it.'

Perversely, the young man was well-spoken, intelligent and relatively 'matter-of-fact' about his crime. Another handwritten article stated: 'If it is a boy (under 3) the penis is cut off.' Russell Street detectives recalled the case of Glebe toddler Simon Brook, who was abducted and murdered in Sydney in May 1968. The similarities between the Brook and Tuohy crimes were striking—both victims had material placed in their windpipes, their carotid arteries cut and were mutilated after their deaths. Percy fantasised in another entry about pitting two children against each other in a fight to the death. He wrote, 'Death must be caused by a bite. The best place is the cargotid [*sic*] artery or the windpipe in the neck.'

Furthermore, Percy's parents lived in NSW and his car had NSW licence plates. Had he been there at the time of the Brook murder? Seven-year-old Linda Stilwell had been missing from St Kilda pier for almost a year. Was he involved in either or even both of these crimes? And how many others?

CHAPTER 4:
Incarceration

The day after he was apprehended for the murder of Yvonne Tuohy, Derek Percy was visited in his cell at the city watchhouse by his former Mt Beauty school friend Ron Anderson, who was then a probationary constable stationed at Melbourne's Homicide Squad. Anderson could not have imagined that his friend, the shy boy he had stood up for in the school playground, could have been arrested for such a terrible crime. Seeking to exploit the friendship between Anderson and Percy, detectives asked the young constable to speak to Percy and 'find out what made him tick'. Anderson's only motivation was to help his friend 'own up' to what he had done.[1]

'I had run into him earlier in the year when I visited HMAS *Cerberus*,' Ron Anderson told me in an interview for this book. Percy had aged incredibly, Anderson recalls. 'He looked at least ten years older than I remembered him.'

Inside the city watchhouse Anderson found Percy sobbing on the bed of his cell and when he entered the darkened room his friend looked up and said, 'Looks like I've fucked up this time, Ron.'

This time? All Anderson could do was to reply, 'It certainly looks like it, Derek.'

'What am I going to do, Ron?' Percy was starting to panic now. Anderson thought that somehow Percy wanted him to 'get him off' the charge. Anderson went another route.

'I really don't know what's the best thing to do, Derek. Maybe you could ask to see a doctor or psychiatrist; they may consider that you were sick at the time. I don't think they will consider this is normal anyway.'

'Would that help?' Percy asked.

'Best that I can think of, Derek.' Anderson then added, 'Were there any others, mate?'

Percy put his head in his hands and began to sob. 'I cannot remember.'

Anderson pushed him. 'If you can remember it's best to say now, [rather] than after you are released and have to serve more time. It would assist in deciding your mental health at the time.'

Percy said, 'I know, I just can't remember.'

'Well look, Derek, I'll ask you about some of the ones that I know about. You don't have to say anything. If you remember I will jot it down and it could be used in court. I will try and get it heard all at the same time.'

'I simply cannot remember.'

Anderson started to make a list in his head of recent, unsolved crimes involving young children—Stillwell, Brook, Beaumont—and took out his police notebook and wrote down Percy's responses.

'What about Linda Stilwell, she went missing in St Kilda?'

'Yes, I drove through St Kilda that day,' Percy said. 'I had been at *Cerberus* in the afternoon and was driving along the esplanade on the way to the White Ensign Club for some drinks.'

'Did you kill Linda Stilwell?'

'Possibly, I don't remember a thing about it.' But he did not deny it.

Anderson asked Percy about the murder of Simon Brook in Sydney in May 1968. Percy said that he was driving his brother to work that day in Sydney. 'We turned off at the railway cutting where [the victim] was found. I came back home that way.' Percy appeared familiar with the Glebe area where the little boy was murdered—the railway line cuts across Victoria Street and goes underground there. Simon Brook was last seen heading up toward Victoria Street on the day he disappeared.

Anderson tried to clarify the point. 'So you drove past the same spot in Sydney on the day Simon Brook was killed?'

'Yes,' Percy replied.

Anderson said: 'Do you remember if you killed him?'

'I wish I could. I might have. I just don't remember.' Again, Percy did not deny anything.

'But clearly you remember being in the area at the time?'

'Yes,' Percy said.

'What do you know about the Beaumont children in South Australia?' Anderson asked.

'I was in Adelaide at the time.'

'You were what?' Percy had placed himself at each crime scene. 'You remember being in Adelaide when they went missing?'

'Yes.'

'Whereabouts were you when they disappeared?'

'Near the beach. But nothing else.'

At that moment, the watchhouse keeper walked past and told the probationary constable that he had no business being in the accused man's cell. Anderson said he was on 'homicide squad business', but he had to leave Percy's cell and phone detectives upstairs to clarify the issue with the watchhouse keeper. When Anderson returned and tried to speak to his friend again, Percy's demeanour had changed—it was like a curtain had descended over him. Perhaps Percy no longer saw his former school mate as a friend but someone who was working for the police. Yet, Ron Anderson believes to this day that if he'd been left alone to talk to Percy he may have confessed to all three crimes.

The hurried conversation between two former friends was not taped by police or written down verbatim. Notes based on Percy's responses to these unsolved crimes were scribbled down by Anderson in his police notebook and even though this was handed to the police it was later lost. The only record of Anderson's discussion with Percy was a reference to Anderson's police ID number, which was recorded in the Tuohy case file and not found for another 35 years.

Ron Anderson took two other former Mt Beauty schoolmates, Kim White and Bill Hutton who were waiting in another room, to speak to detectives about the 'gorge incident' but the Homicide Squad felt that there was no need to interview them—they had their man and he was going to be locked away for a very long time. Any sympathy Anderson may have felt for Percy disappeared that night when he was confronted by the crime-scene photos of the murder of Yvonne Tuohy. Anderson remembers telling White and Hutton, 'They'll hang the bastard.'

⊠⊠⊠

As the 1960s drew to a close capital punishment was still 'on the books' in Victoria—it had only been two years since Ronald Ryan was hanged for killing a prison warder in a daring escape from Pentridge gaol. Such was the horrific nature of the abduction and murder of 12-year old Yvonne Tuohy—possibly the most shocking and callous murder of a child in Victorian criminal history—

Melbourne detectives who worked on the original investigation believed the state's 'pro-capital punishment Premier', Sir Henry Bolte, would have considered executing Derek Percy if he was found guilty of murder. If Percy did not hang for this crime, they believed, it would have been the end of the death penalty in Victoria.

Derek Percy stood trial for the murder of Yvonne Tuohy in the Melbourne Supreme Court on Thursday 2 April 1970 before Justice Pape.[2] The trial was conducted in front of a jury but the only matter for consideration was the 'issue of sanity or otherwise of the accused at the time of the incident in July'.[3] The mountain of evidence against Percy and his signed confession on the day after the murder, meant that there was no possible defence to the charge except on that sole point—was Derek Percy not guilty by reason of insanity?

Graham Berkovitch, Percy's solicitor, had found the young sailor 'quiet and uncommunicative', making his defence that much more difficult, but realistically, Derek Percy was never going to take the witness stand. Before the trial began, Percy's counsel, the distinguished George Hampel, had no objection to the judge's ruling that the Crown's witnesses could be 'led' throughout the trial. Normally, counsel are not allowed to lead the witness—to put questions to a witness in a form that suggests the answer—but this was waved in order to get to the crux of the case. Was the now 21-year-old former naval rating insane either before or at the moment he murdered Yvonne Tuohy?

The court was told of certain undisputed admissions—Percy had attempted to abduct two children from Warneet; he grabbed 12-year-old Yvonne Tuohy and took her to a remote area and then killed her. The jury were informed of the sequence of events that led to Percy's capture—Shane Spiller, Bill Little and several detectives and constables who worked on the case and interviewed Percy also gave evidence. The Tuohy family was thankfully spared the trauma of giving evidence but the court heard distressing details of the shocking crime. Forensic pathologist Dr James McNamara stated that the little girl had died as a result of 'asphyxiation and lacerations' but was alive when her throat was slashed. The cut to the stomach had been conducted post mortem and although there was a slight bruise in the lower right quadrant of the vaginal canal, there was no sign of rape. Semen and human excreta, however, were smeared on the victim's body.

Dr Allen Bartholomew, the Psychiatrist Superintendent in the Department of Mental Hygiene at Pentridge Gaol, examined Derek Percy in July 1969 as a matter of routine when he was first detained. Dr Bartholomew also had access to crime scene photographs, Percy's handwritten notes and drawings, the various records of interviews and all written and signed statements relating to the investigation. He was later asked by the Crown to assess Percy in regard to his fitness to plead at his trial. Percy was given a psychological test, investigated 'electro-encephalogically'—the recording of brain waves—and even given a karyotype test to determine any chromosome abnormality,[4] but none of the information gained gave any insight into his psychological condition.

Dr Bartholomew stated that he had no previous experience of a person with Percy's unique sexual condition, which was described as 'sadistic paedophilia' and as the chief psychiatrist attached to Pentridge he had reviewed more than 1500 cases in Victoria. He could not speculate upon the cause of Percy's apparent 'disease of the mind'—there was no evidence of head injury, alcoholism or drug addiction. Percy did not volunteer one word more than was absolutely necessary in his interaction with the psychiatrist; in fact, he did not tell him too much more than was already in his record of interview with the detectives. Dr Bartholomew did, however, comment on Percy's 'extraordinarily flat emotional state and coldness'.

Reviewing Percy's childhood history Dr Bartholomew stated that there was nothing of any particular relevance that might give an indication of his current mental state until the age of 16–17 years when he began 'generating violent sexual scenarios' involving children and wrote these down in his diaries and notebooks. There followed two instances of sexual deviance while he was still at school—the 'gorge incident' at Mt Beauty in the summer of 1964–65 and the assault on two children in a caravan at Khancoban in 1966, but because he had never been treated for any psychological condition, nothing was documented apart from anecdotal evidence from family and friends. Percy acknowledged these incidents because there were witnesses—and his parents knew about them—and the doctors were bound to find out about them but he did not disclose any other matters.

Three psychiatrists testified during Percy's trial that he suffered from an 'acute psycho-sexual disorder'. Although Percy maintained that he was sitting in his car on the day he abducted Yvonne Tuohy and was suddenly overcome by a feeling—'almost a compulsion' he said—to murder a child, he admitted that he had this thought on many occasions over the previous four years. 'It might be once per week when he was not busily occupied,' Dr Bartholomew reported, 'but [these] thoughts would dominate his mind of having intercourse, humiliating and killing children—both male and female.'

Dr Bartholomew was of the opinion that Percy suffered from 'hysterical repressive mechanism'—a condition that explained why the young man might have been unable to remember the murder when first interviewed by police. Dr Bartholomew explained that memories may be repressed when 'something causes acute pain or embarrassment or demeans him in the face of others'. This is different to merely stating 'I don't remember'—it is a state of mind that 'represses, buries recollections that are totally abhorrent and unpleasant to others'. Dr Bartholomew further maintained that if Percy had not been found by the police for another week, instead of on the night of the murder, he could have repressed all knowledge of the crime, not deliberately, but be unable to recall the crime at all. Dr Bartholomew conceded, however, that at times Percy deliberately chose not to provide information because the facts were 'too horrible' to talk about.

One of the three doctors who observed Percy, Dr Richard Ball, told the court that sexual deviants can be placed into two groups. In the first group, the act is satisfying—such as exhibitionism, in which the act of exposing oneself is the sexual satisfying activity. In the second, smaller group the act is not satisfying. In this group there is a tendency toward inner conflict and the acts of deviancy escalate. Initially, Percy would have had a degree of self-control in dealing with his fantasy life but as time passed and he became increasingly independent of his family, his self-control decreased.

There were elements of voyeurism in Percy's teenage behaviour—he fixated upon naked images, for example when he was the 'peeping tom' at Khancoban and he stripped naked his victims in the caravan. There was also transvestitism—Percy wore women's clothing at the gorge at Mt Beauty, stole women's underpants from clothes lines and wrote about his fascination with knickers in his diaries. Although he never admitted it, psychiatrists believed Percy stole the underpants to wear them, but he also slashed them with a knife and fantasised about forcing children to urinate, defecate and finally bleed in them.

Percy had both the potential and the predisposition to act out his violent fantasies during the four years (the time that he was known to be writing the fantasies) before he was captured in 1969. In fact, Percy's writings indicated a strong probability of 'progression' in acting out his fantasies. In the summer of 1964–65, Percy was acting out some sort of fantasy during the 'gorge incident' in Mt Beauty and within months of moving to Khancoban in 1966 he had quickly involved other children in his fantasies. In 1967, while living in Newcastle, he was fervently writing about the abduction, mutilation and murder of young children. It wouldn't be long before he was acting out these gross fantasies—or perhaps, he already had.

Belatedly, Derek Percy provided Dr Bartholomew with an important insight into his psychological condition while waiting in a holding cell attached to the Supreme Court on the first day of his trial. Driving back from Cowes on the day of the murder, Percy told Bartholomew, he put on five pairs of underpants. He then deliberately defecated in his pants and had an erection. This had happened on previous occasions, Percy said, and he knew that defecating in his pants was associated with sexual gratification. That is why he brought the extra underpants with him on his 'hunting' trip that weekend. Once sexually aroused, he admitted to Bartholomew, 'I think I was probably off my head when I saw the kids.'

Derek Percy was a coprophiliac. In psychiatric terms coprophilia is defined as 'a morbid attraction to, and interest in (with a sexual element), faecal matter'.[5] However, Dr Whittaker knew of no psychiatric term where a person suffering from the condition forces it upon another person. Percy admitted that his writings and drawings provided him with a form of 'sexual gratification' but at the onset of puberty while still at school, he began wearing plastic underpants so that he could deliberately defecate and become sexually aroused. The smearing of faeces on his victim was an extension of perverse sexual fantasies.

Dr Richard Ball, wrote of Percy: 'The smearing with faeces is to me an expression of a tremendous degree of emotional disturbance.' Dr Ball believed that this was proof that Percy had lost his ability to reason; he lost control and composure after abducting Yvonne Tuohy and killed her while in 'a prolonged and orgastic state'.

Percy showed his lack of personal insight when he told his doctors that growing up he was 'different from other boys but not that much'. At no time did he ask or was taken to see a specialist about his 'little differences'—his highly sexualised 'jottings', his deviant sexual interest in children and his 'excretory satisfaction'. His writings were also dotted with references to 'uro-genitalia' sadism. In one piece Percy wrote about forcing children to eat laxatives and filling them up with beer so that they physically suffer a rupture of the bladder. Dr Whittaker remarked, 'I don't know what they call that in psychiatry… [it's] so rare nobody has bothered to put a name to it.'

Percy was adamant, however, that he had not hurt any children before 1969. Defence psychiatrist Dr Howard Whittaker argued that Percy had 'many psycho-sexual abnormalities' and it was 'difficult to believe that he had not killed other children'. In Percy's mind, as evidenced by his writings and his actions, 'killing is the ultimate sexual act… this man's instinct is expressed through destruction'.

Of particular concern to Percy's 'insanity' defence was the very clear evidence that he did not 'instinctively' or 'impulsively' kill Yvonne Tuohy after abducting her from the beach as he had maintained. Dr Bartholomew stated that 'notes seized from Mr Percy's car after the killing of the young girl disclosed that her abduction and death were not spontaneous events, but occurred very much as the notes anticipated.' Percy hid the little girl under the eiderdown in his car so that she would not be discovered and when he was disturbed by another family during his first attempt to molest her, he drove his victim to a more secluded location. After he killed her, he hid the body behind some bushes.

'Why did you find it necessary to kill the girl?' Bartholomew had asked Percy in one interview.

'Just panic I suppose. I thought if she got away she would tell on me.' The words 'I suppose' gave Bartholomew the indication that Percy was searching for a reason. The fear that she would 'tell on me' shows the absence of personal insight and his retarded emotional maturity. The real reason he killed Yvonne Tuohy is that Percy obtained sexual satisfaction from killing her, although he could never openly admit that.

'You knew what you were doing was wrong?' Dr Bartholomew asked, to which Percy responded affirmatively.

But the three psychiatrists argued that while Percy immediately realised after the murder that what he had done was wrong, he could not reason during the actual murder. Dr Bartholomew stated that, 'it is appropriate to say that there was overt evidence at this point of a gross mental disturbance which, in fact, is of such a degree that I think it proper to call it a mental illness. I think perhaps one should make a point to clarify matters, that like many things in psychiatry, and also, I imagine in medicine, you are not either normal or abnormal, like turning on a light. The whole business is a continuum.'

In this way, Percy could appear 'a normal chap'—in Dr Bartholomew's words—but still be quite ill. Even though he drove his victim to a second spot when he was interrupted—a rational act in the circumstances—Dr Bartholomew argued that events were hurtling toward a tragic outcome that Percy had already constructed in his head, fantasised about and even written down in his diaries. As Dr Bartholomew explained to the jury, 'I suppose one could argue he could reason about [the crime], but only as an insane man can reason about it.'

It was almost a Catch 22 situation in reverse—Percy had to be insane because only an insane man could have committed this crime against an innocent little girl. Justice Pape also had 'great difficulty' in instructing a lay jury to pass judgment on Percy's sanity, remarking that they 'tend to evaluate the actions and thoughts of a man who is suffering a disease of the mind on the basis that he is a sane man'.

Justice Pape instructed the jury not to be so concerned with 'medical terms' or even 'laymen terms' of insanity, but whether Derek Percy suffered from 'a disease of the mind' which produces 'certain results and disabilities'. The jury had to be sure beyond a reasonable doubt that 'the act that resulted in death was a voluntary or a conscious act on [Percy's] part'. Interestingly, the Crown called no witnesses to rebut the evidence of the three psychiatrists called by Percy's defence counsel. The issue was moot.

After a six-day trial Derek Percy was found not guilty on the grounds of insanity and on 9 April 1970, Justice Pape, pursuant to Section 420 of the Crimes Act (1958), ordered that Percy be kept in 'safe custody until the governor's pleasure was known'. On 10 May 1970 the Governor made known his pleasure, that Percy be confined in custody for an indefinite period. The relatives of

Yvonne Tuohy and Shane Spiller and his family were assured that he would never be released back into the community.

※※※

Throughout his trial, Percy was supported by his mother while his father, who continued to run the family business in Wallsend, made occasional trips to Melbourne. His parents visited their son every year, but after retiring to Queensland the frequency of their visits diminished over time. Mrs Percy maintained regular contact with her eldest son over the ensuing years, especially after her husband died in the 1990s. Percy's younger brother, who was still a teenager when the 20-year-old was apprehended in 1969, told detectives that he had heard about the murder from his mother but 'didn't want to know any of the details'. It was his way of coping with the enormity of what his eldest brother had done. The two brothers, who had not been particularly close at school, corresponded for a time and played long distance chess by mail but then drifted apart. Percy's youngest brother has had no contact with him.

Percy, who described himself as 'a loner, not lonely',[6] was a model prisoner. Throughout his incarceration, which in the first ten years was in 'G' Division at Pentridge gaol—a division that had psychiatric services—Percy received little to no treatment. He showed no inclination to be involved in any rehabilitation program, although it must be said that no existing program would have been suitable to treat his unique psychiatric condition. Dr Bartholomew hoped, over time, to learn more about Derek Percy. 'At present one can only wait and observe, and later attempt to further investigate the prisoner. I hope that he may be allowed to remain in 'G' Division for the next few years—he is a rare and interesting case.'

A routine search of his cell on 28 September 1971, however, found that Percy had hidden 'comprehensive notes describing even more horrific fantasies concerning the abduction, imprisonment, torture, rape and killing of children'.[7] Percy had also constructed a complex chart, with first names given to his proposed victims, in which he outlined 'a pattern of activity' involving the rape, torture and killing of the named children that would take place over many years. 'Among the first names of children referred to in these 1971 notes,' forensic psychiatrist Dr Ruth Vine revealed, 'were some names that coincided with those of children of a family known to him, which he had occasionally visited at the time of his arrest.'

'Go down below the lake and meet her on way,' Percy wrote. 'Tell her my car is bogged down there and I want help. Get her in car and take her to place.' Having watched the movements of the younger sisters of a friend at Mt Beauty, Percy was going to park and wait for one or both to return from basketball or church and lure them into his car.[8]

Percy claimed that he compiled the material at the request of a psychiatrist who had asked him to write down his fantasies for 'therapeutic purposes'. Whether this was true or not, the fact remains that the work was solely the product of Percy's sick imagination and the notes and collage demonstrated that he was still a very dangerous man. Dr Bartholomew observed that 'the prisoner was behaving in a manner very similar to the year or more prior to the killing with which he was charged: apparently normal behaviour to the ordinary onlooker, but a grossly disturbed sexual fantasy life.'

Dr Bartholomew spent the best past of the next two decades observing Derek Percy. In April 1975 he wrote of Percy: 'He is efficient, undemonstrative, quiet, and never forms a relationship with anybody. He is the nearest thing to a robot I have met. I have to say that I can think of no valuable indices for release, and tend to wonder whether any really exist other than old age and or gross physical disability.'[9]

Outwardly, Percy functioned effectively, as this parole report shows:

NAME: PERCEY [*sic*], Derek Ernest
PRISON: 'O' Division Pentridge

> DATE: 23.5.75
> Percy has been in custody now for just over five years... He has undertaken a number of correspondence courses; he keeps himself fit by playing tennis and table tennis, he operates the 'G' Division radio receiver; and has learnt to play the guitar, play chess and makes miniature sailing ships of high quality. In general he is a 'model' prisoner and consistently receives excellent reports for conduct and industry... He continues to be employed as a writer in 'G' Division and is obviously highly regarded by staff for his efficiency and the role that he fulfils in assisting the division function. The chief Prison Officer said, 'Derek would be a difficult man to replace'.[10]

Richard Ball, now a professor of psychiatry, re-interviewed Percy in January 1977. 'He volunteered nothing, and extracting information was like pulling teeth. I doubt that he is entirely without sadist fantasies.' A decade later Professor Ball added: 'I think this man has always been very secretive about his fantasies and his actions. It is very clear of, course, that for many years prior to his apprehension he had successfully hidden these from public scrutiny, even when living in a communal setting such as the navy... In a formal sense I suppose he could be regarded as without psychiatric illness. I think he must be regarded as having an abnormal personality with major sexual deviation and I cannot assure myself that this has changed for the better.'

In 1984, Dr Stephens, the Pentridge co-ordinator of forensic services, reported that Percy 'said that he has matured a lot in his years in prison but was not able to offer more'. Dr Stephens warned that Percy had 'a dangerously abnormal personality, but [is] not mentally sick in the accepted sense. He is not certifiable, neither is he psychiatrically treatable and he is totally unsuited to a mental institution. If Percy is ever so transferred, he will, in all probability, earn some degree of freedom as the result of reasonable and conforming behaviour. The consequences of such freedom could well prove tragic.'

Psychological testing conducted in 1988 could not determine if Percy was still experiencing his grossly abnormal sexual fantasies, but given his lack of cooperation and the limitations of the tests, it was doubtful that this could be established anyway. Dr Christopher Drake, the author of the parole report based on the psychological testing, stated that Percy appeared to have 'limited insight into his offence' and demonstrated 'a reluctance to accept responsibility for the killing' of Yvonne Tuohy.[11]

As he became increasingly institutionalised, Percy developed 'well-rehearsed responses' and so prison psychiatrists tried new ways of 'drawing him' out. In 1991 Professor Ball attempted to take a different approach. 'Why do you think society takes such a dim view of people murdering children?' he asked.

Percy laughed, 'Why, there would be nobody left, would there?'

Two years later, Professor Ball put Percy under emotional pressure by bringing up the details of the torture and murder of Yvonne Tuohy. Percy said he did not think about it and callously added that his victim could have been 'hit by a bus a week later and died'.

'He did not appear distressed in any way,' Professor Ball observed, 'and there was no evidence of sweating, raised pulse rate, his respiratory rate remained unchanged, his colour was no different, his eye contact remained exactly the same. I might simply have been talking about the kinds of cheese that one eats.'

But psychiatrists over the years—and Percy was formally interviewed 17 times by ten different doctors between 1971 and 1993—finally agreed that despite the jury's finding in 1970, Derek Percy was 'clearly abnormal' but 'not insane'. In 1993 Professor Paul Mullen wrote of Percy: 'The wisdom or otherwise of the court's finding in Mr Percy's case may be open to question, but it is not open to modification.'

Percy's record in prison was largely uneventful—he was fined $60 in November 1995 when he was found to have too many educational tapes in his cell. However, in 1988 he was stabbed in the chest by another prisoner who wrongly believed Percy had murdered his niece. While he did not make any 'friends' in prison, Percy allegedly liked the company of a volunteer Salvation Army officer who visited him regularly in Ararat Prison but had retired, as had prison officers and psychiatrists over the course of thirty years. He also outlasted three of the gaols in which he was an inmate—Beechworth, Castlemaine and finally Pentridge all closed over time.

Having moved to Ararat Prison, Percy spent his time working in the silk workshop, compiling cricket statistics on computer, building model boats and reading. Percy was the prison chess champion and despite being a heavy smoker, he was a more than capable tennis player. He also liked carpet bowls and organised intra-prison competitions. 'He's highly intelligent but you could never get a real handle on what he was thinking,' stated one prison officer who spent ten years guarding him.[12]

Each year between 1990 and 1997, Percy's ongoing incarceration was reviewed by the Adult Parole Board. Records disclose that Percy continually expressed his 'keenness' to be transferred to the Forensic Mental Health Centre at Mont Park (now known as the Rosanna Forensic Psychiatry Centre) and talked about his 'willingness' to cooperate with doctors in discussing his problems so as to facilitate treatment. Percy was clearly intelligent and his main objective in seeking a transfer to a mental hospital was not for treatment, his doctors believed, but for eventual release. Doctors noted that the majority of patients at the Rosanna/Mont Park facility had 'reasonable prospects' of being granted extended leave.[13]

The lack of any alternative secure facility, however, coupled with Percy's reluctance to be involved in any real exploration of his mental state, led the Adult Parole Board not to recommend that he be transferred from prison to a psychiatric unit. The assertion that he would, if transferred, cooperate with treatment programs had to be weighed against the fact that he had not been open in his conversations with mental health professionals in the past.

In short, Percy's 'rather modest indication' of his interest in treatment was taken 'at face value' by his doctors.[14]

In 1997, however, a change to the Crimes (Mental Impairment and Unfitness to be Tried) Act meant that all 46 'governor's pleasure' detainees in the Victorian prison system would have their cases reviewed by the Supreme Court. The court sought to determine if these 'forensic clients' were still under the influence of their mental illness and if or not they presented a serious danger to the safety of the public. If not they would be released under a 'non-custodial supervision order' and integrated back into the community.

By the time Derek Percy's custodial supervision order came up for review in late 1998, he was the only person who, having been made the subject of a 'governor's pleasure' order, still remained in prison in Victoria. Already, the media was linking him to the Wanda Beach murders (1965), the disappearance of the Beaumont children (1966), the murder of Allen Redston (1966), the abduction–murder of Simon Brook (1968) and the disappearance of Linda Stilwell (1968).

CHAPTER 5: The Wanda Beach Murders

In the summer of 1964–65 the national moth class regatta was held at Botany Bay Yacht Club—several kilometres northwest of Wanda Beach. Did Derek Percy travel to Sydney that Christmas and stay with his grandmother so that he could attend the yachting championships? Members of the Percy family do not remember being in Sydney that January—either as a family or Derek by himself—nor do they recall the moth class championships holding any special significance for them that year.[1] But a Corryong High classmate has a different recollection.

Wayne Gordes[2] had befriended Derek Percy's younger brother in late 1965 when the family moved to Khancoban in southern New South Wales. After Derek rejoined the family, both Percy brothers were in the fifth form completing their leaving certificate. 'Derek and his brother both stayed at my place during the year,' Gordes recalls. 'I was closer to Derek's younger brother, but his parents went away one weekend and both boys stayed at my house. Derek was different—a loner—he didn't want to mix with anyone.'

Although it was more than 12 months after the Wanda Beach murders Wayne Gordes decided to tease Derek after he noticed a 'resemblance' to the description of the chief suspect in the then-unsolved Wanda Beach murders. 'I jokingly thought to myself "That's Derek", because of the description and I knew that they went to a beach in Sydney,' Gordes says. 'A group of us were standing in the quadrangle when Derek Percy walked past. I said, "We know it was you that killed those girls in Sydney. You have the same haircut and we know you were there." With that Derek went berserk,' Gordes recalled. 'He said, "Don't you say that"… I think he wanted to fight me for what I had said. I had never seen Derek behave like that before. He was off his brain.'

It was 'stupid schoolboy stuff', Wayne Gordes admits, and he forgot all about the incident until early 1970 when he was living in Sydney. Gordes bought a copy of the Melbourne *Herald Sun* at Central Station and read that Derek Percy was to stand trial for murdering a little girl. Gordes was shocked: 'Derek had stayed at my house and I had a little 3-year-old sister at the time. That worried me.' It may have been nothing, but he decided to contact Sydney detectives who were still investigating the unsolved murders of Christine Sharrock and Marianne Schmidt at Wanda Beach more than five years before and tell them of the 'playground' incident involving Percy.

Sydney detectives took a statement from Gordes and added it to the Wanda investigation running sheet that by then numbered more than 80,000 pages.

✻✻✻

In the early afternoon of Tuesday 12 January 1965, teenager Peter Smith took his three young nephews for a walk along the sandhills north of Sydney's famous Cronulla Beach.[3] Smith, from the New South Wales Central Coast, was staying with his married sister at nearby Caringbah while he looked for work over the summer school holidays. The teenager took the young boys more than 2 kilometres past the Wanda Beach Surf Club before he turned around and headed back toward Cronulla. Smith carried his youngest nephew in his arms as he walked behind the first row of sandhills, about 150 metres from the water's edge. The other boys, aged 8 and 7, raced ahead of him, running in and out of the dunes.

About 2 kilometres north of Wanda Beach, as one of his nephews stopped in the hollow between two sandhills, Peter Smith saw what he originally thought to be a store mannequin partially buried in the sand. As he moved closer, he could see feet sticking out of a mound of sand, an elbow and a partially exposed forehead. Smith slowly scraped away some of the sand around the head and realised it was the body of a young woman. He quickly gathered his three nephews and ran back toward the Wanda Beach clubhouse and raised the alarm. When local detectives arrived at the clubhouse the teenager led them to the crime scene. On closer inspection detectives soon realised that there were two victims in the makeshift grave. The sand had been merely piled over the victims, rather than being dug into the hollow of the two dunes, and the wind had partially exposed the bodies of two young girls.

The victims were quickly identified as 15-year-old neighbours—Christine Sharrock and Marianne Schmidt of Brush Road, West Ryde, in western Sydney. The previous day, the girls had taken Marianne's four younger siblings—Peter, Trixie, Wolfgang and Norbert Schmidt—to Cronulla Beach by train. During the afternoon the older girls led the children on a walk through the Wanda sandhills. Some distance north of the Wanda Beach clubhouse, Christine and Marianne left the children sheltering behind a sand dune and continued into the hills. After several hours had passed, and with Christine and Marianne failing to return to the spot where they had left them, the younger Schmidt children went back to Cronulla Beach and collected their belongings before catching the last train back to West Ryde. The Schmidt children arrived home at about 8.00 pm and police were quickly contacted. At this stage Christine and Marianne had only been reported as missing—the full horror of what happened to them in the Wanda sandhills that afternoon was not discovered until the following day.

The body of Marianne Schmidt was lying on her right side in a semi-foetal position, her left leg bent at the knee at a right angle to her body. Christine Sharrock was lying face down in the sand, her right arm bent at the elbow, her forearm close to her face as if shielding it. The bodies were in line with each other, with Christine's head touching the soles of Marianne's feet. Christine had been stabbed multiple times and her eyes were blackened by a vicious blow to her head. The killer then attempted to rape her, despite the fact that she was menstruating—her sanitary belt and napkin had been removed with her shorts and shoved into her crotch area. Just as shocking, Marianne's throat had been cut and there were signs of multiple stabs wounds and an obvious attempt to rape her. Her swimming costume had been cut down the side and rolled up around her breasts exposing the lower half of her body.

Detectives noted a drag mark—about 34 metres long—extending north in the sand and down an incline into a gully between two sand dunes. Blood was found in the sand and on grass stalks along the drag mark and it appeared that Christine had been dragged toward the grave. Police theorised that at some point Christine had run away from her killer, most likely as Marianne lay dead or wounded, but had been overtaken and hit on the head with a piece of pipe, rock or wood, subdued with a blow to the jaw and repeatedly stabbed in the back. Although it was not possible to determine the order of her injuries, post mortem results confirmed that the killer had fractured Christine's skull.

'At intervals of about 10 ft [3 metres] along the drag marks,' wrote one police report, 'there were heavier concentrations of blood, consistent with the person who dragged the body up the slope having paused at these positions.' Christine Sharrock was a petite girl, only 160 centimetres and barely 55 kilograms—the killer may not have been significantly bigger or stronger than his victim if he struggled in the sand with her body.

Forensic pathologists found scratch marks on the inside of the thighs of each victim and the presence of spermatozoa on Marianne's body (although rape had been attempted both girls died with their hymens intact). It was also ascertained that the girls had died within half an hour of each other, but the hot sand had delayed the onset of rigor mortis and it was difficult to determine the exact time of death. All police would say was that the victims had died between 2.00 pm and midnight on 11 January. An examination of the contents of Christine's stomach detected only vegetable matter, such as a 'Chinese meal'—which is not what the other children had eaten for lunch—while Marianne's stomach was empty. Interestingly, Christine had a blood alcohol level of 0.015 in her system—enough to have consumed a large glass of beer. The professional opinion was that the alcohol had been consumed orally and was not just a case of the vegetable matter fermenting.

That revelation in itself was extraordinary—had Christine shared part of a meal and some beer with her killer? This information went against everything that was known about the quiet Catholic teenager who had recently left school to start work, and her shy, intelligent German immigrant friend who lived next door.

Christine Sharrock and Marianne Schmidt were inseparable in life and in death. Christine had opted to live with her grandparents, Jim and Jeanette Taig, in West Ryde after the death of her father and the remarriage of her mother. In March 1963, the Schmidt family moved into the modest war service home next door. Helmut and Elizabeth Schmidt had arrived from Germany as part of Australia's postwar 'assisted passage' immigration program with their six children—Helmut, the eldest, followed by Marianne, Hans, Peter, Trixie and Wolfgang (a seventh child, Norbert, was born in Australia). The family had lived in Unanderra and Temora migrant hostels before moving to Sydney when Mr Schmidt contracted Hodgkin's disease—a form of cancer that attacks the lymph glands—which ultimately claimed his life in June 1964. Christine and Marianne, whose birthdays were separated by only a few weeks, shared a love of pop music, an innocent attraction to boys their own age and a special bond in each having lost their fathers at a young age.

In January 1965, Marianne's mother was convalescing in King George V Hospital at Camperdown after undergoing a major operation. Mrs Schmidt's eldest son Helmut, then 16 and an apprentice with New South Wales Railways, and Marianne looked after the children while she recovered. On Saturday 9 January, Marianne took her friend Christine to visit Mrs Schmidt in hospital. While they were there they asked Mrs Schmidt if they could take the younger children to Cronulla Beach on the following Sunday. Cronulla had been a favourite picnic destination for the Schmidt family when their father was alive and Christine and Marianne had spent New Year's Day there. Helmut and Hans Schmidt had taken the family there again the following day (2 January) but Christine, who was feeling the effects of sunburn, did not go on that day.

Mrs Schmidt allowed the two girls to take the children to Cronulla but it rained on Sunday and the children decided to go to the beach the following day—Monday 11 January. The eldest

Schmidt boys, however, stayed home that day—Helmut to paint the kitchen and Hans to mow the lawn—and Marianne and her friend Christine took the younger children to the beach. As she packed for the journey to Cronulla, Christine Sharrock remarked to her grandmother that it would be 'fun to walk across the sandhills again'.

'Don't go today, love,' Christine's grandmother 'Nan' Taig told her. 'You have got the four little ones with you; it's too far.' Christine and Marianne must have walked across the dunes behind Wanda Beach on New Year's Day and the lure of the sandhills would ultimately prove too strong.

Christine Sharrock packed a thermos of cold lime-green cordial inside a white and gold beach bag along with a red and white towel, a plastic purse containing a £1 note, a pair of sunglasses and a transistor radio. She did not take any food with her; Marianne made marmite, tomato and cucumber sandwiches for them to eat, and took along some fruit as well. Christine did not wear a swimming costume because she was menstruating and did not intend to swim. Shortly before 8.30 am Christine, Marianne and the four youngest Schmidt children walked to the bottom of Brush Road and on to Victoria Road to catch the bus to West Ryde railway station. When a bus did not arrive they walked to the station, caught a train to Redfern and changed platforms for the trip to Cronulla.

The party of six arrived at Cronulla some time before 11.00 am. They then walked through Munro Park, past the life-saving club and onto the path that led to the surf beach and found that Cronulla Beach was closed because of dangerous seas whipped up by the weekend weather conditions. The older girls led the younger children to the southern end of the beach where they left their belongings on the rocks. Seven-year-old Wolfgang was determined to go for a swim so Marianne took him to a shallow end of the beach away from rocks. After a quick dip, the group shared the sandwiches and fruit they brought with them before Marianne suggested that they walk to the sandhills past Wanda Beach. The children hid their beach bags behind some rocks at South Cronulla and walked along the promenade to the North Cronulla Beach and down onto the sand past the unpatrolled Elouera Beach.

At about 1.00 pm, some 200 metres past the Wanda Beach Surf Club, the younger children complained that the wind was whipping up the sand and stinging their legs. Wolfgang found a place between two dunes where the children could shelter and the older girls covered the younger children with their towels and gave them Christine's transistor radio to keep them company. It was assumed that Marianne and Christine would return to the southern end of the beach and retrieve their belongings for the trip home. Inexplicably, the teenage girls headed in a northerly direction toward Kurnell. The boys called out to them that they were going in the wrong direction but Christine and Marianne 'just laughed' and headed off over the dunes.

It is not clear why the older girls persisted in their desire to walk further into the sandhills. Detectives have long speculated that they may have arranged to meet someone there that afternoon but none of the younger children were privy to these plans. What the teenage girls also didn't realise was that the Wanda sandhills were a well-known haunt for 'nudists, male perverts and exhibitionists' and the dunes allowed anonymity for casual sex at a time when homosexual acts were still a crime. Cars could be parked behind the sandhills on nearby Captain Cook Drive, which allowed easy access to the isolated area via a number of bush trails, and potentially provided a quick getaway. It may have just been a spur of the moment decision by the girls to head off on their own for a while but it was a decision that ultimately cost them their lives.

On the afternoon after the bodies of the victims were discovered, detectives from Cronulla Police Station travelled to Brush Road to obtain a more detailed description of what the girls were wearing when they disappeared. Marianne's black, one-piece swimming costume with white lace front and multi-coloured sleeveless blouse; Christine's green and white patterned sleeveless blouse, white brassiere and white shorts, confirmed the identity of the two victims but it was Christine's uncle, Les Taig, who was given the task of formally identifying the bodies. The Schmidt children still did not know that the girls were dead. Mrs Schmidt was released from hospital for the afternoon on 13 January to tell them the grim news.

But it was while one of the detectives questioned the Schmidt children that afternoon that 7-year-old Wolfgang revealed that he had seen the teenage girls walking into the sandhills with an unknown youth. When the girls were about 36 metres away from the younger children, Wolfgang said that they were joined by a 'fat boy' who was asking them to tell him their names. The youth was described as being of high school age 'like my brothers'; with fair hair and an 'unshaved' face. He was wearing light grey trousers and carrying a towel.

And so the chief suspect—a blond teenage 'surfie' type—was cast in the media from the outset. Thousands of teenagers immediately became suspects and the police were swamped with leads, theories and erroneous information.

In the conservative 1960s, news that two Sydney schoolgirls had been raped, mutilated and buried on a popular Sydney beach shocked and outraged Australia, and realised parents' worst fears. New South Wales Police Commissioner Norm Allen made an appeal for public assistance to solve the case. A record £10,000 (approximately $20,000) reward was offered for information leading to the arrest of the person or persons responsible. That reward is still in existence.

On 13 January detectives took Peter, Trixie and Wolfgang Schmidt back to Cronulla Beach and retraced the steps the children took on the fatal day. Slowly the final movements of the two victims became a little clearer and with increased media coverage many people on the beach came forward to offer information. Dennis Dostine, a local fireman, was walking south toward Wanda Beach with his 5-year-old son when he noticed two girls walking between the sandhills, about 200 metres inland from where he was walking at the water's edge. It was about 12.45 in the afternoon, 600 metres from the Wanda Beach Surf Club and about 400 metres south of the eventual murder scene. The girls, who matched the general appearance of Christine and Marianne, were walking alone in a northerly direction. Dostine noted that one of the girls was looking behind her, as if being followed, and they were walking at a fast pace, but he did not see any other person near the girls. This was the last official sighting of the two victims.

Dostine also told police of several other people he had noticed along the beach that day—two separate groups of horseback riders; a 19-year-old man—tall, wearing khaki shorts and white short-sleeved shirt; an older 'leathery' man—shorter, wearing black briefs; a man and a woman fishing; and a group of youths sliding in the sandhills. Although the girls riding horses were identified, the two men who were heading in a northerly direction never came forward. The pairs of young girls riding horses told police that they had separately seen several strangers on the beach as they rode back toward Wanda that afternoon—a naked man, aged about 35 to 40 with dark hair and sunglasses, carrying a bundle of clothing and walking between the dunes 400 metres north of the murder scene at about 1.00 pm. They also sighted a man wearing grey trousers and a bright coloured shirt surveying the dunes about 400 metres south of the murder scene at about 3.45 pm.

But little Wolfgang's statements bothered investigators—the young boy's recollections seemed to change every time he was questioned. First he said that the 'fat boy' was walking into the sandhills with his sister and her friend. Two days later he told detectives that it was the same boy the family saw on the beach earlier in the day hunting for crabs with a homemade spear. Christine and Marianne had spoken to this boy just before the group ventured into the sandhills. A month later Wolfgang added that the boy had a knife in a sheath around his waist; and he said that when he saw the boy walking back along the sandhills about ten minutes after the girls had disappeared the knife was missing. Further, he claimed that the 'fat boy' had light brown hair the same colour as Christine's—not blond, as was originally reported in the media. Wolfgang had even spoken to the youth as he walked back alone between the dunes and he observed that the boy had 'an angry face'. 'Where are the girls?' Wolfgang asked the boy. The youth walked straight past him.

The problem remained that no other members of the Schmidt family saw the youth with the girls that afternoon. When Christine and Marianne had been gone about ten minutes Peter Schmidt sent Wolfgang to look for them but at the time the little boy didn't say anything to his brother about seeing the 'fat boy' walking back alone toward Wanda Beach. Police attempted to build an identikit sketch of the 'fat boy' suspect but when they tried to interview Wolfgang they found that the 7-year-old agreed with every suggestion they made. When Helmut Schmidt was asked to help his brother, Wolfgang merely agreed with everything Helmut suggested.

Helmut Schmidt told police that Marianne had walked across the sandhills on their visit to Cronulla on 2 January and had been missing from the family group for some time. Marianne's brothers had not seen her talk with anyone in particular on that day but police felt this may have explained why the girls were so keen to venture there again nine days later. Had she met someone with whom she promised to meet up with at a future date? The problem with this scenario is that the girls had not intended to go to the beach on Monday—they were supposed to take the children on the previous day but the weather didn't allow it—and the likelihood that someone had kept a secret rendezvous on another day when the beach was again closed seems remote to say the least. Rather, if the girls had arranged to meet someone that afternoon it would have been with someone they had met that day.

In Trixie Schmidt's statement to police on 10 March 1965, she recalled that the group caught the train to Redfern Station, where they had to change trains for the trip to Cronulla. While on the train, Trixie told police, a 'tall, 15-year-old boy' talked to Christine and Marianne. Trixie could not hear what they were talking about. When the train stopped at Redfern, Christine and the Schmidts exited and the boy stayed on the train. The group then went to another platform and waited for the connecting train to Cronulla. Trixie stated that no person spoke to the children while they were on the train to Cronulla.

During the original investigation, the dunes surrounding the crime scene were sifted with a front-end loader and dotted with police markers where particular items were found. Old clothing, three knives and a striped towel were recovered but two of the knives were traced back to local fishermen while the other was too broad to be the murder weapon. On 19 January, while sifting through one of the sandhills, a section of a knife blade was found. Measuring 9/10 x 8/10 inch [2.3 x 2 cm], the section of steel was stained and when examined gave 'positive presumptive tests for blood'. The piece of steel was described by a Sydney University metallurgist as 'high quality stainless steel used for carving knives or surgical instruments' and was probably manufactured in Europe or the United States. Was this part of the murder weapon that had fractured when plunged into hard bone?

⌘⌘⌘

The murder of the two girls received worldwide publicity and investigations were conducted throughout Australia and internationally. There were a number of 'suspects' the police could not find or interview in connection to the murders including several 'beach pests' seen at Wanda on the day the girls were murdered and in the weeks leading up to that fateful day. Several local women complained about a man, aged 25–30, with a 'solid, flabby' appearance and a 'round, boyish face', who on occasions had a 'noticeable growth of stubble on his face'. The man had approached several women on the beach, shown them a magazine with explicit photos and asked them for sex. In several instances he said that he was from South Australia on holidays but the man was spotted at Cronulla and Wanda in the two years before the murders and on the day the girls were killed. He often wore dark trousers, a white singlet or shirt and carried a towel, a rolled-up newspaper and a radio. Detectives labelled this suspect 'the fat man'.

During the next decade more than 14,000 people were interviewed and more than 80 volumes of police reports containing 10,000 pages of notes were accumulated. Some 5000 'persons of interest' were interviewed over the course of the investigation, with the greater majority quickly eliminated as suspects. Several people, some emotionally disturbed, admitted to committing the murders but due to a lack of knowledge of the crime and specifics relating to the crime scene, the authenticity of their admissions were not accepted by police. A number of other suspects had their inquiries suspended because there was no further information available to detectives to continue their investigations.

On 22 April 1966, a coronial inquest into the Wanda Beach murders was held at the City Coroner's Court in Sydney before Mr JJ Loomes, the Stipendiary Magistrate and City Coroner. Loomes found that Marianne Schmidt had died from 'haemorrhage, the result of a cut throat and four penetrating wounds of the chest'; and that Christine Sharrock died from 'haemorrhage as the result of penetrating wounds of the chest associated with injuries, namely a fracture of the skull and injury to the brain'. Loomes also stated that he did intend to canvass the evidence presented or to comment on it. 'To do so,' he said, 'can serve no purpose and could perhaps hinder the [ongoing] inquiries.'

The murders of two more women the following year were originally linked to the Wanda Beach investigation. On Saturday 29 January 1966, the body of Wilhelmina Kruger was found in the basement of a Wollongong car park. The 57-year-old cleaning woman had started her shift at the Piccadilly Arcade in Crown Street in the early hours of the morning and was found bludgeoned and knifed to death at the base of a stairwell shortly before 6.00 am. Kruger had suffered multiple stab wounds, numerous other injuries including a ruptured heart and had been strangled with her own stockings. The ferocity of the attack shocked hardened detectives, several of whom had worked on the Wanda Beach investigation, and Detective Dick Lendrum stated at the time, 'On the information available to us we cannot discount the possibility Mrs Kruger… met her death at the hands of the same person who is being sought for the murders at Wanda Beach.'

Then, on 26 February 1966, the decomposed body of Sydney prostitute Anna Dowlingkoa (born Elizabeth Anne Dowling in Perth) was found on the side of the Old Illawarra Highway at Menai south of Sydney. The woman's body remained hidden for several days before the killer returned and moved it closer to the highway so that it could be discovered. Detective Inspector Cec Johnson, who compiled the official police resumé of the Wanda case, wrote that 'the viciousness of [the Wanda crimes] is equal and similar to the mutilation murders of Mrs Kruger at Wollongong in January 1966 and Anna Dowlingkoa at Lucas Heights in February, 1966'. The discovery of a third murder victim in the Wollongong district later that year heightened police fears that they had a 'multiple murderer' in their midst; the term 'serial killer' had not even been invented yet.

In June 1966, the naked body of 19-year-old Carolyn May Orphin was found on Mount Ousley (by-pass) Road. The young woman had been raped, strangled and beaten to death with a large rock after leaving a Wollongong dance with a local man, Alan Raymond Bassett. The 21-year-old English immigrant was later charged with Orphin's murder and sentenced to life imprisonment. He was subsequently diagnosed as a schizophrenic and gaoled in Morisset Psychiatric Hospital in Newcastle. Detective Inspector Cec Johnson, who was investigating the Wanda case, became convinced that Bassett was involved in the deaths of Christine Sharrock and Marianne Schmidt and for the next decade, until he retired as a detective, he pursued a confession from Bassett.

Cec Johnston would regularly travel to Morisset Hospital and discuss the unsolved cases with Bassett but the patient was non-committal about his involvement in any of the unsolved crimes. On one visit, Bassett gave Johnston a painting that he had done of a bush scene but the detective thought it was 'bloody awful' and put it away in storage. After he retired from the police force Johnston took a closer look at the painting and could see the bodies of four women hidden in the bush landscape. The former Sydney detective saw the painting as a 'confession' to the murders of Sharrock, Schmidt, Kruger and Dowlingkoa and went to the media with his suspicions. Johnston lost his life in a pedestrian accident in 1980 but went to his grave believing that Bassett was involved in all four crimes but several Sydney detectives believed that the murders were not connected and that Johnston had become obsessed with solving the Wanda case.

Alan Bassett was finally released from prison in 1995 but has steadfastly maintained his innocence. In 2000 he offered to provide a DNA sample in order to prove his innocence and today he is not regarded as a suspect in the unsolved Wanda case. The same year the clothes Christine Sharrock and Marianne Schmidt wore were tested for DNA profiling. The presence of a foreign DNA profile, and the current status of the other crime scene forensic samples, cannot be confirmed by the New South Wales Police.

New South Wales detectives still working on the case looked into the movements of 39-year-old Australian-born Christopher Wilder who was killed by troopers in Massachusetts in 1984 after committing a murder spree across several American states.[4] Wilder, the son of an American World War II sailor and an Australian mother, was born in 1945. Blond and thickset, Wilder was charged with gang rape on a Sydney beach in 1962 and was later treated with shock treatment for a sexual disorder at Sydney's discredited Chelmsford Hospital. He married briefly in the late 1960s but the marriage ended because of allegations of sexual abuse. Wilder returned to America where he made his fortune as a building contractor and racing car driver. He was also treated by an American psychiatrist as part of his sentence for the rape of a teenage girl in the late 1970s.

While in Australia to visit his parents in 1982, Wilder kidnapped two teenage girls from a Sydney beach and forced them to pose for pornographic photos. After his family posted $350,000 bail Wilder escaped prosecution when he returned to America for business reasons and, in 1984, murdered at least eight young women while posing as a fashion photographer. His potential involvement in the Wanda Beach murders has never officially been investigated.

The circumstantial evidence linking Derek Ernest Percy to the Wanda Beach murders, however, has continued to stack up against him during the past ten years:

- in January 1965, Percy was a 16-year-old school student who was about to enter Form Five (Year 11) at Mt Beauty in country Victoria—the same age as the 'Wanda' suspect—and was known to carry a knife in a sheath similar to the style described by witness Wolfgang Schmidt
- the 'gorge incident' at Mt Beauty, where Percy demonstrated his fascination for women's underwear and had violently slashed them with his knife, had recently occurred—Marianne Schmidt had her swimming costume briefs cut in a similar fashion
- Percy was a school student and would have been on holidays in January 1965; his family was interested in moth class sailing and the national championships were held in Sydney that summer for the first time since the late 1950s and it was the only time the championships were held in Sydney during the decade
- if they were in Sydney that January, the Percys would have stayed with Mr Percy's mother in Denistone, which was the neighbouring suburb to West Ryde where Christine Sharrock and Marianne Schmidt lived

- Percy would have caught the train at West Ryde, the same station from which the Schmidt children caught the train to Cronulla Beach, in order to watch the regatta at Botany Bay—was he the teenage boy the girls spoke to on the train that day?
- some detectives believe that Percy's diary entry concerning the kidnapping of 'two girls at Barnsley' is linked to what happened at Wanda Beach
- Percy also wrote about feeding his victims beer—Christine Sharrock had a blood alcohol level of 0.015 which is enough to have consumed a 10 oz glass of beer
- when Percy was arrested for the murder of Yvonne Tuohy in 1969, he had three knives in his possession—one of them had been filed down to make a smaller blade; detectives believe this may be the knife that splintered on Wanda Beach in 1965
- finally, despite being highly intelligent and a capable student, Percy's grades deteriorated in 1965—after the Wanda Beach murders had been committed—and he inexplicably failed his Leaving Certificate.[5]

Derek Percy, however, does not match the general description of the 'surfie' suspect seen with the girls by Wolfgang Schmidt on the day they were murdered—he would never have been described as a 'fat boy'. All this could be easily solved, of course, by matching the sperm sample found on Marianne Schmidt's clothing with a profile of Derek Percy's DNA. But, as is explained later in this book, there are inherent problems with this simplistic solution.

If only 'cold case' investigations really were like those seen on television.

CHAPTER 6: The Disappearance of the Beaumont Children

In 2006, I wrote the first definitive account of the disappearance of the three Beaumont children from Adelaide's Glenelg Beach on Australia Day, 26 January 1966.[1] Several authors had written about the unsolved case—devoting chapters in anthologies on infamous Australian crimes—but most had only succeeded in reinforcing many of the myths and misunderstandings about the matter. My book *Searching for the Beaumont Children* looked at the 40-year history of the case in light of the impact charlatans, clairvoyants and subsequent 'persons of interest' have had on the still ongoing investigation. 'More than any other crime,' I wrote, 'the disappearance of three siblings from a crowded Adelaide beach in January 1966 seems to have permanently damaged the Australian psyche. For the generation of baby boomers growing up in the mid-1960s the subsequent investigation into the abduction and probable murder of the Beaumont children has both repelled and haunted us.'

On the day after he was captured in 1969—three and a half years after the Beaumont children disappeared—Derek Percy was questioned about the unsolved case by probationary constable Ron Anderson and allegedly told his former school friend that he was at Glenelg Beach on the day they disappeared.[2] Whether Percy was trying to confuse the young constable—refusing, perhaps, to deny any assertion put to him to support his insanity plea—to this day he has not denied involvement in any of these unsolved cases.

❋❋❋

On the morning of Wednesday 26 January 1966, Jane Beaumont, aged 9, her sister Arnna, 7, and their 4-year-old brother Grant travelled to Glenelg Beach for a morning swim. The actual day on which Australia Day fell was not a public holiday in 1966—the holiday was celebrated the following weekend—and the children's father, war veteran GA 'Jim' Beaumont, was away on business as a linen goods salesman. When the children woke in their modest Somerton Park bungalow they asked their mother Nancy if they could again travel to nearby Glenelg Beach by bus. The children were persistent—the temperature was expected to top 100°F (38°C) and the children had safely caught the bus home after being dropped off at the beach by their father the previous day. Finally, their mother allowed them to make the short bus trip to Glenelg alone—she was not one for 'beach outings'—as long as they returned on the midday bus.

Nancy Beaumont gave the children eight shillings and six pence (about 85 cents) to buy some pasties for lunch. The children left their home at 10.00 am and caught a bus ten minutes later from the corner of Diagonal Road and Peterson Street, which is 100 metres from their Harding Street home. The bus route took the children past Glenelg Oval on Brighton Street and left into Jetty Road. The bus driver, Mr ID Munro, remembered seeing the children get on the bus—the eldest girl was carrying a paperback copy of *Little Women* under her arm and a blue-green airlines type shoulder bag—but he did not remember seeing the three siblings get off the bus. Police believed that they alighted in Moseley Street, a short walk away from the beach and the place from where they were to catch the bus home.

At 11.00 am a 74-year-old Glenelg woman sitting behind the Holdfast Sailing Club noticed three small children playing on the lawn of adjoining Colley Reserve. Fifteen minutes later, a man wearing a blue swimming costume with a white stripe down one side had joined them. 'The three children had gone over to him and he was laughing and encouraging them as they played,' she told police. 'The boy was jumping over him, the younger girl too, and the older girl was flicking him with a towel.'

The man was described as being in his late 30s or 40s, 5 feet 11 inches to 6 feet 1 inch tall, with a thin face and athletic build.

His hair was light brown, parted on the side and long at the back. Although he had a fair complexion, he was sun-tanned and generally described as a 'surfie type' or 'beachcomber'. A Broken Hill man who had come to Adelaide to watch the fourth cricket test between Australia and England later came forward and said that the man seen with the children had 'fairish to light brown hair', dispelling the earlier 'surfie' description of the man.

Another elderly woman, who was sitting on a park bench with her husband and teenage granddaughter, had a conversation with 'the stranger' around midday. The man approached them and asked if they had seen anyone going through his belongings, which were placed besides the children's clothing on a white bench, as some money was missing. 'Have you seen anyone messing with our clothes?' the man asked. 'Our money has been pinched.' The children appeared friendly toward the man, the woman later told detectives, and the reference to 'our' money and 'our' clothes gave them the impression that he was with the youngsters.

Just after midday a middle-aged woman saw the man dressing the three children for their trip home. This witness thought it was strange that the man was dressing the oldest girl, who appeared to be old enough to dress herself. Nancy Beaumont said that this was especially unusual because Jane was a shy child and would never have let a stranger dress her. The police wondered, then, had the man befriended the children on previous visits to the beach? The man certainly had gained the confidence of the children; the woman noticed the man pick up his towel and trousers and walk with the children to the Colley Reserve change rooms and there, the children waited on a seat for him while he dressed. The group then walked behind the Glenelg Hotel and disappeared.

Tom Patterson, a local postman, later told police that he saw the three youngsters walking east along Jetty Road towards Mosely Street 'holding hands and laughing'. The children knew the postman by sight and called out to him, 'it's the postie'. The postman could not remember if it was at the start of his round or at the end, but he did not see any other person with them. Police later determined that this sighting was actually in the morning at around 10.30 am. There was no other sighting of the children after midday when Jane, Arnna and Grant went to Wenzel's cake shop near the bus stop on Mosely Road and bought some pasties and a pie. Although Nancy Beaumont had given her eldest daughter some coins to buy lunch, it was later discovered that Jane paid for the food with a £1 note. This was a lot of money in the mid-1960s and police kept this information out of the media for the next twelve months. Did the man offer to buy the children lunch to gain their confidence and to ensure that they returned to him with the pastie and change? Where did the children go after they bought their lunch?

Police believed at the time that after missing the midday bus the children attempted to walk home and accepted a lift in a car by person(s) unknown. The problem remains, however, that no witness saw them walking home or getting into a car and the man seen with them on the beach was never identified. Was he a local man who lived close to Glenelg Beach? Did they walk to where he was waiting for them?

When the children did not arrive home on the midday bus Nancy Beaumont was not immediately concerned—she presumed they would be on the two o'clock bus. Family friends dropped by and the group of adults shared an afternoon drink in the hot conditions. When the two o'clock bus came and went, she felt she should go and look for them—perhaps they missed the bus and were walking home. But the children could be walking several different ways back to Harding Street, so she decided to stay and wait for the three o'clock bus. Jim Beaumont arrived home at 3.30 pm and when told that the children had not returned, he immediately went to Glenelg Beach and frantically searched for them. Doubling back to the family home, Jim and Nancy went together and searched the beach area. Their children could not have met with an accident on the beach, the parents reasoned, as there was always 'safety in numbers' and any of the children could have given authorities the family details if one or two of them had been injured. In the early evening the Beaumonts went to the Glenelg Police Station.

Jim Beaumont spent the night searching for his children while his wife Nancy was comforted by friends before being sedated by her local doctor. Hundreds of citizens joined the search, as did members of the Suburban Taxi Service [Jim Beaumont was a former owner-driver]. By the end of the following day, a huge search of the Glenelg area had been completed but no trace of the children or their belongings were found. The Police Aqualung Squad searched the Glenelg boat haven, but the sediment in the water hampered any detailed search. At 5.00 am the police launch *William Fisk* had set out and searched close to the shoreline all the way to the coastal town of Aldinga and back to Henley Beach. Hollows and caves in seaside cliffs were thoroughly searched, as were stormwater drains opening out onto beaches.

The police considered three scenarios: the children had run away and were hiding; they had drowned; or they had been abducted. The first explanation defied logic, because the Beaumont children were from a happy family and were just spending a morning at the beach. A note, written by Jane to her parents two nights before they disappeared, reflects her responsible manner and the nature of the tight-knit Beaumont family:

> *Dear Mum and Dad*
> *I am just about to go to bed and the time is 9. I have put Grant's nappy on so there is no need to worry about his wetting the sheet. Grant wanted to sleep in his own bed so one of you will have to sleep with Arnna. Although you will not find the rooms in very good condition I hope you will find them as comfortable as we do. Good night to you both.*
> *Jane XXX*
> *PS I hope you had a nice time wherever you went.*
> *PPS I hope you don't mind me taking your radio into my room Daddy.*

The second scenario was also quickly dismissed. It was impossible that the three siblings could drown unnoticed on a crowded beach, and none of the children's belongings had been found. The third theory also had its detractors at the time—multiple abductions, especially three children from the same family were unheard of. But during that long night the dark reality began to dawn on the Beaumonts and the local authorities. 'There is only one reason the kiddies are not home,' Nancy Beaumont recalled thinking, 'someone is holding them back, stopping them from getting here.'

Adelaide Advertiser sketch artist Peter von Czarnecki drew the first preliminary drawing of the main suspect seen playing with the children at Colley Reserve. The problem was, the sketch was an artistic interpretation, not a police identikit, and relied more on the artist's translation rather than the memory of the elderly witness at Glenelg Beach. From the broad description the woman gave, the artist prepared a rough sketch and while another detailed painting was prepared, the woman could not remember the shape or colour of the man's eyes, nor the shape of his nose or mouth. All she could say was that von Czarnecki's sketch 'resembled' the man. Nevertheless, this image of the wanted man was broadcast Australia-wide and remains the only tangible description of the chief suspect.

On Thursday 27 January police used the resources of ADS Channel 7 and 5AD radio station to appeal for public help and to gather information. Adelaide newsreader Brian Taylor manned the station's outside broadcast unit for the entire day and into the night, providing interviews with police and with locals who had been on the beach the previous day. By the following weekend the disappearance of the Beaumont children had gained national press coverage. On 30 January, the night before the Australia Day holiday Monday, Jim Beaumont again went on national television to appeal to the public for any information that would lead to their return. 'Today is a world of prayer throughout Australia for Australia Day. I hope whoever is holding my children will return them,' Jim Beaumont said. He then broke down and said, 'My wife is not too good. She is still under sedation.'

The investigation stretched the limited resources of the South Australian Police to their fullest, especially as they were swamped with erroneous reports. People claimed they had seen the children in a car, or on a bus in the company of two men at nearby Semaphore Park, but the leads proved negative. A man fitting the description of the main suspect was questioned at Adelaide Airport, but was later released. A 33-year-old labourer telephoned police and said that a man driving a Holden came to his house in the Adelaide Hills and forced him to fill the Holden's radiator at gunpoint: inside the car were three children matching the description of the Beaumonts. The man was later charged with providing a false statement.

On 3 February 1966, Nancy Beaumont held a press conference in the garden of her home. 'I don't think they're alive, but I haven't lost hope, and all I want is that they come back,' the 38-year-old mother told the press. 'I've got to look at it from both sides… I can't be stupid and say they're going to come in with a skipping rope,' she added. 'I've got to feel the little things are huddled up somewhere and nobody has found them.' Jane Beaumont was a sensible, mature girl, her mother told the press. 'They're very affectionate—they're lovely to one another. If the other two were keen to go with someone, Jane would go with them to look after them and wouldn't leave them alone.'

That day, the 28-hectare Patawalonga Boat Haven was searched at low tide: the gates were secured, the lock drained and while divers searched upstream, fifty police cadets waded waist-deep in the sludge. Not a single piece of evidence relating to the children was ever found and the only sighting of the children occurred at Glenelg on the day they disappeared. 'I believe they've just finished the "Pat" [Patawalonga],' Nancy Beaumont lamented to pressmen. 'I'm inclined to think it was all over on the Wednesday afternoon [that the children disappeared]. Whoever it was [who took them] had nothing to lose.'

In March 1966, a Dutchman named Jan Van Schie consulted

Gerard Croiset, a well-known psychic living in The Netherlands. Croiset, who was known as 'the man with the x-ray mind', had allegedly had some success in solving cases in Europe, especially those concerning missing children. Contacted in July that year, Croiset stated that he used his 'paranormal powers' to see that the Beaumont children were buried within a kilometre of where they were last sighted. 'I see an overhanging rock plateau under which there are stones of a nice colour and behind is a cave or hollow,' Croiset said. He then asked for aerial photographs to be sent to him so that he could 'pinpoint' where the children were buried. 'There was no foul play, nor were they kidnapped. The children are dead. I am almost certain they suffocated; smothered alive. There was some sort of collapse.'

Croiset's revelations reignited interest in a case that was already being labelled as 'one of the most baffling mysteries in South Australian police history' but was, using the newspaper terminology of the day, threatening to 'go off the boil'. A local man, Dr Douglas Hendrickson, found some items while digging in dunes near an oval behind the Minda Home for disabled children and Croiset claimed that the children were buried metres from where a straw hat had been found. The Dutchman told the media to look for a 'kinderwagon' (pram) in the rubbish as a marker for their graves. In September 1966 the dunes were extensively searched and investigators were heartened when they found a pram amongst the rubbish but it was later revealed that it was placed there by one of the patients who was just trying to be helpful. The dunes have since been levelled and replaced with a playing field.

Brighton car dealer Barry Blackwell, a family friend of the Beaumonts, and local businessman Con Polites, paid for Croiset to fly to Adelaide on 6 November 1966. Croiset's arrival was the biggest thing that had happened in Adelaide since the arrival of The Beatles 18 months before, but his time in Adelaide was a failure. He declined to nominate Minda as the burial site of the children's bodies and was under increasing pressure from the press to 'point to the spot' where the bodies were allegedly buried. On the night before he left Australia a woman contacted Croiset and told him that the floor of a food warehouse in Paringa Park, not far from where Jane and Arnna Beaumont attended primary school, had recently been concreted. Croiset now claimed that the bodies of the children were buried 'under concrete'. 'My job is done,' the clairvoyant proclaimed. 'The rest is up to you.'

Despite the fact that police had no evidence to substantiate Croiset's claim, this theory that the children were buried under the warehouse floor took on a life of its own. The South Australian Government even debated the merits of digging up the concrete floor before abandoning the issue altogether. A Citizen's Action Committee raised $7000 for the specific purpose of ripping up the concrete floor on the first anniversary of the children's disappearance. Croiset claimed that he was '99.9 per cent sure' that a tunnel would be found under the concrete slab containing the children's bodies. On 8 March 1967, a partial excavation of the floor was completed but no trace of the children was found. A decade later Croiset was still convinced that the children were buried there. It was not until 1996, 30 years after the Beaumont children disappeared, that the warehouse floor was again excavated. Finally, in December 2005, the warehouse was demolished but no trace of the children was found.

Jim and Nancy Beaumont vainly held on to the hope that their children were still alive. On 27 September 1966 Senior Constable Ron Grose of the small Victorian town of Kaniva was on the phone waiting to be connected to police headquarters in Russell Street, Melbourne, when he overheard two women discussing 'bringing back the Beaumont children from Hobart'. Although Grose could not convince either the Victorian or South Australian police that the call was anything but a hoax, newsreader Brian Taylor drove Jim Beaumont the 380-kilometre trip to Kaniva to meet with Grose. The senior constable was genuine in what he had thought he had heard, however, two local women came forward on 13 October and admitted that although they had been talking about the Beaumont children, they had quickly changed the subject and were actually talking about relatives in Hobart.

In February 1968, Jim Beaumont received a letter postmarked Dandenong, Victoria, which was written in a child's handwriting and signed 'Jane'. The letter stated that if Jim went to the post office in Dandenong at 8.50 am on Monday 26 February wearing a dark coat and white trousers, the children would be returned to him there. Although Arnna's name was consistently misspelled as 'Arna' and the writing style did not match a sample of Jane's handwriting, a desperate Jim Beaumont contacted Detective Sergeant Stan 'Tonner' Swaine of the Adelaide Homicide Squad. Despite being told not to keep the appointment by his superiors, Swaine and the Beaumonts conducted the trip to Dandenong in great secrecy. The existence of a letter from 'Jane', however, was leaked to the press and the trip resulted in great embarrassment for Swaine and heartbreak for the Beaumonts.

When Jim Beaumont stood outside the Dandenong Post Office the following morning, two reporters from the *Herald Sun* and five Adelaide newsmen (including two photographers) were also watching as events unfolded. At 9.00 am a postal worker delivered a message to Jim Beaumont; a man had phoned and said that the children would soon be there. Some time later another message was delivered, saying that Grant Beaumont was sick and the children would not be able to come until after lunch. Jim Beaumont waited until 3.00 pm but no one showed. When Beaumont and Swaine returned to their hotel they were confronted by journalists from the *Adelaide News*. Swaine later left the police force following the fall-out from the secret trip but remained obsessed with solving the case for the rest of his life.

Three more letters were sent to the Beaumonts, two from 'Jane' and one signed 'The Man'. While police remained sceptical, Jim and Nancy Beaumont held on to a glimmer of hope that the letters were genuine. Almost 25 years later, improvements in the technology of fingerprint detection allowed police to identify the man who wrote these letters to the Beaumonts. A Victorian man, who was 17 at the time he wrote the letters, told police it had all been 'a joke'. Although he originally refused to admit any part in the writing of the letters, the man was later 'extremely remorseful' and police declined to charge him because of the statute of limitations regarding the offence.

The disappearance of the three Beaumont children has always held tenuous links to several other unsolved crimes. Three days after the disappearance, the *Sunday Mail* stated that 'police are investigating the possibility the man [seen playing with the children] is the same one wanted for last year's Wanda Beach murders'. Detectives believed several aspects of the Beaumont case were similar to the Sydney murders. The timing and place of the two crimes were certainly similar—both occurred in the January school holidays and on a public beach—but the only connection Sydney police had with the Beaumont case was in March 1966 when retired Detective Inspector Ray 'Gunner' Kelly arrived in Adelaide. Sponsored by a Sydney newspaper, Kelly had been hired as a private detective to provide the newspaper with an insight into the case but left Adelaide after only one day.

The fate of the three Beaumont children gradually slipped from the front pages of newspapers and into the collective psyche of the nation. Over the years police received hundreds of leads about possible sightings of the children but each proved baseless. The scenarios were inventive: the children had been brainwashed by a cult, assumed new identities and taken interstate or even overseas. Jim and Nancy Beaumont were encouraged to leave Somerton Park and start again, but Nancy at first refused. 'But I can't in case the kiddies come home,' she said. 'You see, I'm waiting for them to come back here. I never know. Perhaps someone could drop them at the front gate. Wouldn't it be dreadful if I wasn't here?'

Not knowing the fate of their children ultimately took its toll on the Beaumonts' marriage, Jim and Nancy eventually divorced and retreated to the anonymity of private life. Computer-enhanced photographs of what the children might possibly look like as adults were published in newspapers around the country in the mid-1990s but Nancy Beaumont could not bear to look at them.

⊗⊗⊗

A crime committed seven years later was a heartbreaking reminder for Adelaidians, and the entire country, of the unknown fate of the Beaumont children. On 25 August 1973, two young girls were abducted from Adelaide Oval during a South Australian Aussie Rules match. Eleven-year-old Joanne Ratcliffe was at the ground with her parents and was sitting next to 4-year-old Kirste Gordon, who was with her grandmother that day. Although she did not know the toddler, Joanne took a shine to Kirste. During the afternoon the younger girl's grandmother asked Joanne to take Kirste with her when she went to the toilet at the rear of the John Creswell Stand. The pair returned several minutes later, and afterwards the girls went to get straws for their drinks. When Kirste again wanted to go to the toilet at about 3.45 pm, Joanne volunteered to take her. This time they did not come back.

After 15 minutes, Mrs Ratcliffe went looking for the girls but was quickly joined by the other adults in the group when no trace could be found. The Ratcliffes tried to have the children's names paged over the ground's public address system but their request was denied and precious time was lost. Ken Wohling, the assistant curator of the oval later told police that he saw two young girls leaving the ground in the company of a man—the stranger had been helping the girls entice stray kittens at the back of an equipment shed. In the hours immediately after the girls went missing, four different sightings of the man and the two young girls were recorded.

A description of the man, who was wearing a wide-brimmed hat, was suspiciously similar to the suspect in the Beaumont case, although he was slightly shorter, at 5 foot 8 inches, he had the same long, thin face. Just as importantly, the circumstances were similar—two young girls (who could have been mistaken for siblings) abducted from a public place without a trace of them found despite an extensive police investigation.

In the late 1970s and early 1980s a series of crimes shed a faint light on the seedy underbelly of Adelaide—known as 'the City of Churches'. The bizarre series of events started in 1972 when Dr George Duncan, a university law lecturer, drowned in the Torrens River. Duncan, who was openly homosexual, was bashed and thrown into the river by four men at a notorious pick-up area for gay men on the banks of the Torrens. Another man, Roger James, was also bashed and thrown into the river but was saved by a passer-by, 25-year-old Bevan Spencer von Einem. In 1987, senior Vice Squad detectives later stood trial for allegedly throwing Duncan into the Torrens River but were found not guilty of manslaughter after a three-week trial.

Between 1979 and 1982 the mutilated bodies of four young men were discovered in and around Adelaide. The following year, 15-year-old Richard Kelvin was abducted from a bus stop near his North Adelaide home. On 23 July, the boy's body was found in the Adelaide foothills. A post mortem revealed that although he had been missing for seven weeks, he had been kept alive for at least five weeks and his body contained traces of four different drugs. Kelvin, like several of the other victims, had died from blood loss from a shocking injury to his anus. The Adelaide press dubbed the killings 'the family murders' when detectives revealed the existence of a subculture of paedophilia and sexual sadism in the city's network of homosexual activity and the media suggested that members of this network were being protected by high-ranking public officials.

One of the names in that network was Bevan Spencer von Einem, the man who had saved Roger James from drowning a decade before. Von Einem, now a tall, immaculately groomed 37-year-old, was a known paedophile but denied any knowledge of the five unsolved murders. Police searched von Einem's house and discovered three of the drugs found in Kelvin's body and matched von Einem's hairs to those left on the boy's clothing. Von Einem was sentenced to life imprisonment for the murder of Richard Kelvin but when he stood trial for the murders of the other victims sensational allegations were made against him at his committal hearing.

One of the prosecution's 22 witnesses, Mr B, whose identity was withheld for his own protection, implicated von Einem in the death of Alan Barnes. Mr B told a shocked courtroom that von Einem had allegedly told him that he had abducted the Beaumont children from Glenelg Beach in 1966 and had performed some 'brilliant surgery on them'. Their bodies had been buried in Moana or Myponga, south of Adelaide. Although no names were mentioned, von Einem, also allegedly told Mr B that he had taken two young girls from Adelaide Oval—most likely Joanne Ratcliffe and Kirste Gordon. On 11 May 1990, Bevan Spencer von Einem was committed to stand trial for the murder of Alan Barnes and Mark Langley but the trial never went ahead. The following February the Crown's case collapsed when Mr Justice Duggan ruled that evidence tabled in the Kelvin trial would be inadmissible in any other proceedings. Mr B's assertions concerning von Einem's possible involvement in the Beaumont disappearance—among other unsolved murders—were never tested in court.[4]

The unknown fate of the three Beaumont children still has the power to move the nation's media to action. In 1997, Stan Swaine, long retired from the police force, claimed that a Canberra woman was Jane Beaumont. The matter went to court, where it was revealed the woman had been raised by a cult in Victoria and her childhood was only a vague memory but no, she wasn't the eldest Beaumont child. Family and friends verified the woman's identity but the former detective remained unconvinced. A restraining order had to be taken out against him to stop him pursuing what was an obvious case of mistaken identity.

In 2002, the missing Beaumont children hit headlines on both sides of the Tasman Sea when a New Plymouth butcher made the extraordinary claim that a local man had told him that he had once lived next door to the Beaumont children in Dunedin in the South Island of New Zealand. Although the story was relayed third hand, news of this revelation brought a flood of telephone calls from Australia with several press and television reporters quickly dispatched to New Zealand. The matter was quickly resolved through the records of births and deaths—another case of mistaken identity.

After writing my book *Searching for the Beaumont Children* I became convinced that the children were abducted by a local person who may have been known to them, but not necessarily known to their parents. There are several reasons for this:

- the tall, 35–40-year-old man seen 'frolicking' with the children on Colley Reserve was wearing blue and white swim trunks and these are the colours of nearby Henley Beach Surf Club
- Bevan Spencer von Einem remains a chief suspect; he was only 19 in January 1966, but he was prematurely greying; a 1989 confidential police report links von Einem to the Beaumont and Adelaide Oval cases; and the convicted paedophile was interviewed by police regarding the missing children as recently as September 2007[5]
- no witness saw the children get into a car so police cannot rule out the theory that the children walked to the abductor's home; and yet because the distinctive Glenelg mansions and bungalows remain in families for generations, there is the possibility that the children are buried in a private residence within walking distance from the beach
- if the children were transported from the beach to a remote area, such as the Adelaide Hills, 'the man' would have had access to a car and knowledge of a burial site where the bodies would never be found.

Derek Percy was only 17 in January 1966 and although he facially matches the description of 'the man' seen with the Beaumont children on Glenelg Beach the day they disappeared, he is the wrong age and height. Was Percy even in Adelaide in January 1966? He allegedly told his friend Ron Anderson as much but South Australian Police, and his own family, cannot confirm that he was there. If he was on Glenelg Beach that day, could he have befriended the three Beaumont children on the beach and, within a couple of hours, charmed them to go with him from a public beach? Possibly, but then take them where? Even if there is a suspicion that Percy was on holidays with his parents in Adelaide at that time, where does a teenager take three children and hide their bodies when he is on holidays with his parents?

One other major problem remains—Derek Percy was in custody when Joanne Ratcliffe and Kirste Gordon were abducted from Adelaide Oval in 1973. The suspects in both the Beaumont and Adelaide Oval cases look remarkably alike[6]—more so than the teenage Derek Percy once did to the chief Beaumont suspect. There are just too many questions with no logical answer.

CHAPTER 7:
The Death of Allen Redston

While the unsolved Redston case has remained relatively unknown on a national level, it is still very well-known among retired detectives who served with the now-defunct ACT Police[1] in the 1960s and in subsequent decades. 'There is an enormous amount of information involved in the Redston case, including the original case files and a review by New South Wales Police,' says Australian Federal Police (AFP) Detective Sergeant Chris Sheehan, who is now the case officer for the unsolved crime.[2] Sheehan has been able to build on the considerable work performed by Detective Constable Mark Travers who, as a part of this renewed enquiry into the movements of Derek Percy, was first asked to review the original investigation, organise important documentation and recover the crime scene materials.

The most important aspect of the four-decade long investigation into the death of Allen Redston is that the original crime scene specimens have been maintained in pristine condition. 'ACT Police procedures secured the crime scene and the original handling of the exhibits was of a world class standard and normal forensic procedures have been followed over the decades,' Sheehan says. DNA could provide the 'golden key' to solving this case, but as Sheehan points out, 'some of the items got wet at the crime scene, some did not' so this too is still speculative. If DNA technology cannot determine who killed Allen Redston, detectives will have to rely on behavioural experts to compare what happened at the crime scene with what is known about the chief suspects.

❋❋❋

In 1966 Curtin was one of the newer suburbs of the national capital, Canberra. The suburb was named after the 1940s Australian Prime Minister John Curtin and is situated just 6 kilometres to the south-west of Parliament House. Most of the houses in the new suburb were still being built on the old Yamba homestead that had been subdivided into neat rows of streets. There was a distinct absence of trees among the fibro and brick houses when professional soldier Brian Redston moved his young family there the previous year from Bendigo in Victoria. The Redstons—Brian and wife Violet; children Anne Maree 7, Allen 6, Peter 4, and baby Stephen—lived in Macalister Crescent, not far from Yarralumla Creek, which flows into Lake Burley Griffin.

On Tuesday 27 September 1966, Allen Redston arrived home at 3.20 pm from South Curtin Primary School eating an iceblock.[3] His mother asked him where he had got the money to buy the iceblock, knowing that she had not given him any money when she packed him off earlier that day to walk to school with his next-door neighbours—5-year-old Peter Ryan and his mother. Decimal currency had been introduced to Australia the previous February and the new coins were a major novelty with children. Allen told his mother that he had found two cents on a path and that Peter Ryan had given him another two cents so that he could buy an iceblock from the local corner shop.

Mrs Redston gave Allen another four cents and told him to take his younger brother Peter to the shop and buy him an iceblock. The shop was close to the Redston residence and young Peter returned with his iceblock after only a few minutes, telling his mother that Allen was outside playing with his friend. Mrs Redston busied herself making the evening meal for the family, but what Peter did not immediately tell her was that Allen did not take him to the shop. Allen had given his younger brother the money and told him to go to the shop by himself before going next door to play instead. During the afternoon she heard children playing in the front yard of the Ryan house and assumed that Allen was there. He wasn't.

Allen had left Peter Ryan's house almost immediately and met another school friend, 5-year-old Phillip Keenan who lived in nearby Service Street. Mrs Shirley Gibbons, who lived opposite the Redstons, saw the two boys walk past her house at about 3.30 pm and knew Allen and his family well. She called out to Allen to check if his mother knew where he was off to and the little boy called back, 'Yes, Mummy said I could go'. The boys then went down into Holman Street and out of Mrs Gibbons' view. When Phillip Keenan arrived at his Service Street home, which faced open ground where Yarralumla Creek ran, he went inside and Allen Redston continued on down the road to play.

Brian Redston arrived home from his job at the Defence Department between 5.00 and 5.15 pm that afternoon but Allen had not returned home by the time the family sat down for their evening meal at 5.30 pm. Mr Redston later stated that Allen was often late for dinner. 'We didn't particularly take notice of his not being there because he used to go out and play with his friends and he used to come home about half past five when it was time to start eating again. We were actually sitting down to tea before we noticed he wasn't there.' It was then that Mrs Redston informed her husband that Allen had come home eating an iceblock and when she told him to take Peter to the shop, he sent his brother off by himself and went next door to play instead. Mr Redston later recalled thinking that when his eldest son came home he could 'take his choice whether he [got] fed or not'. But Allen was never to return home.

After tea the Redstons sent their eldest daughter to see if Allen was playing with any of his friends and to bring him home. When Anne Maree came back and said that Allen could not be found, Mr Redston got into his car and drove around the local streets looking for his son. Returning home, he went next door and asked the father of Peter Ryan to help him search for the boy. Geoff Ryan suggested they try the rubbish dumps near Yarralumla Creek—it was a popular haunt for local children who liked to play hide-and-seek among the gullies and piles of rubbish left there by building contractors. Mr Redston had recently warned his son and daughter about playing down at the creek, especially as Allen liked to play near the footbridge that adjoined the neighbouring suburb of Hughes. The two men drove down to the creek and looked around the different building sites before returning home some time after 6.45 pm and calling police.

A callout for a missing boy—six years old and 3 foot, 7½ inches in height with fair hair—was broadcast over police radio, local radio and television. Allen was wearing a bright green pullover, a yellow t-shirt with a dark brown collar and a white singlet; long brown and blue checked trousers, grey socks and silver-coloured plastic sandals. Mrs Gibbons heard that Allen was missing and immediately went over and told the Redstons that she had seen Allen walking into Holman Street with another boy. Mrs Gibbons comforted Mrs Redston and stayed with her throughout the night while her husband and groups of volunteers helped police look for the boy.

Throughout that cold Canberra night, police searched the drains that emptied into the creek as well as a local rubbish tip used by building contractors to dump their waste materials and used by local children as a play area. Volunteers searched streets, backyards and bushland—anywhere a young boy could be hiding or be lying injured. As dawn broke, some of the neighbours who had worked throughout the night returned to their homes and had a quick breakfast before continuing the search. Shortly after 8.00 am, the search came to a tragic conclusion.

George Sadewater, another neighbour of the Redstons from Macalister Crescent, worked as a cleaner and did not know about the missing boy until 7.00 am that morning when his next-door neighbour, Mrs Van Lier, told him that her husband Gerhard had been out searching all night. Mr Sadewater took his German Shepherd dog and drove down to the rubbish dump area near Yarralumla Creek to meet up with the search parties. Just before eight o'clock, his dog bounded into the middle of the reeds in the creek bed about 200 metres from Service Street, closer to the junction of Yarra Glen and Melrose Drives, and started tugging at an object. Upon closer inspection, George Sadewater and Gerhard Van Lier could see the head of a little boy protruding from a bundle of old carpet wrapped in an old housecoat. The men called to police—it was Allen. Both men knew Allen as one of the many children who played in their street, but it was clear that the boy was dead.

Detective Constable Ian Broomby from the scientific section of the CIB in the ACT Police Force arrived at the crime scene shortly after 9.00 am that Wednesday morning and was joined by other local police officers. Allen's body had not been visible from the creek bank and would have been easily missed by the search parties. He was wrapped in what appeared to be an old coat and was lying head-first and face-down in the reeds, nearly four metres from the eastern bank of Yarralumla Creek. The front of the housecoat and the face of the victim were lying in about five centimetres of water. Although George Sadewater's dog had moved the bundle, police could easily see the trail the body had left after it had been dragged through the reeds deeper into the creek. It appeared that Allen Redston had been killed somewhere else, his body wrapped in the discarded material found at a local rubbish dump and deliberately hidden from view.

Gerhard Van Lier formally identified the body prior to 10 o'clock that morning. After the arrival of a local doctor and ACT Coroner Mr K Dobson, the body of the boy, still wrapped in the material in which it was found, was placed in a plastic bag and taken to the Canberra Community Hospital Mortuary. The investigation into the murder of Allen Redston then commenced under the direction of Detective Inspector McSpeerin. Fourteen hours had passed from the time the police had been contacted until the discovery of the boy's body—detectives had already lost crucial time in determining who was responsible—but the reality was that Allen was most likely already dead when Brian Redston came home from work the previous evening.

A strip of purple felt, knotted like a bow tie, was wrapped around the lower part of the bundle encasing the little boy's body. The knot was on the left side of the body and the felt was looped and wet. Below the neck the body was wrapped in a green and white, floral-patterned housecoat, the surface of which was also wet with light brown mudstains on the upper front and middle of the back. A strip of khaki cloth—about five centimetres wide—was knotted around the boy's neck with the knot on the left side.

A length of electrical cable and a man's green and gold coloured tie secured the body inside another layer of material—a piece of mushroom-coloured carpet. When the outer layers were removed during the post mortem examination, dried grass was present in and under the knot of the tie. The grass was given to Detective Constable Broomby for bagging so that police might determine where the boy had been killed. The carpet was wrapped three and a half times around the body and was kept in placed by a length of white plastic which was looped and knotted around the boy's shoulders, with a knot below the right shoulder and wrapped to the right side of the ankles. In the second layer of carpet there were a number of items—a piece of glass with white lettering on it, black dirt and some twigs.

Underneath this layer, the full extent of the binding on the boy's body was revealed to police. A knotted loop of plastic was partly wrapped around the left side of his neck. A long, thin plastic bag, stapled at both ends and about two inches in width, was looped loosely around the neck five times; one end of it passed under a double strand of rope, the other wrapped around the front of the left forearm. The plastic was also knotted at the back of the neck. Loosely looped twice around the neck and knotted on the left side of the neck was a strip of white cloth, almost two inches wide. When the carpet was removed pieces of dry brown and white grass as well as twigs were stuck to the boy's bright green pullover.

A strip of khaki cloth was wrapped tightly around the buttocks and knotted at the middle of the back of the trousers. Another similar cloth strip was wrapped twice around the left wrist and once around the right wrist and knotted between the front of the right wrist and the right buttock. A third strip was looped once around the ankles and knotted at the front. A double strand of cotton rope was looped around the front of the neck and then ran down the middle of the back with one end wrapped around the left wrist and the other joining a single strand of rope wrapped around both wrists. The free end of the single strand of rope was knotted behind the ankles and joined another piece of rope which was multi-stranded and cotton in type. This cotton rope was looped twice around the ankles and once around the right wrist.

Police formed the opinion that 'all the items with which he was tied and wrapped were in abundance and did come from the disposal areas in the near vicinity where the body was found'. A local man showed police a position, 120 metres north of the crime scene on the western embankment of a small feeder gully to Yarralumla Creek, where earlier that week he had seen some of those items. A search of the gully found a number of carpet cuttings similar to the piece used to wrap Allen's body along with khaki cloth matching those used to tie the boy's hands. A woman also came forward and said that the floral-patterned housecoat was hers. It was dumped by her husband at the makeshift rubbish site used by builders on the open ground in Holman Street, not far from where the body was found.

Although the body was found face down in about two inches of water, Allen Redston had not drowned; his lungs were clear of fluid. Death was due to 'asphyxia caused by strangulation by a loop of double stranded rope'. The rope was merely looped around Allen's neck, not knotted, but attached to the hands and lower limbs and so any movement of the hands and feet would have hastened the boy's death. This manner of restraint—a hogtie—was an important clue in the original investigation and subsequent reviews that determined that minimal force was applied to the throat and the boy was not manually strangled.

The use of a hogtie to murder a small child puzzled detectives; there was almost a sense of 'overkill'. Although Allen Redston's body had been tied in what seemed to be a complex manner, there was no sophistication to the binding—the knots were not boy scout, truck driver or sailing knots, for example—they were almost like simple shoelace knots. Detectives could not discount the theory that the death may have been accidental—the result of a game with an older boy that had gone horribly wrong. As there were no marks on any part of the body other than the bruising caused by the rope around the boy's neck, there was the suggestion that Allen may have been a willing participant in the 'game' and not fought off his attacker. Perhaps Allen knew the person tying him up, or at least recognised him as a local boy, and played along until something went wrong—the older boy had hogtied him so effectively that the little boy died within minutes. Was the killer a local boy, then? Had the killer panicked when he realised what had happened to Allen and hurriedly concealed the body using any materials he could find?

There was also a complete absence of any sign of physical sexual assault, either before or after the boy died. 'Re-dressing' the victim, which is one physical indicator of sexual abuse, did not occur and poignantly, a small handkerchief given to the lad by his mother before he went to school the previous day was still tucked into the left sleeve of his pullover.

Another telling factor was the use of waste materials found at the local rubbish tip to first bind the victim and then conceal the body—this was a crime of opportunity. The killer had not brought the items with him to tie the boy but either knew of or made use of the materials found in the local area. Detectives theorised that if the killer had deliberately come to the area to murder, why hide the body from view? There was almost an element of shame in what was done; the body was wrapped not once but twice so that the killer didn't have to look at his handiwork.

* * *

Detective Sergeant Dudley Martin later stated: 'Appeals for information were made per medium of television networks, radio stations and newspapers throughout all the other States of the Commonwealth. During the course of the investigation many suspects were put forward by members of the public… [and] a large number of suspects interviewed and eliminated. Particulars of the death of the deceased were circulated throughout every police station… [and] information received from these sources was thoroughly investigated, without success. A reward notice was issued to the extent of $1000 for information regarding the death of the deceased. Certain information given as a result of this reward was investigated, without result.'

But the revelation that a number of similar assaults involving young boys had occurred in the area in weeks before Allen Redston's death was the first and only breakthrough in the case. Unfortunately, the person responsible for these attacks was never identified to the satisfaction of investigating detectives.

On Saturday 27 August 1966, on the first weekend of the school holidays and exactly a month before Allen Redston met his death, three local teenagers were walking towards Yarralumla Creek via Whyte Place. The boys explored the area for a while and then saw a fleeting glimpse of a large boy beside a pile of dirt near some dumped building materials. This boy, whom they later described as being 16 years, with straight blond hair, was bending over what appeared to be a bundle of clothing but as the teenagers approached the boy ran away. When they got to the place where the older boy was bending over they found a young boy tied inside a length of dark plastic sheeting—his hands were tied behind his back to his legs with a length of green string and a strip of plastic was tied around his mouth and neck. The little boy's legs were tied behind his buttocks and linked to his hands and neck by a rope, just like Allen Redston.

The teenagers were quickly joined by some other boys and one of them ripped a hole in the plastic to allow the little boy some air. While two others went to get some help, another boy untied the victim. The young boy was crying and 'breathing hard'. He told his rescuers that he lived in Service Street, which faced the creek area where Allen's body was found the following month.

The boy later told authorities that he had been yabbying near one of the stormwater drains near the old Yamba farmhouse and was walking home when an older boy approached him and asked if he wanted to play 'cowboys and Indians'. He told the boy 'no' but the older boy grabbed him and tied him with some rope that he took from his pocket. Having wound plastic around the victim's mouth and knotting it behind his neck, the attacker momentarily left the boy and returned with a large strip of plastic and told the boy to lie on his stomach. The attacker then wound the boy up in the plastic and tied it off at both ends with green string. The victim could not remember the older boy saying anything else during the attack and when the attacker was disturbed by the teenagers and ran off, the 8-year-old feared that he was merely going to get more materials.

The victim was exceedingly lucky that his rescuers stumbled upon the scene with the little boy only moments from death. Neither the three teenagers nor the victim knew the identity of the larger boy, if he had a bicycle of any kind or where he went after being interrupted. The teenagers took the boy home and his father made a formal complaint to police later that night. The victim told police that the attacker was close to 13 years of age, had black wavy hair and wore a grey jumper with a green, white and brown 'v' around the neck, long grey trousers and white sandshoes—possibly a school uniform. The boy later gave detectives another piece of important information; he had recently seen his attacker again, a week before Allen Redston's death, riding a red and white bike with a carrier on the back which was holding a spade.

On 18 September, two young brothers were also playing in the area when they were joined by an older boy, aged 15–17 years with fair hair over his forehead, who wanted to play 'cops and robbers'. The older boy began playing aggressively, caught the younger brother around the waist and began tying his hands behind his back and around the ankles. The older of the two brothers, who was only aged seven, began charging at the older boy to try and push him away. The attacker then threw rocks at the older brother and took this opportunity to tie a plastic strip around the mouth of the younger brother and knot it at the back of the head. The older brother eventually scared the bigger boy off and untied his distraught younger brother. The brothers later told police that they saw a red and white bike with reddish-brown handlebars and a carrier on the back with a spade in it, near where they were playing. When the boys left the area the older boy and the bike were gone.

Enquiries were made at schools, public places and recreation areas, together with house-to-house canvassing, to identify this teenage boy. The victim of the first attack and the brother of the second victim were taken to local schools and shown photographic records but the problem was, their descriptions of the offender differed greatly and detectives attributed this to the age of the witnesses, the trauma they suffered or perhaps there were two offenders bullying younger boys in the Curtin area. An identikit photograph was compiled from the information offered by the two boys but detectives thought it was 'not a true and accurate representation' of the attacker. Despite this, many teenage boys matching the general description of the attacker were interviewed by police at various schools around Canberra in the presence of their parents and questioned about their movements on the day Allen Redston met his death and whether they owned or had access to a similar-coloured bicycle.

In January 1967, New South Wales Detective Inspectors Keith Paul and Dick Lendrum, who had both worked on the unsolved Wanda Beach murders two years earlier, were sent to Canberra at the request of the ACT Commissioner of Police to carry out a review of the ongoing investigation into the death of Allen Redston. They made a number of technical and operational recommendations but believed that 'an examination of all available evidence strongly suggests to us that the person responsible for the death of Allen Geoffrey Redston, was the boy who had grievously tied up [the other two boys] in the same area'. Despite a thorough investigation, four months after Allen's death New South Wales detectives believed that 'the atmosphere has been lost'[4]—the case was cold.

New South Wales Police suggested that it should be widely advertised that 'police have not dismissed a theory that the boy responsible may not have intended to cause death'. Maybe this would prick someone's conscience and the person responsible—or a member of his family—would come forward and confess that Allen's death was indeed an accident. No one did come forward, however, and charges were never laid in regard to the matter. Authorities later speculated that the killer was actually named in the original inquiry but the boy's parents may have protected him from further incrimination and ensured that no further attacks took place.

At the official inquest into Allen's death in Canberra on 9 June 1967, Coroner KT Dobson formally stated that he 'was found dead in Yarralumla Creek on 28th September 1966 with certain marks of violence on his body' and he further found 'that the cause of death was asphyxia caused by strangulation by a loop of double-stranded rope at or near Yarralumla Creek aforesaid on or about 27th September 1966 by some person or persons unknown to me. The circumstances under which the injuries were inflicted and the evidence deduced, does not enable me to say.' Coroner Dobson then extended the sympathy of the court to Allen's parents but there would be precious little comfort for the Redston family in the years ahead.

Brian Redston summed up the feelings of a whole generation when he said: 'We allowed the kids at that time quite a lot of freedom, rather than being their boss and making them do what we wanted them to do. We were bringing them up to have enough sense of freedom, but so they would still come and tell us if they wanted to go somewhere or if they wanted to do something, just as long as we knew where they were.'

The Redstons kept a close eye on their remaining three children, describing them as 'horribly restricted' in what they were able to do and where they were allowed to go. 'Anywhere they go now,' Mr Redston explained, 'we know where they are. They know that they've got to tell us where they go or else they get some form of punishment because if they're missing for any length of time and we can't find them it's surprising how much it really worries you until they come home.'[5] This is perhaps not surprising, given the circumstances of the unresolved death of their eldest son, Allen.

※※※

During a huge storm in 1971, the Yarralumla Creek flooded and seven people lost their lives at the junction of Yarra Glen and Melrose Drives. Today, there is no sign of the creek, which was reconfigured as an underground drain to make way for the Melrose Drive motorway. Similarly, the suburb of Curtin is nothing like the barren landscape of dotted homes that police door-knocked regarding the death of little Allen Redston in 1966. The streets of Curtin are green and leafy, and the area is a much sought-after suburb for homebuyers in Canberra.

'It is clear that the location where this murder occurred in 1966, on the outskirts of Canberra as it was back then, was not an area that would have been known to the wider Canberra community as a recreational area for local children,' Sheehan says. 'It really wasn't a rubbish "tip" as we understand it today… It was a place where builders dumped their waste supplies and locals dumped trash. It would require some local knowledge of the area to realise that children would have been playing there that day. It was not something that someone who blew in that afternoon would know about.'

Then there is the issue of the earlier assaults on young boys in the area. Sheehan adds: 'The offender has gone to that specific location on a number of times looking for opportunities to bind a child victim… Some of the items used to bind Allen Redston were found at the tip,' he says. 'That would indicate some degree of local knowledge—to know that to tie a child you wouldn't have to bring rope with you.'

The name Derek Percy is not mentioned anywhere in the original investigation into the death of Allen Redston but this does not mean he wasn't involved. 'Detectives in the original investigation weren't to know that Derek Percy was going to murder children,' Sheehan says, 'they focused on the evidence before them. You can't look in the "rearview mirror", if you like, in the light of what we now know about Derek Percy. We also have to look at the available evidence.'

The single most important piece of evidence linking Derek Percy to Allen Redston's death may be the green and gold men's tie found at the crime scene. It has been suggested in some Melbourne newspapers that the tie is Percy's Mt Beauty school tie, the one made by his mother.[6] Why Percy would take only an old school tie, and no other items, to subdue his victim does not make any sense. But then nothing much does when it comes to Derek Percy, except perhaps, his crime scene behaviour. In December 2007, I was shown photos of the crime scene exhibits by the AFP—the tie used to bind Allen Redston is a broad, flat businessmen's tie—not the thick, coarse hand-made school tie Percy wore at Mt Beauty.

It is more likely that the death of Allen Redston was part of 'a series of escalating incidents' involving local boys in the Curtin area in 1966. The absence of sexual activity on or around the body was a particularly important aspect of the behavioural examination of the crime scene. The attack on Allen Redston may not have been murder *per se*, but resulted from the act of binding. Death, therefore, could have been an unintended consequence of the offender's actions—the noose around the neck was held in place by the boy's feet and the accidental occlusion of the carotid artery caused rapid loss of consciousness. A clear suspect was present in the investigation from the first day, namely the older 'boy on the bike', and it was believed that the offender, whoever he was, was responsible for all these incidents.

Not knowing the identity of the 'boy on the bike', however, keeps Derek Percy in the investigation but it also draws in many other suspects—'suspects who lived in the local area and knew about the rubbish tip,' Sheehan says. 'The issue was one of the most focused upon avenues of enquiry at the time. That person (or persons) has never really been identified… it may have been Percy, it may not have been.' Percy also had a bike, although it was dark maroon in colour, not red and white. If Percy was in Canberra, why did he have a red bike with him? And if it wasn't his bike, whose was it and how did he get access to it? And, even if detectives finally place Percy in Curtin on that specific afternoon, was he also there on several other occasions when local boys were bound and assaulted in a similar fashion?

If Derek Percy is excluded from the investigation, then 'the boy on the bike' remains a very real presence in the death of Allen Redston.

CHAPTER 8: The Abduction and Murder of Simon Brook

On Tuesday 22 July 1969—the day after he was charged with the murder of Yvonne Tuohy—Derek Percy was questioned by Detectives Knight, Delaney and Porter about the unsolved murder of Sydney toddler Simon Brook in May 1968.[1] 'I remember the name Simon Brook,' Percy told the detectives. 'There is a Shell training garage at Glebe. That's how I remember the suburb... I could have read about it in the paper.' The Victorian police at first did not realise the significance of this statement—the Shell training garage was in Bank Street, Pyrmont, on the eastern side of Glebe Island Bridge. Derek's father, Ernest Percy, attended the training garage in 1967 and Derek had visited him there on several occasions. This at least indicated that Derek Percy was familiar with the area and knew of the murder. But despite repeated questioning Percy insisted that he 'could not remember' if he killed the boy.

Later that same day New South Wales Detective Sergeant Jack Whelan received a phone call from Victorian Homicide Squad detectives regarding Percy's arrest. Articles obtained from the naval cadet's locker described the mutilation of a 3-year-old boy in similar circumstances to the Simon Brook murder in Glebe, Whelan was informed, and a young constable who knew the accused man confirmed that Percy was in the inner city suburb on the Saturday the boy was killed. It was suggested that the NSW police should interview the 20-year-old naval rating.

Derek Percy was subsequently included as a suspect in the Brook case and enquiries were made into his movements from May 1968 leading up to his arrest. New South Wales Detectives Bradstreet and Whelan travelled to Melbourne on 11 August 1969 but although there is a dated running sheet showing that this interview took place, today there is no record of interview available that documents the conversation. But there is evidence to suggest that Derek Percy was investigated as a suspect in the Brook matter in late 1969.

On 17 August, Detective Jack Lynch spoke with Inspector Campbell of the Naval Dockyard Police to establish if Derek Percy was working on the weekend of 18 May the previous year when Simon Brook was murdered. Enquiries were conducted with both HMAS *Melbourne* and HMAS *Kuttabul* but all duty rosters for that weekend had been destroyed and no other records existed that could be used to corroborate Percy's movements. Meal vouchers handed out to all naval personnel at HMAS *Kuttabul* were checked but these too were unable to assist detectives. Percy told detectives that he was either 'on leave or sailing in Newcastle' that weekend but this could not be supported by his own family—Percy had not been home since the previous Christmas.

New South Wales Detective Inspector Bradstreet, along with Detectives Barry Reynolds and Jack Lynch, travelled to Mt Beauty on 27 August 1969 and interviewed former neighbours, school friends and teachers who knew Derek Percy in the early 1960s. Many of the locals remembered the snowdropping incidents and had heard rumours of Percy's bizarre behaviour at the gorge. But the trail inexplicably went cold and no further investigations were conducted by New South Wales Police in relation to Percy's possible involvement in the Brook case. A running sheet was not submitted, as it was for other suspects, however, detailing any reasons why Percy should be eliminated from the investigation. Derek Percy, therefore, was never excluded as a 'suspect' in the murder of Simon Brook.

❋❋❋

Dr Donald Brook, described by his peers as both a provocative and intelligent art critic, noted in his autobiography that 1968 was the year that changed the world forever. 'John Gorton had become Prime Minister. The Seekers were named "Australians of the Year". Lionel Rose beat "Fighting" Harada. Robert Kennedy was shot and Nixon won the US presidency. France braced itself for more violence, and de Gaulle refused to resign… The fact that this was a watershed year for Australian art was clearly coincidental.'[2]

The year 1968 was a defining year for a generation. It was also the year Dr Brook's infant son Simon was lured from the front yard of his family home in the inner Sydney suburb of Glebe and callously murdered.

Donald Brook had just joined the newly-opened Power Institute of Fine Arts at the University of Sydney with 'a mandate to bring the latest ideas and theories about the visual arts to the people of Australia,' and had also become the *Sydney Morning Herald's* new art critic. Born in Leeds, England in 1927, Brooks was an engineer and sculptor who emigrated to Australia with second wife Phyllis in 1962. The Brooks lived in Canberra for several years where their son Simon was born in 1964. Three years later Dr Brook was one of the original four appointments to the Power Institute. Brook and his young family moved to Sydney and stayed with friends until they found a suitable house to buy. 'We had almost no money at the time,' Dr Brook writes of that period, reflecting upon perhaps the sorry financial state of the academic and arts worlds in the 1960s.[3] The Brooks bought a little Federation-style bungalow in Alexandra Lane, Glebe, several kilometres to the west of Sydney University, for about $15,000. The home faced Jubilee Park and was protected at the front by a small retaining wall and a wire fence at the side.

Not long after he took up his appointment at Sydney University, Dr Brook collaborated with fellow academic and noted sculptor Dr Hubert Flugelman to establish an experimental art workshop, which would allow students 'to practise the art they were theorising about'.[4] Sydney University was convinced to utilise a group of dilapidated corrugated iron sheds on City Road and the 'Tin Sheds' movement was born. The initiative was only in its gestation in the first half of 1968 but it went on to become one of the most 'radical and memorable "alternate art spaces" in Australia' as well as a 'hothouse of art, music, ideas and politics'. But all of this was still very much in the future, and a tragic event would irrevocably bind the Brooks to the past.

At about 1.00 pm on Saturday 18 May 1968, Donald Brook entered Glebe Police Station and reported that his toddler son Simon had gone missing from the front yard of the family home.

The little boy was last seen at about midday playing at the front of the house when family friends arrived from Canberra. The group went inside and had a light lunch but when the visitors got up to leave at about 12.30 pm, because they had another appointment to meet, Simon was nowhere to be found when he was called by his parents. Their house faced Jubilee Park and the Brooks assumed their son had disappeared through a small hole in the wire fence and had wandered down toward the oval. Donald Brook immediately called his friend and colleague Bert Flugelman to help look for the missing boy but following a short frantic search, he contacted Glebe Police.

A police memo was broadcast to all Sydney stations and a radio message circulated to all cars on patrol to be on the lookout for a small, stocky boy—three and a half years old, three foot six inches tall with fair hair cut rather short. Simon was wearing long orange trousers, a predominantly blue tartan sweater, a white t-shirt, blue socks and brand new red desert boots—a combination of favourite items only a child could throw together, but distinctive enough to give hope that he would be easily sighted. A squad of police from No 2 Division was dispatched from Glebe to join in the search, 20 uniformed officers conducted a ground search of the adjoining parkland and the Water Police patrolled nearby Blackwattle Bay. Despite the best efforts of police and volunteers, no sign of the little boy was found that afternoon.

Of concern to police was the reputation Jubilee Park had as a known haunt for perverts.[5] A child-minding centre in the east of the park was a magnet for paedophiles—a three-metre fence separated the centre from prying eyes but the situation had become so bad that supervisors at the centre 'only bothered to ring the police when they saw a new face at the wire'. The surrounding parkland and toilets allowed anonymity for men engaging in homosexual activity, while a nearby underground railway cutting allowed for easy access by rail. On the day Simon disappeared, hockey teams from Glebe, Ryde-Hunter's Hill, St James and Gordon-Wahroonga competed at

Jubilee Oval in the middle of the parkland. The Under-10s through to the Under-14s played from 8.30 to 11.15 am before the senior teams took the field in the early afternoon. Jubilee Oval was a hive of activity and there was the distinct possibility that the person who abducted Simon was drawn to the area because of the number of young children in the park that Saturday morning.

Later in the afternoon Glebe was drenched in a heavy downpour which made the task more difficult but the search continued throughout the night. The disappearance of a little boy from a suburban home was broadcast on Sydney television that night and although several people came forward and provided crucial details of Simon's possible movements that afternoon, a grim discovery the following morning realised the worst fears of police and the little boy's parents.

At dawn the following morning an Italian builder, Felici Lampasona, arrived with his brother at 286 Glebe Point Road to begin work on a new block of home units. The units were being built next to the Royleston Boys Home—the sorting depot to which New South Wales boys were sent if they had been made a ward of the state. At about 7.20 am Lampasona walked to the rear of the construction site to a vacant block of land to relieve himself behind some shrubs. He was walking back to the building site when saw what appeared to be a large doll near a track that ran diagonally across the block. There was a piece of clothing covering the object and it was lying on a piece of rotting canvas. Lampasona removed the clothing and immediately called for his brother—it was the body of a small boy. 'Holy Mother of God, I was frightened. I reeled back and I was sick,' Lampasona later told detectives.[6] 'Such a dreadful, horrible sight... only a raving maniac would have inflicted such cuts.' Police who viewed the scene were equally repulsed by the wounds inflicted on the little boy.

When police arrived they found the body of the small boy lying on his back under the overhanging branches of a small tree. The body was facing the northwest, lying with his arms outstretched and legs apart. He was naked from the waist down, his underpants lying beside his left ankle and his trousers covered his face. His shoes and socks had also been removed but his t-shirt, singlet and jumper remained intact. Detectives were shocked by the level of mutilation that had been inflicted on the victim with a steel razor blade that lay abandoned between the boy's legs with its Gillette 'Super Stainless' wrapper nearby.

Detective Sergeant Norman Merchant of the Scientific Investigation Bureau attended the crime scene and noted that the body had suffered a cut to the throat, the penis severed and left lying beside the body, and the scrotum cut open. There was also a cut along the inner edge of the right leg. There were also several spots of blood on one leg but the absence of a huge amount of blood led Merchant to believe that the boy had been mutilated post mortem. There were marks around the boy's neck, as if he was strangled with a rope or scarf, and newspaper had been shoved into his mouth to stifle his cries and to suffocate him.

Soon after 9.00 am Donald Brook and Bert Flugelman, who had stayed overnight at Alexandra Lane to comfort his friends, went to the site and positively identified the body of the little boy. The crime scene was only 400 metres northeast of the Brooks' home. There was no mystery about how the boy was led there—the killer would merely have had to lure him down Victoria Street to the Nursing College on the corner of Allen Street. The public used the bushland at the back of the units as a shortcut to Glebe Point Road, the main thoroughfare in the suburb, while local children often played there in the shaded, bushy area. There was only a small fence to climb over to enter the block of land and there were a number of informal tracks worn through the bush.

About 9.30 am Dr Edward La'Brooy attended the crime scene and made a number of observations. Dr La'Brooy later conducted the post mortem and removed two wads of paper from the boy's mouth and pharynx—they had been pushed down the throat with some force. Dr La'Brooy stated that he could find no visual evidence that the boy had been sexually assaulted but a rectal swab was sent away for analysis. The direct cause of death was 'asphyxia through suffocation', confirming that the injuries caused by the razor blade had been made after the child's death. The time of death was established as being about 2.00 pm the previous afternoon. Detective Sergeant Merchant examined the two wads of newspaper taken from the boy's throat and compared them to discoloured newspapers found at the crime scene. The pages corresponded with the other newspapers at the site and police formed the opinion that they had not been brought there by the offender.

During that Sunday evening, a canvas of local residents revealed a sighting of the boy on the afternoon he disappeared. Ms Barbara Lrbec, who lived in Alexandra Road, which runs parallel to Alexandra Lane down to Jubilee Park, told police that after walking home from the sandwich business she operated at Surrey Hills on Saturday afternoon she checked her letterbox and noticed a small boy standing on the other side of her fence on the footpath. Ms Lrbec told the boy to go home because it was cold and he ran up Alexandra Road towards Victoria Street. When questioned by police, she was adamant that it was the missing boy because of the brightly coloured clothing he was wearing. Ms Lrbec estimated that the time was about 1.30 pm—more than an hour after Simon went missing. She did not see the boy with any other person.

Eric Barnier, a courier working in the Glebe area that Saturday, also came forward with information. At about 12.35 pm Barnier was driving east along Federal Road on the other side of Jubilee Park when he noticed a small boy walking through the park holding hands with a young man. Barnier remembered the bright clothing the boy was wearing and was able to identify the clothing Simon had on from a photograph. The middle-aged English immigrant then assisted police in producing an identikit picture of the man seen with the boy—20–24 years old, about 5 foot 7 or 8 inches tall, with bushy, brushed back hair. The man had a high and wide forehead, deep set eyes, a straight but longish nose with a narrow bridge, a wide mouth and a long slightly angular chin.

Detectives believed that Simon Brook was enticed by the stranger to crawl through the side fence of the front yard of his home and was then led toward the western side of Jubilee Park. While Donald Brook and his friends searched for the missing boy, the abductor may have doubled back around toward Alexandra Road. A little later, about the time Barbara Lrbec was arriving home from work, Simon may have been told to head up toward Victoria Street where the man could have been waiting for him out of view and after taking a different route. Simon was then taken east up Victoria Street toward the shortcut to the vacant block on the corner of Allen Street where he met his death just 30 minutes later.

The man could have left the crime scene a number of different ways—by car, possibly parked somewhere nearby; by foot as Jubilee Park is only two kilometres from Broadway, which leads into Sydney, or even by rail. There was some conjecture at the time[7] that the person responsible for the murder may have used a nearby railway tunnel as an escape route—heading underground at Jubilee Park, the man would have resurfaced in nearby Pyrmont, on the other side of Glebe Point Road. The murderer would not have been covered in blood, as some press speculated at the time, because the injuries inflicted on the child were carried out after the boy's death and there was a distinct absence of blood at the crime scene.[8]

The Gillette-brand razor blade was a vital clue—the murderer may have been interrupted and had to quickly walk away from the crime scene or maybe he was just plain careless, but the item remained an important lead if it could somehow be traced back to the murderer. The razor blade had the manufacturer's code number 'L4' imprinted on it. A canvas of local retail businesses was conducted but while many of the shops sold that type of blade, the manufacturer's code did not match the ones currently in circulation. None of the proprietors of the local shops were able to provide a description of any person who may have purchased a similar razor blade anyway.

Five days after the murder, information was obtained from Mr

Richards, the manager of the Gillette Razor Blade Company. Mr Richards informed police that the code on the razor blade found at the crime scene meant that it left the factory in Melbourne no later than January 1967. The wrapper found with the blade was the type used to wrap blades contained in packets of three. More importantly, it was established that the type of razor blade was purchased by New South Wales government stores and had been issued to all government institutions in the fortnight before the murder. These institutions included public schools, mental institutions and the Australian Defence Forces.

A colour photograph of a child mannequin doll dressed in clothing similar to the set Simon was wearing on the day he was murdered was circulated in newspapers and magazines, along with the identikit picture of the chief suspect, but no one came forward with a name to fit the image. Thousands of people were interviewed and more than 300 'persons of interest' were investigated but none was charged with the crime. During the course of the investigation, five people came forward and confessed to the murder but, as was the case with the unsolved Wanda Beach murders, they were each ruled out because of their mental background and a lack of knowledge concerning the crime.

Police identified five main suspects—one of them even confessed to the murder and Eric Barnier positively identified the man from an identification parade as the person seen walking with Simon Brook on the day of the murder. Police found evidence that 'Andy'[9] had access to Gillette razor blades and couldn't account for his movements on the Saturday the boy was killed. Two friends told police that Andy was acting strangely in the weeks after the murder and that when he saw a newspaper article with a photo of the little boy he began to cry. When police took Andy to the crime scene he refused to get out of the car and closed his eyes tightly. Although he told police that he manually strangled the boy (which didn't happen) and said that he cut the 'throat, face and body of the victim', police felt that the man was medically disturbed and the lack of physical evidence tying him to the crime would ultimately let them down in a court of law. They did not lay charges against him.

In July 1968, microbiologist Joy Kuhl, who was to gain worldwide notoriety for her work on the Azaria Chamberlain case during the 1980s,[10] provided her findings into the forensic examination of 37 hair samples, newspapers and blood samples from the Brook crime scene. The majority of the hairs examined were found to be of either equine or canine origin—the Brooks had a pet dog, and Simon was described as a being 'fascinated with dogs of every shape and size'.[11] No useful information was provided in relation to human hairs. Blood on the newspapers was found to be human but because of the limited scientific technology of the time, determining a particular blood grouping was inconclusive. Spermatozoa were not detected on the rectal swab obtained from the sample submitted by Dr La'Brooy but Kuhl found 'strong positive presumptive tests for seminal fluid'.

This in itself was disturbing. Had the murderer masturbated after the mutilation? It was the post mortem mutilation, however, that most concerned authorities—there was an element of sadism rarely seen in child murders, which were predominantly the result of domestic violence or sexual attack. 'The mutilation of males is far less common in crime than the mutilation of girls or women,' one report of the period noted. 'There was no exact parallel to this murder anywhere else in the world.'[12]

The New South Wales government also offered a reward of $5,000 but no information was brought to police attention that could identify the person responsible. Norm Allen, the New South Wales Commissioner for Police at the time, took the unprecedented step of assembling a panel of doctors and criminologists whose brief was to help build a psychological profile of the type of person who could have committed this crime. Dr William Rowe, a leading Sydney psychiatrist who had experience of patients with sexual deviance, described in the following interview the type of person he felt could have murdered and then mutilated 3-year-old Simon Brook.[13]

Dr Rowe: To use a more clinical term, the person responsible is a sexual psychopath, a sadist. I think that you could say that [the murderer has] a sexually disordered urge... a sexual urge, if you like, that has gone wrong.
Q: It is an urge to do what exactly?
Dr Rowe: Well to satisfy some emotional desire of which he is not conscious. It's getting rid of some feeling which he just can't put into words.
Q: Are you saying that he could commit a crime like this without knowing that he was doing it?
Dr Rowe: Oh, no, I don't mean that. It's the urge itself which causes him to commit such a crime which he wouldn't be aware of. It's very much the same with crimes of much less importance—like exposure and exhibitionism. A person just has an urge to expose himself to a young girl, without being able to put into words what is causing the urge.
Q: Would you expect him to have graduated, as it were, to the point where he could commit a crime like this? What I mean is, would he have committed a whole string of lesser crimes on the way up to murder and mutilation?
Dr Rowe: This could well be so.
Q: He may already have a conviction for minor sexual offences, then?
Dr Rowe: Yes.
Q: You did say that the man who committed this murder was mad in the medical sense of the word?
Dr Rowe: Yes.
Q: Is it possible, though, that he has never in fact received any psychiatric treatment for any reason?
Dr Rowe: Yes, this is so. I would be more likely to suspect that he had had treatment before; but often these attacks are the first manifestation of the underlying mental disorder.
Q: Are there many people around, then, who are separated merely by a hair's breadth from deviations of this kind?

Dr Rowe: No! Some people may have fantasies along these lines, but would not think of carrying out such a crime as this.
Q: What about the possibility that it was a juvenile? Someone of 14 or 15, perhaps, who was experimenting?
Dr Rowe: I wouldn't have thought so. I would have thought that he would probably be in [about] his 20s.
Q: Why?
Dr Rowe: It's hard just to give an off-the-cuff answer. Past experience has shown us that these people are often in their 20s or early 30s. It is unlikely to be an older person, because this type of disorder usually occurs and makes itself first manifest in the 20s.
Q: Of 11 unsolved child murders [in New South Wales at that time], only two have been against male children. Is there any particular significance in this?
Dr Rowe: Only that the majority of people who commit crimes are males and that most of them, I suppose, are heterosexually orientated. You would expect their crimes to be against the opposite sex.
Q: Would you expect a man who has committed a crime of this gravity to keep it to himself, or would he share it with someone very close to him, say his mother?
Dr Rowe: No, they usually keep it to themselves. This is what makes it so hard to trace them, of course.

Q: The most alarming possibility, I suppose, is that he is going to do it again. How likely is this?
Dr Rowe: There is a strong possibility. Experience shows us that there is often a gap after the first such act; and that they then do it with increasing frequency if they are not caught. In this case, if he is not caught, he may well do it again in one or two years' time; and we can then expect to see his crimes coming with increasing frequency.

The consultation of leading psychiatrists was a bold initiative for a time when very little was known about paedophilia and post mortem mutilation. Professor DC Maddison, a colleague of Donald Brook's at Sydney University, concluded that it was 'highly unlikely that a woman was responsible for committing the crime or that the person was a parent'. The distinguished forensic psychiatrist Dr John McGeorge warned, 'People who molest children are rarely, if ever, cured. Indeed, they are often born with this tendency and have no desire to be cured.' Dr Norwood East, another psychiatrist, added: 'Many offenders refuse psychological treatment because it might cure them of their need for these anti-social pleasures.' In short, most violent fixated paedophiles are never cured because they don't wish to be anything else.

Detectives explored the theory that the child's killer was known to the Brooks, or worse still, was someone who had a grudge against Dr Brook. 'The possibility that the murderer was known to us did not weigh particularly heavily (that is to say, as if it had seemed to be probability, rather than a mere possibility),' Dr Brook writes. 'It would have been, of course, an unattractive possibility. The police were routinely interested in whether I had enemies, and the suggestion was raised that I might have an "enemy" among those artists whose work I had reviewed unfavourably (I was the *Sydney Morning Herald* art critic). This seemed to us preposterous.'

⊗⊗⊗

The Brooks replaced the flimsy wire side fence that their son had crawled through with a large brick wall that secured their privacy but there was an overwhelming sense of futility that this home improvement had come too late for their son.

On 15 January 1969, Justice JJ Loomes delivered an open finding to the official inquest into the death of Simon Brook. Over the next 30 years the Brooks remained publicly silent on the subject of their son's death, not wishing to explore their grief in public or be drawn on potential theories. Intensely private, Dr Brook has only recently confirmed that his wife later suffered a miscarriage and another child, a girl, died in infancy before he and his wife adopted a baby boy.[14]

The Brooks remained in Sydney until 1973 when Dr Brook took up a position at Adelaide's Flinders University and where he earned a worldwide reputation as 'a philosopher on art theory and criticism'[15] and was made an Emeritus Professor of Visual Arts. Brook also has a Fine Art degree from Durham University, a PhD from the Australian National University and is a noted sculptor in his own right. After living in Cyprus for several years, the Brooks returned to Australia and today live in Adelaide.

'During my period as Professor of Visual Arts at the Flinders University (1974–89),' Dr Brook wrote to me vial email, 'I had been deeply affected and my career adversely impacted by a rumour that I discovered—only after several years—to be in circulation, to the effect that I was responsible for Simon's death and that the police were aware of this but lacked sufficient evidence to prosecute. A distressing defamation action ultimately ensued, which was finally settled out of court by the University. There were the usual non-disclosure clauses built in to the settlement, although it is public knowledge that one of my colleagues resigned and I took retirement, upon being awarded the title of Emeritus Professor and being the recipient of a generous letter of apology from the Vice-Chancellor. The wretchedness of that period at Flinders,' Dr Brook writes, 'has nothing to do with the investigation proper (or, at that stage, the lack of investigation) into Simon's death. It just makes over again the already familiar point that victims of crime are curiously exposed to further chastisement in the court of public opinion.'

In the late 1990s the Brooks returned to Australia from Cyprus, where they had been living and studying, and settled in Perth. Dr Brook wondered if advancement in DNA technology could possibly provide some sort of breakthrough in the now three-decade-old investigation into the murder of his son. He continues, 'I wrote to [the then New South Wales Police Commissioner] Peter Ryan in October 2000 to ask whether the file was still open and whether any progress had been made.'

When police went to review the crime scene exhibits for the unsolved Brook case, they discovered that all the physical exhibits seized by police during the original investigation—one pair of trousers, one pullover, one t-shirt, one singlet, one pair of underpants, one pair of red boots, one pair of socks, one razor blade and wrapping paper and newspapers—all except for the biological samples (hair, swab and smears) were deliberately destroyed in 1988.[16] It was common administrative practise at the time to destroy physical exhibits—even those of unsolved cases—because of a lack of storage space. The post mortem samples relating to the murder were later found to be missing from the Government Records Repository at Kingswood in Western Sydney and attempts to locate other copies of the samples at the Government Analyst Laboratories or Glebe Police Station were unsuccessful. These developments, which meant that a renewed investigation into the death of their son to determine DNA profiling was now highly unlikely, was relayed to the Brooks.

Dr Brook maintained a rigorous academic life, even in retirement. As with most academics, he also maintained extensive personal records. Dr Brook ended his brief but generous correspondence with me with the sentence: 'I had a telephone call from [Sydney Detective Sergeant] Adam Barwick at approximately 3.00 pm on 8th July 2004, in which he told me about the inter-state inquiry and of two other likely victims, with Derek Percy as principal suspect.' It was the first time Donald Brook had heard the name Derek Percy.

CHAPTER 9: The Disappearance of Linda Stilwell

In August 2007, 39 years after Linda Jane Stilwell disappeared from the St Kilda foreshore, Melbourne magistrate Susan Wakeling granted her family an application for crimes compensation after ruling that the missing girl had been abducted and murdered. The order was made because an inquest into Linda's disappearance was still to be conducted and crime compensation was not available to victims' families in the 1960s. Under the Victim of Crime Assistance Act, a victim's family could now receive up to $100,000 compensation, but the Stilwell's lawyer, Stephen Schembri, said: 'They are not motivated by money. It has been extremely important for it to be recognised what happened to Linda.'[1]

Older brother Gary Stilwell said that the court decision was 'a huge relief. It is an acknowledgement of what happened,' he stated, before admitting, 'I have been angry for so long because I have always felt we have been let down by the system.'

'For 36 years we, her family, heard nothing,' Karen Stilwell wrote on a website she maintained to honour the memory of her little sister.[2] 'If a child is hit by a car and dies the ones left behind can mourn and visit their resting place. Linda has no such place—she is wherever the animal who abducted her disposed of her body. We have all suffered for so many years a myriad of emotions and feelings… loss, guilt and anguish are just a few. Our lives would never be the same. The loss of a daughter/sister in such an evil act destroyed us all in different ways. Over the years, we had glimmers of hope when different police departments delved into what happened to Linda but nothing came of it and our hopes were dashed again.'

'We have never seen Linda again or know what happened or who was responsible, but I will always hold out hope that we will find her and finally she will rest in peace. I don't believe in a God, but I do believe in a person's soul. I believe a person's soul lives on in the ones left behind. Linda's memory will always live on. She didn't get to go through puberty with all its highs and lows; she didn't experience her first boyfriend or first kiss... no joy of motherhood for Linda... but her memory lives on in all who knew her. We have nowhere to mourn her, so this is my memorial to my sweet little sister who was my best friend. I will miss her always and think of her everyday... she will forever be in my heart.'

Linda Stilwell was 'a happy, carefree little girl' looking forward to her eighth birthday when she went missing from St Kilda in August 1968. Her disappearance sparked a massive search but the tragic events of that Saturday afternoon remained relatively unknown outside of Melbourne. Her family and friends, however, have never forgotten her; nor have the Victoria Police. Since 2004, members of the Melbourne Homicide Squad had been reinvestigating what happened the day Linda Stilwell went missing all those years ago in light of what they now know about Victoria's longest serving inmate—Derek Ernest Percy.

❖❖❖

The Stilwell family came to Australia from England in 1965 as part of the 'assisted passage' program that brought thousands of '£10 poms' to the country after World War II. Brian Stilwell, wife Jean and their three children—Karen, Gary and the youngest, Linda, who was born in 1960—travelled to Australia on the *Fairsky* and lived in a number of migrant hostels before settling in Avondale Heights, a suburb of Melbourne. Brian Stilwell was employed by Vickers Detroit Hydraulics, the firm he had work for in England, while his wife found work in an office. Their marriage, however, was in trouble and not even the birth of a fourth child—daughter Laura in 1967—could improve their relationship. According to one report at the time Brian wanted to 'sit in front of the television' while his wife wanted to 'go out and enjoy life a bit'.[3] It was the 'swinging sixties' and Mrs Stilwell wanted to live a bit. Jean Stilwell quit her office job and gained employment as a barmaid and their relationship soon became violent.

In July 1968, Brian Stilwell left the family in Melbourne and immigrated to New Zealand to live in Otahuhu near Auckland. He took his youngest daughter, Laura, with him while Jean and their three older children moved into an apartment in Beaconsfield Parade, Middle Park, in southern Melbourne. At about 1.00 pm on Saturday 10 August, the three Stilwell children asked their mother if they could walk to nearby St Kilda pier. It was only two weeks after their father had left the family. There was plenty to do at St Kilda—the St Moritz ice skating rink or Luna Park and boats moored at the pier and along the foreshore—would take their minds off the departure of their father and baby sister. Although the Stilwells had next to no money, the children had a knack of making their own fun and the day promised an afternoon of adventure and exploration in their new neighbourhood.

'The 1960s were considered safe for children to roam, so we weren't afraid,' Karen Stilwell later recalled.[4] 'I was considered responsible for my age and was in charge… the three of us were close and, being the eldest, I enjoyed the responsibilities of helping take care of Gary and Linda. Mum was working full time, sometimes two jobs to make ends meet, so we were left to our own devices a lot. Being kids, we always found things to do.' Karen's 7-year-old sister, Linda, was especially open to new adventures. The tomboy of the family, she was drawn to older children and adults—most ominously, she made friends more easily with males than with females.

The Stilwell children met three other boys that winter's afternoon—older boys with fishing lines and rods who were heading off to the pier with a plan to fish off one of the boats moored on the pier. The only problem was—none had permission to be on a boat that afternoon. Later that day a man wearing a striped jersey arrived and told the children to get off his boat. He confiscated the fishing tackle the older boys were carrying and told them they could pick it up from St Kilda Police Station. He then wrote a quick note for the boys to give to the police, admitting that they had been trespassing on the boat.

The confrontation with the boat owner scared the then 12-year-old Karen Stilwell. 'I thought we'd get into trouble,' she said at the time.[5] 'I tried to get Linda to come with me, but she said she was going with the boys to get their lines back.' Gary stayed with her for a little while but was adamant that he was not going with the boys to the police station. Linda told her brother that she would go. 'I told her that she wouldn't be able to find her way back home,' Gary informed authorities, 'but she laughed and said that she would ask someone the way.' When Gary left his sister she was still playing with the boys, who were arguing whether they had the courage to go and confront the police. They never did go to the police station.

Gary eventually arrived home at about 4.00 pm that afternoon, an hour or so after his eldest sister. Jean Stilwell sent her children back out to bring their younger sister home but she was not unduly worried at the time. The Stilwells had only just moved into the area and if Linda wandered from the direct route back to the family unit it might be easy for her to become disorientated. Mrs Stilwell remembered reassuring herself at the time, 'She's a bright little girl and she would be able to find her way back home.'[6]

Jean Stilwell waited until 6.30 pm and went to the pier to look for her daughter but there was no sign of her. Karen recalls: 'Mum was frantic and rang the police. We had no phone so she went to the shops four times to call them. Finally they came out at around 10.00 pm…'[7] The Stilwells had no other relatives living in Australia and their father was on the other side of the Tasman Sea and could not be contacted. They felt alone and abandoned.

Throughout the night police carried out a search of the St Kilda foreshore and even drove around the streets of Avondale Heights in case Linda had tried to return to the family's old address. A description of the missing girl was quickly circulated throughout the state. Linda was seven years old and 4 feet 6 inches tall; thin with light brown hair, cut slightly longer than a page boy cut with a fringe; with blue eyes and a fair complexion. She was wearing a mustard coloured, crew-necked pure wool jumper, light blue jeans, black shoes and odd socks—one fawn and one white. As dawn broke, police had to entertain several scenarios—that the little girl was lost; she had deliberately run away because she missed her father and sister; she had fallen off the pier and drowned, or she had been abducted.

'She had a liking for boats and ships,' her mother told journalists who descended on the family home to cover the story, 'and may have thought she could follow her father.'[8] Mrs Stilwell conceded that 'she is a compulsive wanderer. Several times she has not come home until 7.00 or 8.00 pm after spending the whole day outside... I chastised her for coming home late from school, and even went as far as offering her presents every fortnight if she managed to arrive home on time each night. Sometimes she would make it a few minutes late on one or two days, but I always overlooked that.' Understandably, Jean Stilwell often broke into tears as she tried to remain positive with so many strangers in her home. She told how Linda 'was looking forward to her birthday next Thursday [22 August] and I had promised to take her to the pictures. I had even bought her a new pair of shoes which she was keen to show off at school on Monday.'[9]

Police conducted a doorknock search of the area, scores of volunteers dug up St Kilda beach and a thorough examination of tidal movements was undertaken but no trace of the missing girl was found. A special squad of police cadets searched an area covering six square miles centred on the Luna Park area, along the St Kilda foreshore and in drains that emptied into the sea. Although Linda could not swim, police discounted the theory that she had fallen into the water—the tides of Port Phillip are predictable and a body was not found washed up on the shore in the week after her disappearance. Search and rescue squad skindivers searched nearby Albert Park Lake and the Elwood canal without success.

On Monday, 12 August, the *Herald Sun* reported: 'Police hold grave fears for the safety of Linda Stilwell, 7, who disappeared from Little Luna Park (St Kilda) on Saturday.'[10] Melbourne D24 was inundated with reported sightings of the missing girl and all were thoroughly checked. Detectives received several reports of a man and a little girl getting into a taxi at St Kilda but the taxi driver was not located and the report could not be verified. Another report of a man with a little girl getting into a HR Holden at a Dandenong service station provided the first real lead but the man heard the report and went to the police and cleared the matter. He was travelling with his daughter. A 'scruffy looking man'[11] seen hitch-hiking with a little girl in Horsham was later located in Adelaide—the man had hitch-hiked with his 8-year-old stepdaughter to visit her mother who had been injured in a car accident.

Patrol officers throughout the city were issued with photos of the missing girl but as the days passed, fears worsened for her safety. Police urged people to search backyard sheds, old refrigerators or piles of rubbish that could hide a child's body. By Tuesday, newspaper reports carried an ominous tone. 'Hopes of finding alive South Melbourne girl Linda Stilwell, 7, are fading fast as the search enters its third day,' wrote the *Herald Sun*. 'One of the most intensive searches in the state's history yesterday failed to uncover any trace of the lively child... Police think it is remotely possible that Linda might have run away from home and is hiding somewhere in the St Kilda or South Melbourne area.'[12]

During that long week Melbourne detectives received a telegram from Auckland, simply signed 'Stilwell', saying that Brian Stilwell had heard of his daughter's disappearance but knew nothing about her whereabouts. The 33-year-old father had yet to find work, the telegram said, was currently 'unwell' and unlikely to return to Melbourne. A concerned local woman offered to pay his fare back to Australia but he declined to return and asked police not to publish his new address. It would not be until the end of November, with his daughter still missing, that Mr Stilwell returned to Melbourne to visit his family. He was promptly sued by his ex-wife for maintenance and the case was settled out of court with an undertaking that neither parent would take the older two children out of the state.[13]

Police learned that Linda was seen asking attendants at Little Luna Park at St Kilda for a ride on the dodgem cars—she had no money that afternoon. In the ensuing days, at least ten people were identified as possible witnesses to Linda's final movements that Saturday afternoon. A woman from the East Melbourne suburb of Kew had been walking along the upper esplanade of St Kilda beach at about 5.15 pm when she walked down the stairs leading to the lower esplanade and saw a little girl playing 'roll downs' on the lawn between the two levels. She was positive that the girl was Linda Stilwell. The woman also told police that three teenage boys on the lower esplanade had passed by Linda as they called out to three girls on the upper esplanade. Two middle-aged men who were sitting in parked cars, possibly Holdens, would also have seen the little girl and another younger man with a dark complexion was sitting on a park bench at the time, reported the woman.

Police tracked down the six teenagers and the two men parked in cars but the 'dark man' was never identified and became the chief suspect. There was a further report that at 6.00 pm a man answering the suspect's general description was seen in nearby Carlisle Street, walking away from St Kilda Beach, and Linda was with him. One sighting suggested that 'he was walking so fast that [Linda] had to half-run to keep up with him',[14] but she was laughing and appeared happy. Asked whether her daughter would have gone off with a stranger, Mrs Stilwell said: 'She was very trusting and would have believed any story an adult would have told her. She might have told the man she was missing her little sister Laura and the man could have convinced her that he would take her to see her… She is the most trusting little girl you can imagine. She just wouldn't believe me when I told her that some strangers are bad people.'[15]

The 'dark man' was described as being of slim build, 5 foot 10 inches tall with short, dark curly hair. He was said to be wearing a check, open-necked shirt, a brown or maroon v-neck jumper and dark trousers. The original description of the man having a 'dark' complexion led police to Port Melbourne on the Wednesday after Linda's disappearance. It was a long shot, but police interviewed the crew of a visiting West African ship, the *Veille Etoile*, most of whom were black Mauritian sailors. Police found nothing related to the little girl's disappearance.

By the sixth day, and with no trace of the girl found, the *Herald Sun* reported: 'Detectives heading the search for Linda Stilwell, 7, who disappeared from St Kilda last Saturday now say that there is little doubt the child has been the victim of foul play.' A Homicide Squad detective said at the time: 'We must keep an open mind so that we can follow every angle... it certainly looks bad. We have a hundred theories and we just have to keep following them all.'[16]

One of the 'theories' Melbourne CIB would have considered was the seemingly tenuous link to the disappearance of three children from Adelaide's Glenelg Beach two and a half years before. Adelaide detectives who investigated the disappearance of the Beaumont children in 1966 asked for details of Linda's disappearance to be sent to them. Detective Sergeant Stan Swaine, who was then head of Adelaide Homicide, felt that despite the distance and the passage of time there was an 'uncanny resemblance'[17] in the two crimes. Linda Stilwell, it was said, had 'vanished in circumstances almost identical with those surrounding the disappearance of the Beaumont children'.

The Stilwell family tried to remain optimistic. Jean Stilwell tried to keep it all together, for the sake of her children. 'I will never give up hope,' she said at the time. 'I will keep thinking that at any moment she will walk in the door... until they find her, dead or alive, I will keep hoping.'[18] So on Sunday 18 August, with Linda missing for eight days, the family celebrated Gary's tenth birthday. 'Birthdays were important,' a red-eyed Jean Stilwell told Don Sharpe of *The Age*. Even though Linda was still missing, this was no reason for Gary to miss out on his party, she said. Karen and Gary Stilwell had been staying with family friends, the Noble family in Flemington, while their mother helped police with their enquiries. The Stilwells celebrated Gary's birthday along with Linda's friend, 8-year-old Lorraine Noble. When Lorraine blew out her candles she whispered, 'I wish Linda was here'. During the week her mother had told Lorraine that Linda was 'out playing' and had got lost but even the little girl knew that her friend could not have been playing all this time. Something had happened to her.

On Thursday 22 August, Linda Stilwell would have turned eight. Her mother, Jean, took the day off work, instead of her usual Saturday because she said she just wanted to 'run away and hide for the day'.[19] Linda's disappearance took its toll on the family. Three months after her daughter disappeared, Jean Stilwell took an accidental overdose of sleeping tablets. Oldest daughter Karen told reporters, 'Mummy took the wrong tablets. The police came and switched the lights on in our room to see if we were all right. Mummy was rubbing her hands over her face and hair. She looked real tired.'[20] Mrs Stilwell recovered, but her family had been ripped apart.

Although one of Victoria's top murder investigators, Detective Sergeant Doug Baker, took over the Stilwell investigation there was no breakthrough in the case. A mobile caravan was established at St Kilda so that Linda's disappearance still had a public profile and to make it easier for anyone who wanted to pass on information, no matter how insignificant. Almost 500 people were interviewed and more than 2000 statements were taken down by investigating police but no trace of Linda was ever found, nor was the identity of the 'dark man' established. But gradually the investigation went cold and detectives were assigned to other cases.

In 1969, a local man consulted international clairvoyant Gerard Croiset about the unsolved case of Linda Stilwell. Several years before Croiset gained a dubious notoriety with his involvement in the search for the Beaumont children. John Berkers, a 51-year-old Alphington man, took it upon himself to contact the Dutch clairvoyant despite the fact that Croiset's 'predictions' regarding the Beaumont children had shed no light on their fate in the three years they had been missing. Croiset told Berkers that he 'saw' Linda standing on a wooden bridge leading into the sea. She then slipped, he said, and was 'sucked into the water'.[21]

The clairvoyant asked Berkers to send him a map of the area and a picture of Linda to verify his 'visions'. Croiset was certain—there was no question of Linda being abducted or murdered – she had a met with an accident in the water but the clairvoyant maintained that there was 'no chance of her body now being found'. He refused to provide any further details because he did not want to raise the hopes of the Stilwell family. Berkers took the information to the authorities but Victoria Police dismissed the claims—they did not entertain the 'visions' of clairvoyants in their investigations.

What Berkers did not know is that that such 'visions' were part of Croiset's own *modus operandi*—part of his pattern of public predictions upon which he had built his international reputation. If a child went missing Croiset either said that the child was 'under the ground' or 'in the water'[22]—the celebrity seer was clever enough to know that if a child fell in water, the body would float to the surface after several days. If there was no water in the vicinity where the child went missing, he would say that the child fell into a tunnel or cave and was buried underground—which is why he always asked for maps. If the search party never found them, that didn't mean that he was wrong—they were merely looking in the wrong place. In the disappearance of Linda Stilwell, Croiset was simply covering all the bases—the child was in the water but her body would not be found.

Years later, Karen Stilwell recalled: 'My memories of what we did that day have dimmed and merged with others, but I do remember all three of us were on the pier talking to some other kids, it was getting late and I knew Mum was expecting us. I told Gary and Linda to come home, they didn't want to leave yet so I said I was going home… the first major mistake I made was leaving the two of them. Gary later told us they had gone to little Luna Park, which was just down from the major park. He came home a little while later and said he and Linda had gotten separated so Mum sent me to look for her.

'This was where I made the next mistake... I didn't go all the way to the park to look for her. The guilt I have felt for playing on the swings and thinking she would come home any minute like she had lots of times before has haunted me for so many years. The next weeks were a nightmare. I wanted to die. I thought it should have been me that was taken, not Linda. Mum was a mess, understandably. [Until] I was grown and had counselling I thought Mum blamed me but she never had, but it forever affected our relationship. I look up to her; she is a strong wonderful woman.'[23]

In the ensuing years Jean Stilwell kept in contact with police; whenever she moved house, she would go to the Homicide Squad offices and pass on her new address in the hope that one day she would get the call that there had been a breakthrough in the investigation. But over the years she found the new generation of detectives no longer recognised her or even her daughter's name.

***

Before Operation Heats was formed in 2004 to investigate the movements of Derek Percy in the late 1960s, Melbourne 'cold case' detectives contacted Jean Priest, the former Mrs Stilwell, and informed her that they were reviewing a number of missing person cases and were prepared to reinvestigate the disappearance of her daughter Linda. 'Our role was to put an inquest together—at that stage it was a brief that had never been to inquest—and the coroner would revisit the case,' Detective Wayne Newman remembers. 'Jean Priest was both shocked and relieved when we contacted her.'[24]

Mr Brian Stilwell has since passed away but the remainder of Linda's family have obviously taken a keen interest in the renewed investigation. 'Do these matters help in that there is still a lot of pain to go through first?' Detective Newman asks rhetorically before answering his own question. 'I think it helps the family in that it gives them confidence that certain police are involved 40years down the track... that Linda hasn't been forgotten.'

But there is also a lot of pain and grief associated with delving into unresolved issues from the past. 'It's easy to see the impact on the parents of missing children,' Newman says. 'The crimes remain unsolved and the pain never goes away. I speak to Jean Priest quite regularly and she's an extremely strong woman but... Linda's disappearance has impacted on all the family. When I speak to Gary Stilwell, I can still hear the sadness in his voice. Karen Stilwell has written about it... there's a lot of guilt involved. They all went looking for her and never found her.'

St Kilda was a place where children were entertained— 'a magnet for kids', Detective Dave Rae says—and despite the countless adults in the area it was also a magnet for anyone wanting to prey on lost children. 'The person responsible doesn't have to be a local... he doesn't need to know the area... he could have just been driving through the vicinity at the time.' Newman adds: 'You look at where the Stilwell family were living at the time, in Beaconsfield Parade—there is nothing left there today of the apartments, it has all been developed—but it really was only a short distance to St Kilda pier... it wasn't as if Linda had wandered kilometres away from her home.'

'The original investigation was extremely thorough,' Newman says. 'We've only progressed to this stage today because of the work done by the original members—both uniform police from the first time she was reported missing to when it was passed on to the homicide squad very early on. The actual physical search was extreme ... the military was involved; police scoured blocks of the area and the Bureau of Meteorology was consulted regarding tidal movements. On the first night Linda went missing the entire area was lit up overnight... it was a phenomenal effort by the uniform branch.'

The detectives identified the boys with the fishing rods who were with Linda on the afternoon she went missing and reinterviewed them. While Newman admits that the passage of time can work against 'cold case' investigations, he says: 'I have been astounded at the recollections the witnesses have in this matter.' The reality remains, however, in that there is no forensic material at the moment that can advance the Stilwell investigation. This is why Operations Heats was formed in 2004 to build a behavioural profile of the prime suspect in Linda's disappearance—Derek Ernest Percy.

When Percy was arrested in 1969, police found maps in his car of Melbourne's CBD with routes marked in texta. One map included a line drawn past the spot where Linda Stilwell was last seen on St Kilda esplanade. Ron Anderson, the young policeman who went to school with the suspect in Mt Beauty, talked to Percy in the city watchhouse on the day after his arrest. Asked if he had killed Linda Stilwell, Percy said: 'Possibly, I don't remember a thing about it.' But he also volunteered that he drove through St Kilda on the day the girl disappeared. 'I had been at *Cerberus* in the afternoon and was driving along The Esplanade on the way to the White Ensign Club for some drinks,' he said.[25]

The White Ensign Club was founded in the 1950s to cater for sailors stationed in Melbourne and its premises, at the time, were in South Melbourne. Percy volunteered that he was driving through St Kilda that day and obviously knew the area where Linda Stilwell went missing—HMAS *Cerberus* is only 90 minutes away by car. Had Percy scouted the area on previous visits, parked his car nearby and sat on a park bench waiting for an opportunity to present itself? This, of course, is purely speculative, but it led Melbourne detectives to review the 35-year-old investigation into the murder of Yvonne Tuohy and look for similar patterns of behaviour in the Stilwell matter.

Wayne Newman says: 'We were of the view that in order to get a good picture of the Stilwell matter we really had to look at the other matters'—Tuohy, Redston, Beaumont and Wanda— 'in order to bring the investigation to inquest'. That created the first dilemma. 'It's one thing to investigate,' Newman says, 'but it's no good if you're unable to present it before a competent jurisdiction. David Rae and I met with Melbourne Coroner, Mr Graeme Johnstone, and he had an open mind and took a very commonsense approach and essentially said that he would be happy to hear all these matters' in support of an inquest.

'Although the "rule of evidence" does not apply at an inquest we are very mindful not to go off on witch hunts and we were grateful to the Coroner to allow us to gather evidence so that he can get a full picture of what happened to Linda Stilwell,' Newman says. 'We have a brief to introduce evidence from other crimes that Percy may have been involved in to show a pattern of behaviour.'

Operation Heats has given Jean Priest new hope. 'It has helped me to know that people like [Senior Detective] Wayne Newman have cared so much and done so much work,' she told *The Age*. 'You learn to live with what has happened but you can never forget.'[26]

Melbourne detectives have sent their report to the Victorian Coroner and continue to build their profile of Derek Percy while they await a date to be set for the coronial inquest into the disappearance of Linda Stilwell. The mystery of what happened to Linda may one day be determined, and could also provide the catalyst for charges to be laid against a 'known person'.

CHAPTER 10:
Custodial Review

I mention one final matter. Prior to, and during the course of, my hearings several articles appeared in the newspapers which speculated that Mr Percy may have committed more killings than that of Yvonne Tuohy. There is no evidence before me to support that assertion. Amongst the materials placed before me was a statement by Detective Senior Constable KS Robertson of the Victoria Police, dated 5 May 1970. In that report Robertson referred to an interview conducted with Mr Percy about the deaths and disappearances of other children, both in New South Wales and Canberra. I did not hear evidence from Mr Robertson.

At its highest the statement of Mr Robertson records Mr Percy's agreement that on other occasions prior to the death of Yvonne Tuohy, whilst on beaches in New South Wales, he had sordid thoughts towards children, and his agreement that he might have committed other offences had not the children been in the company of their parents. The note records that police had no evidence to connect Mr Percy to any other killings. Only one item of evidence was advanced. When questioned about one killing in Sydney he is recorded as having said 'I could have done it but I can't remember'. The statement of Mr Robertson merely reports that that alleged comment had been conveyed to him by an unidentified police officer. The circumstances in which the comment was made (if it was) are unknown. There is no other evidence, at all, to link Mr Percy to any other killings.

I have considered this material, as I am entitled to do because in conducting a major review I am not bound by the rules of evidence (Section 38), but, having considered that material, it is apparent that I could give little weight to it. It is not surprising that there was such speculation at the time of Mr Percy's arrest and trial, but it is

> important that speculation based on so little evidence should not distract the court from the task of evaluating the credible evidence which is available for scrutiny.[1]
>
> —*Justice Geoffrey Eames, 1998*

⊠⊠⊠

The custodial review of Derek Percy was heard from July to September in 1998 in the Supreme Court of Victoria before Justice Geoffrey Eames. Because Percy had been detained at the 'governor's pleasure' for almost 29 years, he was defined as an 'existing detainee' within the terms of the new Crimes (Mental Impairment and Unfitness to be Tried) Act which made him subject to a 'custodial supervision order'. The purpose of a custodial review is to determine whether the person subject to the order is able to be released from it. The over-riding consideration in making this decision is whether the safety of the person subject to the order, or members of the public would be seriously endangered as a result of the release of the person on a non-custodial supervision order.

Although the news created barely a ripple in the national media, the prospect that Derek Percy could be released from custody created a media storm in Melbourne in 1998 with speculation that Percy might be freed. Newspaper articles in the *Sunday Herald Sun* on 23 August and in the *Herald Sun News Pictorial* on 2 September were later deemed to have been 'plainly prompted' by Percy's custodial review and found to be in 'contempt of the court'.[2] The *Sunday Herald Sun* article flew the banner headline 'Don't Let Him Out' while the second article, demanding 'Never Let Him Out' began:

> *The detective who first questioned Victoria's longest serving prisoner believes the killer should never be let out of jail. Derek Ernest Percy was jailed at the governor's pleasure in 1970, when he pleaded insanity over the mutilation murder*

> *in July 1969 of 12-year-old Yvonne Tuohy.*
>
> *A Supreme Court judge is considering whether to release Percy, now 51 [sic] following a review of the case under the Crimes (Mental Impairment and Unfitness to be Tried) Act.*
>
> *Mr Bernie Delaney was a senior detective with the homicide squad when he questioned Percy hours after the killing of the girl. He also prepared a brief for the coroner which involved compiling evidence, interviewing witnesses and gathering exhibits.*
>
> *Mr Delaney and another homicide detective who has since died, Sgt Dick Knight, arrested Percy at* Cerberus *Naval Base and carried out the first of many interviews there and at Frankston police station.*
>
> *Earlier in the day Percy attempted to abduct Yvonne Tuohy and a friend from the beach at Warneet on Westernport Bay. The friend, Shane Spiller, who was 11 at the time, escaped and raised the alarm.*
>
> *Percy's car was later identified by uniformed police at* Cerberus, *and detectives Delaney and Knight were called in to make the arrest… Mr Delaney said Percy would still be a danger to the community.*
>
> *'If I am wrong and he still has to stay in jail for years, well I can live with that. The risk is too high,' Mr Delaney said.*
>
> *Mr Delaney has not been called to give evidence at the review.*
>
> *Percy has been questioned over the years by detectives investigating other infamous child killings in the '60s which happened when he was known to be in the same area. He has been a suspect in the disappearance of the three Beaumont children in Adelaide in 1966, the Wanda Beach killings of two schoolgirls south of Sydney in 1965, the killing of a schoolboy, 6, in Canberra in 1966 and the mutilation murder of a three-year-old boy in the Sydney suburb of Glebe in 1968.*[3]

A more sober and correct view of the custodial review exercise was given by Justice Eames. 'It is important to note that a major review is not a sentencing exercise,' he said.[4] 'Mr Percy has been found not guilty, on the ground of insanity, by verdict of a jury, and his detention for 29 years has not been pursuant to a sentence. The task set for the court under Section 35 is not to determine whether the circumstances of the killing which led to his detention were such that any, or any additional, punishment should be imposed by extending the period of his detention. The issues before me focus on the question of present and future danger, not on punishment for events of the past.'

The opinions of several experts were relied upon in the review. Dr Ruth Vine, the authorised psychiatrist attached to Rosanna Forensic Mental Health Centre; Professor Paul Mullen, the Clinical Director of the Victorian Institute of Forensic Mental Health; and Dr Lester Walton, consulting clinical psychiatrist all agreed on the same key point—Derek Percy did not suffer from a mental illness. However, Justice Eames addressed this point in stating that 'the fact that Mr Percy does not suffer a recognised mental illness is important for a number of reasons, not least because it means that he *cannot* be transferred from prison to a mental health facility, such as the Rosanna Forensic Psychiatry Centre ... [which is] only for a person who "appears to be mentally ill". The fact that such a transfer is not open to Mr Percy under that provision means that so long as the diagnosis remains that he is not suffering a recognised mental illness his only prospect of transfer from prison to an approved mental health service is by order of the court by way of this major review.'

Dr Vine described Mr Percy's condition as being 'a highly unusual one, not being a condition now understood as constituting insanity or mental impairment, but being a disorder which fell into a category of paraphilia,[5] being a paedophilic attraction to minors of both sexes, with sadistic features.' In addition, Percy had demonstrated a grotesque preoccupation with faeces, and excreta generally. Aspects of Percy's behaviour such as deliberately soiling his pants to obtain an erection, putting excreta on his penis and forcing his victims to eat biscuits soaked in urine were characteristics of his particular paraphilia. 'Mr Percy has a schizoid personality and is extremely guarded as to what he states,' Dr Vine said. 'He has an abnormal personality with prominent traits of isolation from others.'

Dr Vine considered that it was difficult to make a more definitive assessment because of Mr Percy's reluctance to discuss the sexual fantasies. Therefore Dr Vine conceded that she could not prove that Derek Percy held the same fantasies as were exposed at his trial in 1969 and in 1971 when written articles were confiscated from his cell at Pentridge. While she acknowledged the difficulty of predicting future behaviour in any person, there was no evidence at that time [1998] that Percy had said or written anything that would support her contention. It was clear, however, that Percy had avoided all attempts to enter into 'a frank dialogue' with any treating psychiatrist or mental health professional. 'He has simply denied that he does hold such fantasies,' Dr Vine told the court.

It was Dr Vine's opinion, however, that given that the dangerous sexual and sadistic fantasies which had been present since Percy's teenage years had been acted upon in 1969 and had been re-asserted in his 1971 writings, it was likely that 'his dangerous proclivities were deeply entrenched' and that the clinical experience and literature suggested that there was 'a risk that such entrenched attitudes may remain with the person for life'.

Derek Percy, however, told Dr Walton that his fantasies had 'abated soon after the killing... and had not recurred'. Dr Walton stressed that unlike other known paedophile offenders—even those who have killed—it was the 'very fact of killing which was the end which had been sought by Percy'. In his particular case, killing was not an unintended result, but would continue to be 'the essential purpose of his behaviour' should his condition not be controlled. This was, Dr Walton said, despite Percy's assertion in an interview with him that the murder was 'an unplanned event, which had occurred after he had attempted to rape the young girl,' and had not been the reason why the abduction occurred.

Professor Mullen said his expectation was that Percy's fantasy life continued to this day. As to Percy's statement to Dr Walton, Professor Mullen said that if such 'abatement' occurred it would make his situation most unusual, if not 'unique'. Professor Mullen said there were few cases with which to compare Mr Percy for purposes of making any prediction as to future behaviour, because his situation was that of a man who had 'fantasised, planned, articulated in his own mind a system of hurting, humiliating and torturing a child, ending with killing it as the direction and source of that sexual gratification. That is extremely rare, fortunately.'

The problem remained that, because so little was known about Percy's fantasy life and sexual behaviour, if he was released into the public there would be no 'warning signs' should he intend to murder another child. In fact, Percy was known to have been functioning normally as a naval cadet at the time he murdered Yvonne Tuohy in 1969. In many ways, he was just as much a danger now as he was on the day he was captured.

Justice Eames noted that Percy's sadistic paedophilia 'is a condition which must produce killing and torture were it not controlled (which would seem likely to be the case if Mr Percy were to seek to obtain gratification by indulging in the fantasies produced by his condition); the fact that any planning to cause death would be unobserved; the fact that no community resources exist, which could prevent a killing should he, while free, succumb to the same urges to indulge in such crimes; are all factors which suggest that great care needs to be taken in assessing the question whether his release would constitute a serious endangerment for the public.'

Mr P Tehan, senior counsel for Percy, outlined 'a range of factors', which suggested that Percy would not seriously endanger the public, if released. 'He has been a model prisoner for nearly 30 years; there is no evidence since 1971, either in any writing or in any interview with the many departmental and professional people with whom he has had dealings, that he harbours abhorrent fantasies; his parents and siblings have offered positive support should he be released; and he was very young when the killing occurred.' As to the suggestion that he has been evasive about his memory of the events leading up to the killing, and the killing itself, Mr Tehan submitted that there are reasons why, over time, he might have forgotten many of the details of the killing and may not necessarily be refusing deliberately to discuss them with consultants.

By contrast the psychiatrists agreed that Percy's 'psychiatric situation' is so unique that any treatment program would have to be devised solely for him after assessing and evaluating his situation. As to whether any such program could be developed and be successfully delivered, Professor Mullen expressed a 'very tentative' opinion that it might be possible, if approached carefully, over time. In her evidence, Dr Vine said that although Percy may have 'asserted a willingness to cooperate with treatment programs, he has not, in practice, demonstrated the willing cooperation which is required for any program.'

Justice Eames was equally unconvinced: 'In my opinion, an examination of the 1969 and 1971 material, together with knowledge of the facts surrounding the killing, tend to confirm that not only was Mr Percy very dangerous at that time, he remains so, because the underlying sadistic condition was then, and remains now, deeply entrenched. He has received no treatment of any kind which might have changed that situation. He has shown no real interest in having such treatment. He has demonstrated no significant remorse or anxiety, at least none which I find credible, as to the circumstances which caused him to kill. He has not sought to gain insight into those matters, save, to a very superficial degree, in an attempt to satisfy or divert those seeking to explore the issues with him for the purpose of writing reports which he knows might assist his attempts to gain transfer out of prison, as a step toward ultimate release.'

This was a telling consideration—did Percy express a desire to 'get help' only so that he could transfer to a minimum security mental hospital? Was this the 'first step' in his eventual release or even extended leave as an out-patient? Was he asking for a transfer so that he could have closer access to the outside world—and children?

Percy did not give evidence before his review, and his assertion that he no longer held violent sexual fantasies could not be tested. 'There may well be good reason why Mr Percy would be reluctant to participate openly in such an exploration of his inner thoughts and motivations,' Eames noted. 'He might fear that should he acknowledge that he continues to have such fantasies then it may well harm his prospects of eventual release. His dilemma is that without such cooperation the psychiatrists decline to merely accept his word that his fantasies have changed, and they also take the view that any treatment regime would be extremely difficult to devise or successfully conduct without his full and frank cooperation.'

The fact Percy did not give evidence made it much more reasonable to draw the inference that his deep-seated sadistic-sexual fantasies had continued since 1971. 'Because I am satisfied that Mr Percy holds those fantasies,' Justice Eames ruled, 'in my opinion, the conclusion is irresistible that he remains as dangerous now as he was in 1969 and 1971. Once that conclusion is reached then… I must confirm the custodial supervision order, but I may vary the place of custody.'

Mr Tehan asked Justice Eames if he could be satisfied that the safety of the public would not be seriously endangered if he reduced Percy's status to that of a non-custodial supervision order on condition that he resided at Unit M5 at Rosanna, and obeyed the directions of the Clinical Director of the Centre. In effect, what was proposed was that Percy would be subject to a 'non-custodial order' but would still be 'in custody' because he would not be permitted to leave M5 without approval of the Director or the Court. Unit M5 at the Rosanna Centre is a low security ward, however, it is one where he would mix with mentally ill patients and out-patients and was 'a quite inappropriate placement' for Percy.

Dr Vine noted that in the 'changed environment' which would accompany his release, or even his detention in a low security mental health unit, Percy would undoubtedly constitute 'a serious danger'. Dr Vine's assessments were generally shared by Professor Mullen and Dr Walton and their reports were consistent in the assertion that, in whatever terms Percy's condition could be diagnosed or described, he still presented 'a serious danger to the public and should not be released'. On the basis of these opinions, Justice Eames ruled on 2 October 1998, 'that the safety of members of the public would be seriously endangered were Mr Percy to be released on a non-custodial supervision order.'

❋❋❋

The Herald & Weekly Times—publishers of the Melbourne newspapers which carried the two articles regarding Percy's potential release—were later found to be in contempt of the Supreme Court. The court ruled that the articles 'had a tendency or was calculated to interfere with the due administration of justice' and fined the proprietor and editor of the newspapers a total of $12,000 pending an appeal. In September 2001, Justice Phillips upheld the appeal, stating that the headlines 'Don't Let Him Out' and 'Never Let Him Out' expressed the views of private citizens, were not directions by the newspapers toward the court and therefore 'contempt' was not proven.

All this legal attention put Derek Percy's name back in the public domain and he was being readily linked to five other unsolved crimes involving children. Another controversy also raged. It had been revealed that Percy was one of the wealthiest inmates in the Victorian prison system. After he was retained at the 'governor's pleasure' Percy received $1270 in back pay from the navy and continued to receive a fortnightly pension cheque from the government. By the late 1980s he had more than $30,000 in a bank account and had bought his own personal computer. Eventually he invested his pension fund in gold and had accumulated almost $200,000 in 2003, by which time the situation of a sadistic paedophile amassing a small fortune had caused a public furore.[6] The law was reformed in 2007 but because Percy was not found guilty of an offence, he was not made to repay the money.

In one of those peculiar 'six degrees of separation' situations that often permeate criminal cases, Tim Attrill, a high-ranking Victoria Police Inspector at the time, served with Derek Percy when they were both cadets on the training frigate HMAS *Queensborough*. Attrill told the press that 'many former sailors were disgusted that Percy still received a pension from the navy and had accrued nearly $200,000 since his arrest. "I know there will be a submission to the government to cancel his pension. Why should taxpayers support that animal?" ... I have no doubt that if he ever gets loose he will do it again,' Inspector Attrill said. 'He is a disaster waiting to happen. He is highly intelligent, one of the most intelligent people I've met. He is cold, without emotion and looks straight through you with his crazy eyes. The only way he should be allowed out is in a pine box.'[7]

Derek Percy, though, had other ideas. The Crimes Act (1997) was amended in 2002 to provide that major custodial reviews are to take place at intervals not exceeding five years following the expiry of 25 years as a detainee.[8] Thus in November 2003 Percy initiated his second custodial review before Justice Murray Kellam in the Supreme Court of Victoria. The issues raised during this review were the same as in 1998: his mental health status; his risk of reoffending; and whether he still suffered gross sexual fantasies. In preparation for this second tribunal, Percy was interviewed by forensic psychiatrist Dr Lindsay Thompson on 20 August.

Percy told her that his fantasies 'may have ceased pretty soon after or straight away after the index offence'[9]—but he was patently lying. Dr Thompson challenged Percy that it was well-known that he was still writing about these fantasies in 1971. Percy denied having any such interest in writing down and generating sadistic fantasies and even denied a number of aspects of the fantasies which were clearly reported by Dr Bartholomew in his 1970 trial. Dr Thompson stated that, although Percy engaged 'very well' with the interview process, he did so only until such time as the issues of his sexual history, sadistic fantasies and the murder for which he was captured was raised with him by her. Dr Thompson observed 'an immediate change in his presentation and he became passive and unforthcoming when such matters were raised. It was as if a curtain descended' she said. Dr Thompson's opinion was that if Percy was released into the community on a non-custodial supervision order there would be the potential for serious risk to the community.

Another important insight into Percy's fantasy life was provided by Professor James Ogloff, the Director of Psychological Services at the Victorian Institute of Forensic Mental Health:

> *It is an understatement to say that this is a unique and disturbing case. Mr Percy was found Not Guilty by Reason of Insanity in 1970 for an offence that involved the abduction, sexual assault, mutilation, and killing of a 12-year-old girl. He also tried to abduct an 11-year-old boy. The horror of the situation cannot be overstated and is amongst the worst I have seen in almost 20 years of work with adult offenders.*
> *It is agreed that contemporary approaches to forensic crimes mental health would not result in clinicians finding that Mr Percy ever met the criteria for a major crimes mental illness and that he would not have been found Not Guilty by Reason of Insanity if the offence occurred today. Mr Percy does not have a major mental illness at the present time.*
> *It is apparent and not disputed that Mr Percy has a paraphilia, namely paedophilia and sadism. He demonstrated disturbing and entrenched aberrant sexual fantasies that were in existence for at least five to eight years surrounding the time of the offence. Although he denies the presence of such fantasies at this time, the likelihood that they abated entirely is unlikely.*

> *Mr Percy has never received long-term ongoing treatment of his sexual disorder.*
> *Mr Percy has been described as a loner and he is emotionally withdrawn and distant. He engages in activities in isolation and does not engage with others. His range of emotions is restricted. The information suggests that these conditions have been present over the course of his life… It is likely that Mr Percy has a personality disorder, namely Schizoid Personality Disorder.*
> *Without concrete evidence to the contrary, Mr Percy continues to present a high level of risk for violent sexual re-offending. As such, he requires ongoing detention in a secure facility… Mr Percy requires an ongoing period of treatment with an experienced psychologist or psychiatrist to begin to address his sexual disorder and level of risk it represents. As such, it is my recommendation that Mr Percy be offered the opportunity to engage in such treatment…*
> *Of concern, Mr Percy now denies or is unaware of any relationship between the aberrant fantasies and sexual arousal, yet considerable evidence exists that Mr Percy very clearly obtained sexual gratification from the fantasies. When pressed, Mr Percy states that he simply does not know or does not recall the relationship between the fantasies and his sexual arousal…*

Professor Ogloff concluded his report with the comment: 'Taken together, it would be very unlikely that the fantasies would have simply disappeared.'

Professor Paul Mullen noted that Percy's 'sexual desires have been directed toward children. He has engaged in extensive sadistic fantasies and tragically acted out those fantasies. He suffers a number of sexual anomalies, including sexual excitement in relation to excretion.' The murder of Yvonne Tuohy in 1969 'arose out of a long period of detailed fantasies, which involved the killing and maiming of children,' and that it was now clear that Percy acted on fantasies which he 'had already articulated and written down… That leaves us with obviously very grave concerns about the possibility of that scenario being repeated,' Professor Mullen said.

The evidence given by Dr Thompson, Professor Mullen and Professor Ogloff led Justice Kellam to form the opinion that there was a high degree of probability that the 'grossly aberrant fantasies which were, beyond doubt, suffered by Percy in 1971, continue to be a significant factor in his thinking'. The unanimous opinion of the three psychiatrists was that Percy 'does not now suffer from any identifiable mental illness', but does suffer from 'a gross abnormality of sexual orientation and desire'.

After a two-month hearing Justice Kellam ruled in March 2004: '… the submissions made by both the Attorney-General, through his counsel, Mrs Morrish, QC, and by the reviewee, through his counsel, Ms Randazzo, SC, are that I should confirm the custodial supervision order and, in doing so, confirm that the reviewee is to continue to be held in custody in a prison. In such circumstances, it is beyond argument, in my view, that his release from custody would seriously endanger the public.'

Close to the end of the proceedings and after all of the evidence was presented to Justice Kellam, Ms Carmen Randazzo, on Percy's behalf, submitted that he should be transferred from prison to the Thomas Embling Hospital. Then suddenly, before Kellam handed down his final ruling, Percy changed his mind and withdrew the request to be transferred to a psychiatric hospital. 'In the circumstances of this case, it is, in my view,' Justice Kellam ruled 'certainly not appropriate that an order such that was sought by Ms Randazzo be made.'

'Certainly I accept the evidence given before me by Professor Mullen and by Professor Ogloff that the Thomas Embling Hospital has the capacity to provide a sophisticated sex offender program on an individual basis,' Justice Kellam explained. 'I accept that there are good reasons as a matter of principle why a person who has been found not guilty of the serious crime of murder on the grounds of mental impairment should not be detained in a prison. However, taking into account the fact that Corrections Victoria will provide such a program, and notwithstanding the serious issue of principles the reviewee being now the only person in a Victorian prison who has been found not guilty of the crime of murder on the ground of insanity, the transfer to the forensic psychiatric facility at the Thomas Embling Hospital is, in my view, not appropriate or justified.'

It was Dr Thompson's contention that because Percy suffers from no psychiatric condition, he should be subject to a sex offender program provided by a prison rather than a psychiatric hospital. She gave evidence that he suffers from paraphilia and that condition can be treated by the prison sex offender program. Percy is, she said, 'manifestly different from the vast majority of patients at the Thomas Embling Hospital who are clearly unwell and psychotic'.

Justice Kellam demonstrated that the court also had Percy's well-being in mind when he ruled: 'It must be remembered that the reviewee is now stable and happy in the prison system having been there for many years already. It should be observed that the unanimous view of all of the highly qualified psychiatrists and psychologists who gave evidence before me is that, both as a matter of humanity, and of principle, and as a matter of professionalism on their part, the reviewee should be provided with an opportunity to undergo such a therapeutic program.'

Justice Kellam was also aware of Percy's past behaviour in prison. 'There is ample evidence before me that in the past the reviewee has been reluctant to engage in psychological discussion of his offence, or of his sadistic fantasies. Nevertheless, there is some evidence before me that, irrespective of what has happened in the past, the reviewee is now willing to undergo such a program and to engage in it. Whether that is a genuine desire or is manipulative behaviour designed to open the possibility of his release in the future is, of course, far from clear. There is evidence before me, that Corrections

Victoria is prepared to provide such a program.'

To a limited degree, Percy had already begun to engage with a therapist and there was ample evidence that resources for providing appropriate therapy were available to him in the prison system. The advantages of the sex offender program being provided in prison, Justice Kellam noted, is that this was where Percy resided and therefore he could engage in a program without disruption to his life, in terms of hobbies and prison employment.

'If the reviewee genuinely engages with those who are now prepared and, as I have said, have in effect undertaken to this court to provide, both psychiatric and psychological assistance to him in the nature of a sex offender program, it may well be that at some further review it will become a matter of serious consideration as to whether such a transfer from prison to a psychiatric hospital should take place.' Justice Kellam, however, firmly closed the door on any chance of an early release for Percy. 'I do not consider a transfer from prison to be appropriate at this time. In all of the circumstances I do not propose to direct that there be a further review in a lesser period than an interval not exceeding 5 years.'

Justice Kellam also addressed the role of the media during the custodial review process. Percy's counsel had wanted all coverage of the review proceedings suppressed in the newspapers but although it would be unreasonable to do so, Justice Kellam ruled, it was 'arguable that the public was not entirely accurately informed about the nature of the application before the court.' Kellam dryly noted in allowing media coverage of the review: 'It should not be assumed that the public are not discerning about the media or that they do not scrutinise what is put before them.'

Nor was it practical to suppress the name of the victim, Justice Kellam ruled, because Yvonne Tuohy's name had been reported for 35 years. But he took the time to acknowledge the grief of the Tuohy family: 'No doubt, a day does not pass in the lives of the family of the deceased child when they do not remember the dreadful events which occurred now so many years ago. The pain that those families suffer is clearly exacerbated by the review process, as is so amply demonstrated on the material before me.'

Kellam then ruled: 'There are, however, good reasons why the name of the then boy who accompanied her should not be published. Those reasons are related to his health and his wellbeing and the material which is before me demonstrating the deleterious effect upon him of previous publicity, which matters are of great concern to me.'

The tragic irony of this decision was apparent to all the media covering Percy's second custodial review. Shane Spiller, the brave little boy who wielded his tomahawk at a sadistic paedophile and had run away to alert authorities of an impending tragedy, had been missing since August 2002 and was presumed dead.

CHAPTER 11:
The Troubled Sleep of Shane Spiller

Young Shane Spiller demonstrated enormous bravery when he confronted Derek Percy with his small tomahawk and managed to escape. He showed considerable maturity in being able to give police a detailed description of the attacker and his car—even identifying the naval badge. He was similarly courageous when asked to identify the killer of his friend, Yvonne Tuohy, in a line-up at the police station, or when he attended the trial of Percy on 7 April 1970 in the Supreme Court in Melbourne.

> *His Honour: Before the boy is sworn, do you have any views about his ability to be sworn, Mr Hampel?*
>
> *Mr Hampel: Well, Your Honour, it only occurred to me when I saw the boy get into the witness box. I assumed he would be capable of giving evidence on oath. I have nothing to put to the contrary, Your Honour, and I would have little hesitation in suggesting he probably can, but, of course, it is a matter Your Honour has to satisfy yourself about…*
>
> *His Honour: I would have thought he is sufficiently orthodox Christian to be said to understand the nature of the oath. Yes, you may be sworn.*
>
> *Mr Fitzgerald: Your name is Shane Gregory Spiller, it that right?*
>
> *Shane Spiller: Yes…*
>
> *Mr Fitzgerald: Did you have any trouble picking [the man who took Yvonne Tuohy] out?*
>
> *Shane Spiller: No worries.*

Mr Fitzgerald: You pointed him out, did you?

Shane Spiller: Yes.

Mr Fitzgerald: Do you see that man in court?

Shane Spiller: Yes.

Mr Fitzgerald: Will you point him out?

Shane Spiller: Over there, sitting next to the policeman…

His Honour: Thank you Shane. I suppose you want to go back to school, do you?

Shane Spiller: No.

His Honour: If he wants to go back to school, he can go back to school; if he does not… well.[1]

⊗⊗⊗

In August 2002, 44-year-old Shane Spiller suddenly disappeared from his home on the south coast of New South Wales. Local police investigated a number of scenarios—Spiller had been murdered; he had suffered an accidental drug overdose and his body had been disposed of by friends; or perhaps, he had committed suicide after decades of suffering from post traumatic stress disorder. No trace of Spiller's remains were ever found. Almost five years later, with media attention focused again on Derek Percy via Operation Heats, *The Age* journalist Gary Tippet went to the small hamlet of Wyndham in southern New South Wales and delved into the troubled sleep of Shane Spiller, and wrote:

> *Twice in the winter of 1969, a little boy looked deep into the eyes of a young man called Derek Percy and got lost there forever. The first time, that crisp Sunday in July, Shane Spiller was 11 and strolling down a dirt track at Warneet, on Westernport Bay, with his friend, Yvonne Tuohy. When*

> *they got to the beach at the end of the trail, they were going to make a little fire of driftwood and have a picnic lunch. The second time was at Russell Street police headquarters... detectives needed Shane to look into those killer's eyes again. They put him in a room where the 21-year-old naval rating with the long, narrow face had been placed in a line-up. 'And for all the world,' remembers former police victim liaison officer Robert Read, 'that was the end of Shane Spiller.'*[2]

'What happened stuffed me,' Shane Spiller had told journalist John Silvester when he tracked him down in 1998. 'In the line-up at Russell Street... I had to walk up and point right to his nose. The look he gave me. I can still remember it.' For years Shane Spiller feared that Derek Percy would one day come after him. 'It's really knocked me around, mate,' Spiller confided. 'I still get nightmares. I spin out... I'm going through a rough trot now. I think about it every day of my life.'[3]

After Derek Percy's trial in 1970 Shane Spiller went home to Armadale and tried to resume his life. 'He went back to school after the holiday and seemed to be doing all right,' says his Melbourne lawyer Michael Clark. 'The effects didn't really catch up with him until he was about 14 or 15.' Spiller grew afraid of the dark and suffered from night tremors. His parents were told that their son would 'get over it' and not to 'mollycoddle' him. 'These were the days before trauma counselling,' says Clark. 'Back then, if you saw something you didn't like you bit your tongue and took it like a man. He wasn't able to do that.'[4]

'The events of that day have destroyed my son's life,' Frank Spiller admitted. 'It ruined many people's lives.' Shane had been estranged from his family for some years before he finally disappeared. 'At the time, if you had asked me whether it was going to affect Shane,' Frank Spiller recalled, 'I would have scoffed and said that in a couple of years he would get over it and move on... But the enormity of what he went through and the loss of his friend, the nightmares and a fear of Percy being released have taken their toll. As he has matured I think he has become concerned that he did not do enough. He has terrific feelings of guilt... I think he still hears and sees his little friend calling out to him to help, please help.'[5]

Lost in his guilt and fear, Shane began drinking at 14, turned to drugs in his teenage years and finally sought the help of a psychiatrist at 18. 'He'd been a pretty good student but very quickly his results went from good to pathetic,' Michael Clark says. 'He fell out with his parents, left school and basically went walkabout... from that time on, he was a wandering, lost soul.'[6] Shane Spiller battled alcohol and drug problems for most of his adult life, was unable to hold down full-time work and lived on a disability pension.

Sometime in the mid-1990s, life blew Spiller into the little township of Wyndham, 30 kilometres west of Pambula on the New South Wales South Coast and some 100 kilometres from the New South Wales–Victorian border. Wyndham has 'a pub, a general store and a couple of dozen modest houses tucked into the dips and folds of the Mount Darragh ridgeline, between Whipstick and Rocky Hall,' Gary Tippet noted when he visited there to write his article on Spiller in 2007. 'In the 1860s, it was gold country but now yields mainly cattle and timber, with some sidelining in small plot cannabis plantations hidden in the surrounding national park.'

With a population of less than 100, Wyndham is a mix of 'long-termers, logging workers and alternative life-stylers'—just the place where Shane Spiller could try and 'find' himself. 'The problem was,' Tippet poignantly observed, 'he took Derek Percy with him.'[7]

In August 1998, Shane Spiller was informed that Derek Percy's custodial order as a 'governor's pleasure' detainee was to be reviewed by the Supreme Court of Victoria. The media speculated that Percy might win his freedom, although the consensus of professional opinion would ultimately make this impossible. On 23 August 1998, the *Sunday Herald Sun* published a photo of Derek Percy beside one of Spiller as a frightened 11-year-old boy in 1969. The article began:

> *For almost 30 years, Shane Spiller has been tormented by memories of the man who abducted and murdered his childhood friend.*
> *In every nightmare, he relives the chilling day he narrowly escaped the clutches of Victoria's most vicious child killer. His deepest dread is the fiend will be set free.*
> *The ferocious mutilation murderer was Derek Ernest Percy—and this week Mr Spiller's worst fear might be realised.*
> *A Supreme Court judge is expected to decide on Wednesday whether Percy, 51, Victoria's longest-serving prisoner, will be released from custody.*[8]

It was just too much for Shane Spiller. 'It brought back all the memories and he went into stupefaction again,' says Michael Clark.[9]

The fact that the newspapers also published a photo of him made Shane all the more paranoid that Derek Percy would be able to somehow track him down. Looking much older than his 40 years with his bushy beard and a gaunt face, he still had that wide-eyed look but now appeared focused on an imaginary point somewhere beyond the camera. 'I was promised back then that he would never get out,' Spiller told the media. 'I hope people don't forget what he was like and what he did.'[10] Shane Spiller could not forget.

❋❋❋

Detective Sergeant Mark Winterflood from Bega Police first met Shane Spiller in 1997. Spiller lived on a property at Wyndham with numerous cars, motorbikes and boats in various states of disrepair littered about the yard and in his garage workshop. Even then 'Stick' Spiller, as the lean, anxious loner with the wide hazel eyes preferred to be known, was scared that Percy would one day come after him.

'Shane was a real local identity and very well known,' Detective Winterflood recalls.[11] 'He was also the sort of person who would tell you his life story the first time he met you. He told me that he had witnessed a murder as a child… he didn't tell me the full story, but later, in phone conversations, he said that he had witnessed Yvonne Tuohy's murder and that Derek Percy was the perpetrator.'

Winterflood believed that Spiller may have suffered from a slight intellectual disability that could not be explained by his years of drug and alcohol abuse. 'I was aware that he was diagnosed with PTSD, which was related to his witnessing the Tuohy murder. He also had significant problems with anxiety, depression and substance abuse. While his fear of Percy may have been ill-conceived and at times delusional, from my observation he was never free of the fear that Percy would be released and seek revenge for the evidence he gave as a child.'

Shane Spiller lived in that constant fear even though it wasn't based on any degree of logic. It was nevertheless very real for him. 'I'd hear from him once a week,' Winterflood recalls, 'and then not receive a call for another six months. He would ring just to have a chat… he was not so much lonely, it was only when thoughts of Percy and the stress of dealing with his fears impinged on him that he'd ring and talk about it.'

It was also a story Spiller regularly told and retold patrons at Wyndham's only pub—the Robbie Burns Hotel. Barman Peter Cox says, '"Stick" was a nice bloke, he fitted in and everyone accepted him.' Spiller was well-known to locals for his 'fearlessness' on his GSX1000 Suzuki—a talent no doubt, handed down by his father Frank, a noted motorbike racer—and he also rode several unregistered dirt bikes around town and into bushland where he had his cannabis crops. 'He was a manic rider,' recalls general store owner Bryan Hunter. 'He'd scream past here standing on the seat, arms spread wide. He came off a few times, scraped off a bit of bark, but never really hurt himself. He was a normal bloke in many ways, just a larrikin motorcycle rider who liked a beer and smoked a few cones too many.'[12]

'But there were times his melodramas and paranoia could give you the shits,' one female Wyndham resident told Gary Tippet. Spiller was having a whinge in the general store one day when she called him 'a drama queen'. He quietly walked out and went home. 'He came back a little while later and plonked a file down in front of me and said, "This might explain why I'm like I am,"' she recalled. 'It was full of cuttings about this bloke Percy and what he did. I sat down that night and read it all. After that I was a lot more sympathetic.'[13]

Andy Morris, Spiller's next-door neighbour, recalls him asking friends to note down the number plates of cars parked outside his home. Spiller also cut a trapdoor into his living room floor and slept with a baseball bat by his bed because he was convinced that Percy had put out a contract on his life and would come after him. 'He was the most paranoid person I've ever met,' Morris says. 'There was this overwhelming dark cloud over his life and he was basically self-medicating with drugs and alcohol.'[14]

Detective Winterflood also developed a good rapport with Spiller. 'Shane was harmless, considerate and for the most part honest,' he says. 'He was an unusual sort of bloke. But he lived on the fringe—and he didn't pick his friends very well. He mixed with this circle of substance- abusing people. Anywhere he could get morphine, through shonky scripts or other friends who could scam it, he'd grab it. People took advantage of him.'[15] Spiller had a son from a brief relationship but after cutting off all ties with his family, he found himself in the 'company of strangers'. But even Winterflood admits, 'These sorts of characters were the ones who gave him the time of day and a sense of connection and affirmation as a person.'[16]

Having contacted Spiller and obtained a statement from him for Percy's custodial review, Crown barrister Richard Lewis recommended him to Robert Read, the head of the Victoria Police victim advisory unit. 'He was a knockabout sort of fella, a wild and woolly little character, very thin, with this big Ned Kelly beard,'

Read recalled. 'There wasn't much of him, probably more beard than anything. He was quintessentially a little Aussie bloke from the bush. But that was the facade. Underneath that he was a shattered individual and Derek Percy still controlled him. He was vulnerable and he was extremely fearful.'[17]

Robert Read found Spiller in a state of utter distress: 'In fact, he was almost out of control. He was utterly petrified of Percy [who] took a young innocent and turned him into a runaway—and it was Percy that he was running from.' Read agreed to counsel Spiller and help him to apply for victim's compensation, which was not available in the 1960s. Spiller was awarded just $5000 but this was increased to the maximum $50,000 on appeal. Media commentators noted that Derek Percy had almost four times as much from his accumulated naval pension in his bank account.[18] But the compensation helped; it was the most money Spiller had seen in his lifetime and gave him hope of a better lifestyle. He put a deposit on a modest, two-bedroom shack and bought a new Nissan Patrol four-wheel-drive. But it wasn't enough to buy peace of mind. On Monday 9 September 2002, Shane Spiller suddenly disappeared.

Mark Winterflood says, 'Wyndham is a small hamlet—a pub, a general store—Shane's lifestyle was to rock down to the pub at eleven o'clock and talk to people. Shane was a 'people person' so once he disappeared we knew it wasn't a 'fake' thing where he was trying to draw attention to himself... he couldn't survive without his contact with people he knew so we knew there was something wrong from early on.'[19]

'It's a real mystery. Everyone still talks about it,' says Bryan Hunter, who was possibly one of the last people to see him alive.[20] The morning he disappeared, Spiller walked to the store from his home around the corner to pick up his mail. Neighbours broke into his house several days later and found mouldy food in the fridge and kitchen area, unwashed dishes, Spiller's medication and all his clothing. Local police investigated the home and saw that there was no suicide note and none of his vehicles were missing. Soon after squatters moved into his house and helped themselves to Spiller's belongings. Shane wasn't coming back.

❖❖❖

Wild stories, rumours and suspicions spilled out over Wyndham, including one that Derek Percy had 'bumped off' Spiller or had used his naval pension to hire a 'hit man' to do it for him. Mark Winterflood had to look into the 'hit man' rumour as part of his missing person investigation. 'There was a very strong rumour around Wyndham that Derek Percy had taken out a $20,000 contract on him and now he's disappeared,' he says. Winterflood made enquiries at Victoria's Ararat Prison but a list of Percy's visitors showed that he had only been visited by his mother and his solicitor—no 'hit men'. Percy only had several thousand dollars in a 'with-held' prisoner account of which he could only access a nominal amount. There was nothing of his $200,000 naval pension the media had made so much fuss about—he had no access to it.

Percy's cell at Ararat was 'ramped' (raided) by officers of Melbourne's armed offenders' squad on 20 November 2002. Detective Winterflood was forwarded the following message by his Melbourne colleagues: 'By the way, the officers who did [the search] think you owe them a bottle of scotch for putting up with the smell.' It appears that when it came to 'all things excreta', old habits die hard for Percy. But there was no mention of the name 'Spiller' in any of the correspondence or paperwork located in his cell. The officers at Ararat who had contact with Percy over a protracted period said that he was 'a very talkative bloke' but at no time could anyone remember him ever mentioning Shane Spiller.[21]

Derek Percy was never specifically interviewed about Spiller's disappearance and rumours that he was somehow involved—other than psychologically—were laid to rest. There was the more realistic possibility that Shane had been killed for his compensation money but a check of his bank details revealed that no one had drawn money on his account after he disappeared. One theory that didn't sit well with the locals was that Shane had gone off into the bush and committed suicide. 'Not a hope in hell,' says David Thoroughgood, one of the locals who knew Spiller. 'He could have done it 100 times before and he didn't want to.'[22]

'This was a bloke who talked night after night of killing himself, but it never happened,' says Robert Read. 'If I was honest with my emotions and my intuition, I'd have to say I don't believe he killed himself. Something else happened to him.'[23]

It appeared most likely that Spiller accidentally died of an overdose and his body was hidden in the bush by his associates. 'What doesn't fit with that scenario is that Wyndham is such a small place where everyone knows everything and sooner or later the word would have got out,' says Winterflood.[24] What is known about Spiller's disappearance is that in the months before he went missing 'Stick' had become involved with 'a bullshit scene of morphine abusers, junkies and thieves'. 'We've bandied this about for years,' Wyndham local Tony Boller later reflected. 'Somebody "disappeared" him, that's for sure.'[25]

Andrew Paul Kraymaat and Brian Peebles, who lived at nearby Wolumla, would often get drunk at Spiller's home in Wyndham. Kraymaat had spent most of his adult life in and out of gaol for a string of violent offences, and first came into the area from Tenterfield in 2000. One night in August 2000, after a day of heavy drinking at a barbeque at Spiller's home, Kraymaat 'borrowed' Spiller's Nissan Patrol without permission and drove to Pambula to get some more alcohol. Kraymaat rolled the car and completely destroyed it—his blood alcohol level registered .245. Kraymaat checked himself out of hospital and went back to Wyndham with no thought of compensating Spiller for the loss of his car.

A week later, on 23 August 2000, Kraymaat and Peebles went on another drinking binge at Candelo, about 25 kilometres north of Wyndham, with another associate named Lee 'Mick' Petrie.

During the night Petrie was stabbed to death with a filleting knife. 'The murder was basically three drunks in a room,' says Detective Sergeant Mark Winterflood. 'One person ends up dead and the other two are so blind they could hardly remember the sequence of events. Kraaymaat described himself as virtually paralytic.'[26]

Kraymaat and Peebles placed a plastic bag over Petrie's head, drove him to Myrtle Mountain Lookout and dumped his body there. They were only arrested after Kraymaat had 'a rare attack of conscience. He phoned his mother and said he'd committed a cardinal sin. "I've killed a bloke," he told her.'[27] Brian Peebles indicated that he was prepared to become a witness for the Crown and gave a full statement implicating Kraymaat in the murder of Petrie. Peebles was bailed to appear at Bega District Court on 17 January 2001 and pleaded guilty to the charge of 'accessory after the fact of murder' and was given a suspended 15-month sentence.

Andrew Kraymaat's murder trial in 2001 finished in a hung jury but on Peebles' evidence he was eventually convicted of murder at his retrial in March 2002 and sentenced to 15 years' gaol. 'But that was not the end of it,' says Winterflood. 'Peebles owed a lot of people money and while he was in jail for a short period of time, some people went to his home and took his tools, his washing machine and the such.'

Peebles later moved to Southport on the Gold Coast but knew Shane Spiller and how fragile he was. Someone rang Spiller pretending to be a hit man, saying, 'if you don't get me this stuff back I'm going to blow your kneecaps off'.[28] Spiller immediately phoned his barrister Paul Trapp who contacted the police.

'While we were at his house talking to him about it, the "hit man" rang again,' Winterflood remembers. 'Me and my pistol are 15 kilometres away,' the voice said.[29] The calls were traced to a business in Southport, and Brian Peebles and an associate named Craig Archer were interviewed in regards to 'using a telecommunications device to menace'. Archer was charged with the offence, fined $1000 and placed on a 12-month good behaviour bond. Despite

Spiller's insistence that Peebles was heard in the background of the threatening calls, Peebles was not charged.

Police believe Mark Peebles instigated the 'hit man' threats because Shane Spiller had told him of his fears during their drinking sessions together. When Spiller disappeared the following year, the rumour mill at Wyndham resurrected the 'hit man' theories. It is clear that Peebles had no part in Spiller's disappearance other than to undermine his fragile state of mind.

'About ten days after Shane disappeared,' Winterflood continues, 'a friend called Gary McNally went around to Shane's place and attempted to take his fridge... we caught him and he put it back but clearly he knew that Spiller wasn't coming back. He must have known what happened to him.' Two or three months later McNally overdosed and was found dead on the kitchen floor of his home so if he knew anything about Spiller's fate he's taken that secret to his grave.'

'There was a small circle of people out at Wyndham of which Spiller and McNally were part where they would obtain various morphine-based drugs from chemists through various funds and share them around ... that's what killed McNally and we're assuming that's what happened to Shane.' Winterflood's theory is that Shane Spiller overdosed in front of 'friends' and they hid his body in the bush. 'That's my current feeling,' Winterflood says, 'and with wombats and other animals out in the bush, there'd be absolutely nothing left.'

Another scenario was that Shane's body was thrown down a mine shaft. 'We've been down three so far and found nothing,' Winterflood confirms. 'There would be hundreds of old goldmine shafts in the area so where do you start?' Police pumped out one flooded mineshaft at Devil's Hole, off Myrtle Mountain Road; scouted locations where Spiller hid his cannabis crops and conducted all the relevant data searches—banks, Centrelink and Medicare—and even checked immigration.

It was well-known in Wyndham that Spiller had a few marijuana crops growing in bush hideaways for his own use. 'One of those was in a known location where—another tragic story—a friend of his got drunk and was run over by a car at Merimbula back in 2000,' says Winterflood. 'Rocky Hall, where they went to spread the ashes, was a place where Shane had a little crop going—one of his favourite haunts, it was one of the first places where we went to search for him early on—but there was nothing there.'

The suspicion that Spiller went to one of his crop sites or to a remote bush setting and took his own life still has some credence because he had tried to commit suicide on previous occasions. 'Shane was under the care of a local mental health team in August 2002 for severe depression and other health issues,' Winterflood confirms. 'On 15 August, he had been admitted to a mental health institution in Goulburn. Spiller was discharged from there on 23 August and was to be supervised by a local mental health team. On his release his health further deteriorated and on 24 August he attempted suicide by taking an overdose of medication.'

Spiller was then admitted to Bega Hospital on 25 August where he remained until 4 September. 'His health really went downhill toward the end... not just from his fear of Derek Percy but also a lot of his health issues as well,' says Winterflood. When he disappeared, Spiller was being treated for his morphine dependency.

In 2007, Detective Sergeant Winterflood sent a brief to the New South Wales Coroner regarding Spiller's disappearance but the Coroner wanted the case to remain open in case any new information came to hand (seven years is the usual period before someone is certified 'legally deceased'). Spiller's family has never pressured the Coroner for a determination of his fate—as far as authorities know they never came to Wyndham to look at the house or to collect his belongings. Despite a widespread search there has been no further information about Shane Spiller since the day he disappeared in 2002. Winterflood admits, 'there's nothing concrete to even investigate anymore. We checked his phone records ... there's been nothing since 2002 and he hardly used his phone anyway during the last few weeks of his life when severe depression set in.'[30]

After he disappeared, the bank continued Spiller's mortgage repayments by direct debit and whittled away at his compensation money until there was nothing left. They then foreclosed on the house and took possession of it from local squatters. In 2006, the bank sold Spiller's house and the new owners pulled out the ceiling. There was only a small cavity between the ceiling and the flat roof of the shack and it was clear that Spiller had used this space to stash his cannabis. During the renovations several rats' nests were found—they were all made of marijuana.[31]

The locals at Wyndham remain nonplussed about Spiller's fate—it's just another bush mystery—but they remember him fondly. In spite of his fragile mental state and irrational fears, there was a bravery about 'Stick' Spiller, Wyndham barman Peter Cox says. 'He was a very clever boy. Look what he did way back then. If it wasn't for "Stick", that bloke [Percy] could still be killing people.'[32]

Andy Morris says, 'In a sense, Shane was a Derek Percy murder victim as well. To me, he was a very brave man. I like to picture him lying in a hammock with a banana daiquiri, that'd be heaven to "Stick". But wherever he is, I just hope he's happy at last.'[33]

In his summation to the jury in the trial of Derek Percy in 1969, Justice Pape said of Shane Spiller:

> *You may think that this lad was a very observant boy who gave his evidence very well indeed. It is plain that but for his accurate observation of this car and its occupant the police may have had a very difficult task indeed in locating the girl's body and in apprehending the accused...*
>
> *Unless the accused had led the police to the spot... where the child's body was found, it may have been a very long time indeed before that body had been found. The evidence disclosed some very good police work... work built on the observations of the little boy, Shane Spiller... that had a*

> *suspect accused of murder at 3 o'clock in custody by 5.30 pm and charged with murder later that night.*[34]

Forty years later Detective Wayne Newman of Operation Heats was more to the point. 'Shane Spiller solved the Tuohy case,' he says. 'Without him, Derek Percy may never have been captured.'[35]

CHAPTER 12: Operation Heats

On 2 February 2005, the suspect was brought into the interview room from the Melbourne Magistrate's Court where he had spent the previous night.[1] He looked older than his 56 years—a long, stringy beard framed his gaunt face, and where wavy, light brown hair used to sweep back from his broad forehead in boyhood, he was now completely bald. Years of heavy smoking had undoubtedly aged him—he looked like Fagin from Dickens' *Oliver Twist*—but not a hint of expression was betrayed by an unsmiling face and cold steel eyes.

The man had consented to be interviewed; it concerned him that he was being readily linked by the media to other unsolved cases. Percy told detectives that he still held out some hope of being released from gaol but speculation that he had committed a number of unsolved child murders could damage his release prospects. This was the main reason he agreed to be interviewed.

If the detectives waiting to question Derek Ernest Percy expected to find a monster they were faced, instead, by a highly intelligent, cunning individual. He was cooperative—not aggressive or belligerent, certainly not 'anti-police'[2]—and he willingly entered into a casual conversation with the two detectives sitting on the other side of the table. Detective Wayne Newman from Victoria and New South Wales Detective Adam Barwick put more than 1500 questions to Percy over the next two days—questions that had remained unanswered for almost forty years.

Watching proceedings by video link were members of the Australian Federal Police and South Australia Police. Detectives who had been working on Operation Heats for almost a year were determined not to turn the multi-agency investigation into a sideshow, with Percy the main attraction. But with Percy escorted from Port Phillip prison the previous day, there was a media leak and morning newspapers carried the story that a 'South Australian homicide expert has come to Victoria to help New South Wales and Victorian Police in their investigation of Derek Percy'.[3]

Detectives Barwick and Newman hoped to build a rapport with the prisoner and test his memory against the known facts of the Tuohy case. Percy was also asked about the Beaumont, Redston, Brook and Stilwell cases. The Wanda Beach murders were not mentioned at all and the Beaumont case was referred to only briefly. Asked if he was in Adelaide when the Beaumont children went missing in 1966 Percy answered, 'I don't know'. Detectives asked if he was 'blocking out thoughts because something horrible happened in Adelaide and you don't want to remember it?'[4] Percy said it was possible. The South Australian detective had heard enough—he returned to South Australia before the end of the first day.

The detectives noted only two changes to Percy's demeanour during two days of intense questioning. Percy freely answered any questions relating to his family, school and other events, but when he was questioned about details of the Yvonne Tuohy murder he became visibly different in that his 'lip quivered'[5] and he mumbled 'I can't remember'. The show of emotion was revelatory.

On another occasion Detective Sergeant Barwick, in an attempt to show Percy that the murder of Simon Brook was consistent with some of his writings confiscated from his naval locker in 1969, gave the articles back to Percy to look at. For the first time in almost 35 years Derek Percy laid eyes on his fantasy writings and immediately 'zoned out'. The 'curtain' that other interviewers had noted over the years had dropped again and when Barwick attempted to question Percy, he got no response.

At the end of two days of interviews detectives working on Operation Heats were convinced that Derek Percy did not suffer from any long-term or short-term memory loss—he deliberately avoided incriminating himself by saying that he 'couldn't remember'. But, as had been the case since the day he was apprehended in 1969, he did not deny anything.

❋❋❋

After he was contacted by Victoria Police in 2004, New South Wales Detective Sergeant Adam Barwick started researching the archived case files relating to the murder of Simon Brook in 1968. Barwick decided to apply to the New South Wales Police Commissioner to reactivate the Brook case but one of the first things he did was to contact Donald and Phyllis Brook in Adelaide to let them know that New South Wales Police were relaunching an investigation into a suspect in the murder of their son 36 years before.

After travelling to Melbourne and obtaining a copy of documents relating to the arrest, charge and trial of Derek Percy in 1969, Barwick began the monumental task of reading all the relevant material associated with the Brook investigation and wrote a summary of the evidence linking Percy to the crime. It was then Barwick learned that the physical exhibits relating to the case had been destroyed in 1988. Attempts to locate other copies of the biological samples were equally unsuccessful. With the original exhibits destroyed and the biological samples misplaced, the potential for DNA technology to impact on the case was gone. Barwick now had to rely on points of 'similar circumstance' to Percy's known criminal behaviour rather than direct physical or forensic links.

The similarities between the murders of Yvonne Tuohy and Simon Brook were striking. Both children were abducted near the water, both had injuries indicating attempts to strangle them, both had their throats cut, both had material inserted down their throat, both suffered post mortem genital mutilation. The cause of death for both children was asphyxiation and both bodies were concealed among bushes. The number and manner of similarities between the two child murders was so striking they indicated 'one perpetrator, with a "tendency" to commit this type of crime, is responsible for both'.[6]

Derek Percy was stationed in Sydney in May 1968 at the time of the Brook murder and was attached to HMAS *Melbourne* as a fire sentry while it was going through a refit at Cockatoo Island Dry Dock. Naval records could not determine if he was on shore leave on Saturday 18 May—the day Simon Brook was murdered—but Percy intimated that he wasn't on duty when he told detectives that he was either 'sailing out of the navy base at Kuttabul or in Newcastle visiting his parents' that weekend. Percy's fellow sailors who were interviewed at the time stated that they did not associate with Percy outside of work and none could confirm they were with him that weekend. There was no evidence, in fact, that Percy ever sailed in Sydney. It was later established that Percy did not spend weekends at Newcastle visiting his family—according to his father, he spent only one week there between November 1967 and July 1969.

Barwick learned that Percy allegedly told his friend Ron Anderson that he was driving through Glebe on the day of the boy's murder. Percy's younger brother was reinterviewed and stated that it was 'improbable' that Derek would have driven him to work through Glebe in 1968. It was 'unlikely' he was even working in Sydney in 1968, unless he was doing a course for one of the oil companies—Percy's younger brother worked at their father's Shell service station in Newcastle in the late 1960s so this may have been possible. When the young detective tried to determine whether Percy had access to his car, he faced more hurdles. The RTA do not hold any records relating to driver's licences or vehicle registration from 1968—records were only maintained after 1974 and then only for a period of seven years.

But Percy was known to own a Datsun station wagon which was brought for him by his parents when he went into the navy in 1967. Percy had access to the car in Sydney and had knowledge of the Glebe area—his father had trained with Shell in neighbouring Pyrmont and he had visited nearby Wentworth Park to watch the Moscow Circus. When he was captured in Melbourne in 1969, detectives found Shell maps of the Glebe area with routes marked in texta in the glovebox of his car. Glebe is also easily accessed by rail—there is a railway cutting close to the original crime scene—and Percy had visited friends and relatives by rail while stationed in Sydney.

Although the crime scene exhibits had been destroyed, the identification of the razor blade used in the murder remained an important link to the identity of the murderer. Statements were obtained from the Commander of HMAS *Kuttabul*, who was also a naval cadet in 1967, and former navy personnel, including a retired uniform master in the navy, who both said that police photos of the Gillette razor blade found at the Brook crime scene was similar to those issued by the navy at the time of the murder. A former employee of the Gillette Australia Company confirmed that the company issued a basic three-piece safety razor to the defence forces in the late 1960s. As part of the 'kit' issued to Percy when he joined the navy, he was given a safety razor. Further blades were then available from stores on the bases. Initial inquiries in 1968 indicated that the manufacture markings on the blade found at the crime scene meant that it was made 'not later than January 1967'. Percy commenced his naval recruit training in November 1967. But this was all circumstantial.

Derek Percy also bore a striking resemblance to the identikit image completed by witness Eric Barnier in May 1968. Mr Barnier had since passed away, so a visual identification of Percy as the man he saw walking with Simon Brook in Jubilee Park that winter's day was impossible. Barbara Lrbec, the neighbour who last saw Simon in Alexandra Road in the early afternoon, could not be located on any national database so the possibility of her supplying additional information was also gone.

In June 2005, Detective Sergeant Adrian Paterson, the Officer in Charge of Victoria Police's Criminal Identification Squad and an expert in offender identification techniques, identified important similarities between the two images. Now outdated by computer technology, the American facial composition 'identikit' system comprised 365 individual components in 12 categories (hair, chin, eyes, nose etc). Sergeant Paterson compared the 1968 suspect image with Derek Percy's arrest photo in 1969 and immediately drew reference to several comparative points:

Hair: Wavy, brushed up and across, off the forehead, slightly receding, fuller on the top, shorter on the sides
Forehead: High and wide
Eyes: Deep-set, medium close, eyebrows straight
Nose: Straight, medium long, narrow bridge, fuller at tip.
Mouth: Medium-wide
Chin: Longish, slightly angular/oval

Sergeant Paterson was of the opinion that there was 'a high probability that the person depicted in the photograph is the same person depicted in the identikit image.'

In 1968, Professor DC Maddison stated that it was highly unlikely that a woman was responsible for the murder of Simon Brook. The offender could be someone with no previous criminal record and with previous normal behaviour or unknown psychiatric previous behaviour. The normal pattern with this type of crime, Professor Maddison observed, is that the offender is likely to repeat the event but not usually in close proximity to the original crime. This murder will give them some release but if they have not been picked up within five or six days, then they may turn up anywhere. The type of person who committed this crime would be mentally ill in a gross sense but it was clear that the police were dealing with somebody 'cunning and not obviously mad and perhaps even intelligent'.

Percy also fit the psychological profile provided by psychiatrists who assessed the murder of Simon Brook in 1968. Percy had no previous criminal record and had at that time, an unknown psychiatric disorder. According to Pentridge psychiatrist Dr Allen Bartholomew, Percy was not 'obviously mad' as he functioned quite well in the navy and his IQ was measured as 'superior'. Lastly, and possible most tellingly, Percy's writings reveal his inner thoughts and some were consistent with the *modus operandi* in the Brook murder. Articles found in his naval locker described the abduction of a 3-year-old boy and the severing of the penis.

When Adam Barwick finally came face to face with Derek Percy in Melbourne's Homicide Squad interview room in February 2005 he was ready to put a range of matters to the 56-year-old detainee. From the beginning Barwick and Newman attempted to get Percy to talk generally about certain subjects and to move him away from his 'I can't remember' stance. At the start of the interview Percy outlined his family history and travel movements in the late 1960s before his capture and these basically matched the known facts. Yes, Percy owned a bike—one with gears on the front wheels. Yes, he remembered Kim White and Bill Hutton. They were keen sportsmen at school. No, he did not have any knowledge of a Shell training garage at Glebe—the one where his father trained in July 1967 and which he allegedly visited. No, he had no memory of 'the gorge incident' where he was seen wearing women's clothing and cutting the crotch off women's underwear by his two schoolmates. While Percy could recall the incident at Khancoban in 1966 involving two young girls in the caravan, he could not remember their names.

Percy was shown a photograph of the razor blades found at the Brook crime scene. He stated that while attached to the HMAS *Melbourne* in 1968, he would have had a similar type of razor or a cut-throat razor. They could be purchased from the supply store, he told the detectives. Later in the interview Percy stated that that type of razor was 'generally available'—meaning that a lot of people in the community had access to one.

Percy did remember the visit by former school friend Ron Anderson while he was in custody after being arrested for the murder of Yvonne Tuohy and though he did not recall details of the conversation they had, he said 'it was possible that it took place'. This conversation, as recounted by Anderson in 2004, was then put to Percy. He stated that he didn't know what he was doing driving around Sydney in 1968, as he didn't think he had a car at that stage. Although this could not be checked against government records, detectives believed Percy did have access to a car at the time. But this was of little consequence as Simon Brook was not transported out of the area so whether Percy had a car or not, was not the issue. What was critical was whether he knew of, or had visited, the area.

The conversation Percy had with Detective Dick Knight in 1969 concerning the murder of Simon Brook was then put to him. Again, Percy said that he could not remember that conversation but he did remember being interviewed. He agreed that the bizarre fantasies he had relating to children commenced about 1965. The argument was put to him that if he had these thoughts and was fantasising about the mutilation and murder of children, then he would have been aware of the Simon Brook case, considering the massive media attention it received. Contradicting the conversations he had with Ron Anderson and Dick Knight in 1969, Percy maintained that he had not even heard of the murder of Simon Brook.

The detectives tried to test Percy's assertion that he had 'no memory' of the Brook case. He was shown a copy of his handwritten articles concerning the murder and mutilation of children and was again questioned as to whether he murdered Simon Brook:

Q: Alright. I've got through those similarities for you between the crime you did commit in '69 which you have told the authorities that you did commit that crime. We've gone through your history—your behavioural history from when you began having these thoughts roughly around '65, told you that there has been an incident where Bill Hutton and Kim White have given us a statement saying they saw you at the Gorge performing these acts. The next year you actually involved other children and that's the one at Khancoban where you got the girls to pull their pants down. Now, you were in Sydney at the time Simon Brook was murdered. It was a type of crime that does relate to the writings that you say you made in '69 and '68.
A: Yeah.
Q: You say that you don't remember the incident at 'the gorge'.
A: No…
Q: Right. Do you remember what Dr Bartholomew gave evidence about at your trial?
A: No.
Q: He said that he believed you had a type of hysterical repression where an incident is so repulsive to others or may cause you embarrassment in front of your peers that you

won't remember it. You'll repress that memory so that you can't remember it.
A: Mm.
Q: Did that sound like an accurate assessment of you in your mind?
A: Possibly.
Q: Right. So how can we explain that you don't remember the incident at the gorge where you cut up the women's clothing... the crotch from the women's clothing?
A: I don't know.
Q: How can you be so sure then that you didn't kill Simon Brook?
A: I'm just sure that something like that I would remember something about it.
Q: Well, did the incident at the gorge happen?
A: Apparently, but I would consider that is considerably minor compared with the murder.
Q: Right. So you will consent that the minor incident possibly happened, but the murder...
A: If... if... if there are witnesses...
Q: But not only, you're sure...?
A: If... if there are witnesses that said it, said that, then...
Q: What if there were witnesses to the Brook murder?
A: If there were and they're sure that it was me, it must have happened, but I can't remember it happening.
Q: See, I don't want to mislead you and tell you there are witnesses because I can tell you there are no witnesses here that will identify you for the Brook murder, but the point I'm discussing here is that you would accept then that it did happen. You will accept that the incident at the gorge happened because there are witnesses.
A: Yes.
Q: And hypothetically speaking, which is exactly what it is, that if there were witnesses for the Brook murder, you would

> *then accept, 'Well, then it did happen and I just can't remember it.' Is it because one matter is more serious than the other that you're so sure you didn't commit the second one?*
> *A: No.*
> *Q: Can you explain then that if you don't remember either of them why you are willing to accept that one did and not the other?*
> *A: Given the seriousness of the circumstances, I'm sure I would remember something about it.*

Throughout the interview Percy's standard answer to any questions concerning the unsolved murders was that he couldn't remember. He reasoned that he mustn't have committed these crimes because he couldn't remember committing them. It was put to Percy that if he agreed that he was involved in the Tuohy murder and the 'gorge incident' because there were witnesses but that he couldn't remember these events, then it was possible that he committed other child murders without there being witnesses because of his 'hysterical repressive mechanism' defence. Percy would have none of it.

Detectives Barwick and Newman formed the view that Percy was lying when answering these questions. Professor Ogloff had stated in Percy's 2003 review that the prisoner has 'relied on a similar style of responding since 1969'. Was he lying, then, about not remembering his involvement in other murders? Barwick worked for the next two years preparing an inquest brief for the New South Wales Coroner. Despite the destruction of crime scene exhibits, the loss of key witnesses and Percy's memory lapses, Operation Heats believed that of the five unsolved crimes now being associated with Percy the Brook case had the strongest circumstantial links.

About the same time that Percy's interrogation was taking place, the AFP confirmed in the press that it was taking part in Operation Heats. 'Interest in the case of Allen Redston in 1966 has been revived several times in recent years because of new evidence and forensic techniques,' ABC Online reported. 'Commander Shane Connolly says a new approach is being taken by investigators... "ACT, NSW, SA and Victorian Police have all been working together on this particular person".'[7]

The following month the ACT Policing Executive Committee agreed to fund an historical homicide review project to address several unsolved cases committed in the ACT.[8] Professor David Barclay, from the University of Hull and previously Head of Physical Evidence for UK National Crime and Operations Faculty accepted an invitation to provide a series of lectures to AFP staff in relation to current advances in forensic investigations. Professor Barclay's specialty is identifying forensic 'opportunities' within crime scenes that can now be explored more fully by utilising emerging forensic technologies.[9] Barclay had worked in Australia in late 2004, assisting the Western Australia Police in the review of a long-running serial homicide investigation[10] and was invited to review the Redston case in 2006. The recommendations of this review, which was codenamed Operation Kobold,[11] had a profound effect on the AFP's involvement in Operation Heats.

'It is common practice amongst all law enforcement agencies to review cases,' says Detective Chris Sheehan, who has been the case officer in charge of the Redston case since 2006.[12] 'Other police will come in to review an investigation or expert advice is sought concerning aspects of an investigation... it's good investigative practice. The advantage of bringing someone in from outside the law enforcement community is that they're coming at the investigation with a non-law enforcement mindset.' The AFP is like any other police force in the country—open and accountable. 'But more importantly than just appearing to be "open", we want to catch the person who did this,' Sheehan said. 'It may be 41 years down the track but that doesn't mean you give up. You never give up.'

What then, are the known facts about Derek Percy in 1966? Tuesday 27 September was a school day and Percy was a Fifth Form student at Corryong High School some four hours to the south of Canberra. Percy was living at Khancoban with his family and was aged 18—slightly older than the age description of the 'boy on the bike'. He did not have his driver's licence and could not have gone to Canberra by himself. 'There have been exhaustive enquiries—newspaper records, school attendances, travel histories, family enquiries and those of any of his associates,' Sheehan says. 'There is some talk that he may have been visiting an aunt in Curtin but there's no proof that Percy was ever there. That said… he was in close enough geographical proximity at the time so it is an issue.'

Every document relating to the original investigation was read, with the most relevant information annotated in respect of their particular significance and the potential to yield additional information. Discussions were held with retired members of the ACT police and staff from the AFP laboratory regarding the storage and handling of the crime scene exhibits. Chris Sheehan says, 'Almost everything secured at the time, including the majority of the actual bindings and the clothing of the victim, was not only labelled and stored in exemplary fashion over the years, the documentation of the exhibits will greatly assist any future analysis of the exhibits and possibly help identify Allen Redston's killer.'

The British are world leaders in the development of DNA technology, and it is suggested in the review process that LCN (Low Copy Number) DNA may be present on some of the bindings used to tie Allen Redston. Although this technique cannot produce a DNA profile that can be matched against a database, it can be used to determine a 'high probability of association'[13]—that is, to test against a known suspect. The AFP has a number of original suspects and it may be possible to one day match a DNA profile to one of these men, but only if DNA can be extracted from the exhibits. The wet, damp conditions of some of the items and the activity of the dog in dragging the body out of the reeds may make the retrieval of DNA difficult. It will be important to obtain Allen Redston's DNA profile directly from the items (as opposed to an associated DNA profile from his parents), if a partial profile of an unknown person is to be detected. Police believe the hanky Allen had kept in his jumper may be the best source of control DNA.

Potential contact points between the offender and the bindings have been identified. A priority plan for LCN DNA has been devised based on the materials that have remained dry and areas that should give a control DNA profile of Allen Redston have been identified. Consideration was given to obtaining DNA from identified 'persons of interest' named in the original investigation—some of whom still live in the Canberra area—as well as Derek Percy. The ACT offender DNA database is still in its infancy so it is unlikely that even if LCN DNA is extracted from the crime scene exhibits, the offender is going to be identified by a 'cold hit' against the database. Incomplete and degraded mixtures of DNA might also be obtained.

It must be said that there is nothing of Percy's established *modus operandi* evident in the Redston case. The offender may have befriended younger children by playing their games and then bullied them in an accelerating series of events leading to several hog-tying incidents. Although Yvonne Tuohy was gagged and her hands tied behind her back, the binding was 'functional' to stop her from running away after she was abducted in an open area. The main objective in the Redston case was the tying up itself. Percy did not befriend his victim—he tended to use a 'blitz' approach and 'hunted' from his car in areas to which he had legitimate access. Percy used a knife, which was an integral part of his particular paraphilia—there was no use of a knife in the Redston murder. Knowing what we do about just how much of a monster Percy is, he wouldn't have been able to stop himself from inflicting further damage once his victim was subdued.

Chris Sheehan admits: 'You look at Derek Percy's "drivers"—sadomasochism, lust and coprophilia—and you don't see any of that behaviour in the Redston case. In this murder the binding was the objective… the tying, the wrapping him up… there were no marks on the body and no evidence of sexual activity although this does not mean there was no sexual activity external to the body. There was no element of torture, mutilation… in fact he died quickly. But you have to have some starting point in your investigation and while we're working hard to eliminate Percy, at some point we'll need to put some questions to him again.'

It is difficult not to form the opinion that the Allen Redston murder, as with the disappearance of the Beaumont children earlier that same year, was a 'local' crime—not a crime committed by the teenage Derek Percy while opportunistically travelling through the area on holidays with his family. Percy had a bike, but it was dark maroon, not red. Percy cannot be placed in Curtin on the September afternoon that Allen Redston lost his life, or in any of the 'precursor offences' that precipitated the little boy's death. Logic, as well as any standard behavioural analysis of the crime scene, would indicate that Percy was not responsible for the Redston murder.

There was a series of recommendations from the external review conducted by Professor Barclay in 2006 but the AFP cannot comment on operational issues. However, they believe that the 'boy on the bike' may have been passing through or visiting the area as a result of a hobby (such as collecting waste material or using his spade to dig a mound for bike jumping) or minor employment (such as mowing lawns, completing a paper round or working on one of the farms that still ringed the area). One of the pastimes of the local teenagers was to search the dump sites for electrical wire and to strip the copper conductors for resale.

The suspect would have had a history of inappropriate behaviour at his school—aggressive, disruptive behaviour and bullying. The boy may have lived closer into the centre of Canberra and although he did not attend a local South Canberra High School, he was drawn to the Curtin dump as a recreational play area. Police doorknocked every home in South Canberra and although the suspect could not be positively identified, detectives believe that his name was mentioned in the original enquiry and was probably even interviewed by police back in 1966. And it wasn't Derek Percy.

'Until we've exhausted all avenues of enquiry the investigation will remain open,' Sheehan says. 'It would be a major step forward in this investigation if we could eliminate Derek Percy as a suspect. And if it's not Percy, then definitely, who was involved. The first thing we have to do, however, is to try and eliminate Percy as a suspect and the easiest way is to prove that he wasn't in Canberra the day of Allen's murder.'

There is also the Redston family to consider of course. Brian and Violet Redston still live in Canberra and Allen's siblings have grown to adulthood still not knowing who was responsible for their death of their brother. 'Everyone in the AFP who have come into contact with Allen's parents over the past few years say they are the loveliest people you could hope to meet,' Sheehan says. More than 40 years after the tragic event it is just as important for the Redstons to know if their son was deliberately murdered or died through misadventure. They will take no comfort from the theory, if proven, that their son was not one of Percy's victims but died at the hands of an older local boy as the result of an assault that went horribly wrong—but the AFP is continuing to work hard to provide them with a definitive answer. But will there ever be any closure?

The concept of 'closure' troubles Chris Sheehan. 'There is no closure with violent death. You live with it for the rest of your life and the loss leaves a gaping hole. To have the person who did the crime in gaol would be, at times, a comfort but it doesn't close off the grief and pain for the family.'

It is a concept the Stilwell family in Melbourne know only too well.

CHAPTER 13: Australian Psycho

On 20 June 2007, detectives executed a search warrant on a South Melbourne warehouse and found 35 boxes of items belonging to Derek Ernest Percy. The majority of the material found at the storage facility was made up Percy's private belongings, including his stamp collection and model boats, but allegedly included 'newspaper articles on sex crimes, pictures of children, a video with a rape theme and handwritten stories on fresh sex offences involving abduction and torture'.[1] There was also a massive written document numbering more than 300 pages with an index at the back, which itemised hundreds of scenarios relating to the abduction, mutilation and murder of young children.

For decades Percy had denied to psychiatrists that he was generating violent fantasies involving children and writing them down. Despite being one of Australia's most violent sex criminals deemed 'too dangerous' for release, Percy had somehow managed to collect and transfer the material from his prison cell to a city storage unit. Victoria's Police Commissioner, Christine Nixon, acknowledged the potentially incriminating evidence found in Percy's storage unit comprised 'significant information' and 'may lead to many, many matters being dealt with'.[2] Chief Commissioner Nixon was unable to explain how such a notorious prisoner was allowed to send items out of gaol for storage for more than 30 years.

On 27 August, Magistrate Belinda Wallington granted detectives working on Operations Heats permission to question Percy about the seizure of the items. The media speculated that his writings contained 'confessions' of unsolved crimes but realistically there was 'nothing groundbreaking' in them.[3] Just because Percy wrote about certain incidents this didn't mean that he acted all of them out. Razor blades found in the boxes did not match the ones used in the Brook murder, as speculated; they were given to him while in prison and used for building model boats. A lewd cartoon with the heading 'Wicked Wanda' had nothing to do with the Wanda Beach Murders as had been widely reported—it had been ripped from the pages of an old *Playboy* magazine.

Jean Priest, the mother of Linda Stilwell, hoped the discovery of any new information would lead to charges being laid against Percy. 'I am so glad they now have something to have a go at him with. I just hope that he will finally talk.' The evidence could be produced at the coronial inquest into her daughter's 1968 disappearance. 'Then I will be able to put a name to the face,' Jean Priest said. 'I just hope he would finally admit what he has done.'[4]

Gary Stilwell, Linda's older brother, publicly urged Percy to confess. 'Our family has been traumatised enough and all we want is closure. I appeal to any shred of decency within Percy to come forward with any information he has so that we can find the remains of my sister.'[5] Derek Percy, though, had long ago abandoned any concept of human decency.

※※※

Psychologically, Derek Ernest Percy is as rare a specimen as the Tasmanian tiger—as much misunderstood as he is difficult to identify—and remains a walking, talking, breathing, thinking textbook example of a sadistic paedophile. A treatise on sexual predators differentiates between 'seductive' paedophiles—those who charm and groom their victims—and sadistic paedophiles. In the subcategories of paedophilia, Percy would best be described as a 'Mysoped' in that he has 'no concern for his victim's welfare and no remorse for his actions'.[6] Applying well-worn idioms, Percy may well be 'Our Hannibal Lecter', or even worse, he is Australia's Norman Bates—an 'Australian Psycho'.

Percy is unique in that three characteristics—sadomasochism, paedophilia and a dominant fantasy life—combined very early in his psychological development to create a monster. An analysis of Percy's writings indicates his sexual preference for children of either sex—boys, 6–10 years old, and girls, 6–14. In his writings Percy describes both homosexual and heterosexual gratification with children and includes details of cannibalism and ritualistic murder.[7]

New South Wales Detective Sergeant Adam Barwick, who investigated Derek Ernest Percy for three and a half years, explains:

'Some people may develop sadomasochistic traits in their 30s, for example, and never act upon them... Percy was acting his fantasies out as a teenager. To have those compulsions before the age of 20 is very rare. And there can't be any one trigger for his behaviour... there was no abused childhood, his parents were caring if not overly protective, there was no alcoholism or failed relationships. You can't blame someone else for the way Derek turned out. It's just how his brain is wired.'[8]

'He could have had a relatively normal adult life and turned out like [notorious 'granny killer'] John Glover and killed older women,' Barwick opined, 'but he targeted children from the outset. Percy obtained sexual gratification and pleasure from hurting children but not necessarily because he had been abused himself.' There has been some media speculation that Percy may have been abused by a grandparent,[9] but this allegation is not supported by his family and cannot be corroborated.

The inquest into the 1968 murder of Simon Brook commenced at Glebe Coroner's Court—the same suburb where the little boy was found murdered—on 12 December 2005. Barwick arranged for Derek Percy to be flown to Sydney under an assumed name and amid tight security to appear before New South Wales Coroner Mr John Abernathy. 'I had to be careful when I presented the Brook inquest,' Barwick admits. 'I didn't want any connection to those other crimes'—Wanda, Beaumont, Redston, and Stilwell. 'Once you drag in the other crimes, they [the DPP] could say, "Well 'Wanda' involved two 15-year-old girls, the Beaumonts were in South Australia.'[10] The involvement of the 'other' unsolved crimes in any potential court proceedings could create too much of a smokescreen for a jury, Barwick believes, and Percy could get away with any crime that he may have committed.

Not surprisingly, Derek Percy exercised his right not to be questioned during the inquest. Peter Zahra, SC, the counsel assisting said that the Brook case had 'striking similarities'[11] with the 1969 murder of Yvonne Tuohy in Melbourne. Zahra identified ten points of comparison between the two murders.[12] Detective Sergeant Barwick outlined the evidence linking Percy to the unsolved murder and informed the court that in his opinion, based on all the available evidence Derek Ernest Percy was responsible for the murder of Simon Brook. Nathan Steel, Percy's defence counsel, said there was 'no direct evidence at all linking Mr Percy with the murder ... [and] no physical forensic evidence linking him to the crime scene'. On the second day of proceedings, Mr Abernathy had heard enough and terminated the inquest and referred the matter to the New South Wales DPP believing that there was a 'reasonable prospect... that a jury would convict a known person in relation to the offence'.[13]

In June 2007, however, the Director of the New South Wales DPP declined to lay fresh charges against Derek Percy. New South Wales detectives were at a loss to explain the decision: the 'tendency evidence' tabled at the inquest could have been prejudicial; the brief may have contained too many elements that identified differences between the two crimes; or the DPP may have gained legal advice that some evidence might not be admissible in court. It appears that there may have been a reasonable doubt that Percy was in Sydney on the day of the murder—Percy said that he was in Newcastle, but this could not be corroborated—and several other suspects ('Andy') had admitted to the crime. Lastly, despite the unquestioned integrity of Ron Anderson, the legal 'unreliability' of Percy's admissions to him after his capture in 1969 possibly went against the Brook investigation, especially as Anderson's statement relied on his memory of the conversation some 23 years after the fact. Percy's other admissions, including those allegedly made to other prisoners, were equally 'equivocal'.[14] Sydney detectives felt they had enough evidence to charge Percy with murder but whether the DPP viewed the case as too difficult to prove—or too old to try when weighed against the public benefit, given that Percy has been in custody for so long—fresh charges were not laid against him.

'We are convinced, both by the police evidence and by the

Coroner's recent findings that Derek Percy was responsible for Simon's death,' Dr Donald Brook wrote to me via email.[15] 'Our only reason for wishing that the New South Wales DPP would bring on a prosecution is to ensure as an outcome that Percy should not go free while the possibility remains that he might commit another such crime. We do not think that vengeance is a creditable motive, and would not even oppose his release from prison under supervision if [impossible, under the circumstances] we could be assured by a consensus of psychiatric opinion that he has gained insight, is genuinely remorseful, and would not offend again. There is, of course, another possibility,' Dr Brook noted. 'A prosecution for Simon's murder might fail, perhaps on a technicality, and paradoxically his having been found not guilty might actually assist him in making a future parole application.'

The decision of the New South Wales DPP not to charge Derek Percy has serious ramifications for Melbourne detectives working on Operation Heats who have prepared an inquest report for the Victorian Coroner regarding the disappearance of Linda Stilwell. The Brook case had a victim, a known crime scene and photos of some forensic exhibits—the Stilwell investigation has none of these elements. Although Operation Heats has a brief to introduce evidence from these other unsolved crimes, it remains to be seen if the Stilwell case can be linked to Percy on circumstantial evidence alone.

The continued media speculation about Derek Percy's possible involvement in other crimes creates even more issues. News of the renewed investigation into Percy's movements in the late 1960s, for example, prompted a Melbourne woman to come forward in 2007 and inform police that she saw Linda Stilwell at St Kilda on the day she disappeared with a man wearing a dark spray jacket. When Percy was arrested for the murder of Yvonne Tuohy in 1969, he was photographed wearing the same type of jacket. 'I am absolutely sure that the man I saw sitting on the park bench the day Stilwell disappeared is the same man,' she told police.[16]

The problem remains, witnesses weren't picking Percy out of a photo line-up, they were responding to stimulus from the media. Percy's 1969 'arrest' picture was now in wide public circulation in newspapers, on television news coverage and even the internet. *The Age*, for example, constructed a multi-media website devoted to Percy and the unsolved crimes. Not only is this not admissible in a court of law, the real danger remains that even if fresh charges are laid it may become increasingly impossible for Percy to gain a fair trial in Melbourne.

And there are other issues. If Melbourne detectives introduce evidence into the Stilwell inquest from other investigations—the Wanda, Beaumont or Redston cases—and it is later determined that Percy was not involved in these murders, then it could potentially derail a conviction in the Stilwell case. By contrast, AFP Detective Sergeant Chris Sheehan admits that 'even if Percy wasn't involved [in the Redston case] and we end up charging someone else for Allen's murder, any defence lawyer worth his money is now going to throw Percy's name at the jury as an alternative suspect'.[18] But this does not deter Operation Heats. In a coronial inquest all the available evidence, the tested and the untested, is tabled before the Coroner. 'We'll show everything we've got,' says Detective Sergeant Wayne Newman.[17]

South Australian Police has politely and professionally cooperated with Operation Heats during the past four years but it is my understanding that despite being unable to exclude Derek Percy from their inquiry, they believe that he was not involved in the disappearance of the Beaumont children.[19] This view is based on contact with them in researching my 2006 book on the disappearance of the Beaumont children and the absence of any logical evidence tying Percy to the crime. He does not fit the description of the man seen playing with the children on Glenelg Beach; police cannot place him in Adelaide on Australia Day, 1966; and he may have lacked the opportunity to commit the crime even if he was there. And yet the Australian media readily links Percy to the missing Beaumont children as a matter of fact.[20]

And what of the Wanda Beach murders? New South Wales Police did not ask Derek Percy a single question about the 1965 murder of Christine Sharrock and Marianne Schmidt. While their Melbourne colleagues working on Operation Heats included the Wanda case in their multi-agency investigation, New South Wales Police focused their energies on their investigation into the murder of Simon Brook. Operation Heats asked New South Wales Detective Sergeant Adam Barwick to show the school photo of Derek Percy as a 16-year-old to the adult Wolfgang Schmidt to see if he could identify him as the 'surfie boy' seen walking into the sandhills with his sister more than 40 years ago. Wolfgang could not do so.[21]

This book has taken a clinical look at the five unsolved crimes identified by Operation Heats and their relationship to the crime Derek Percy is known to have committed—the abduction and murder of Yvonne Tuohy in 1969. Linking any of these five unsolved cases to Percy relies on establishing points of 'similar circumstance'[22] with the Tuohy case rather than on direct physical or forensic links. Some of the circumstantial links are strong, others threadbare, but having discovered as much as we now know about Derek Percy is it possible to determine definitively what crimes he was involved in?

According to the Behavioural Science Unit of the Federal Bureau of Investigation, the murder of Yvonne Tuohy was 'a lust murder'.[23] In a lust murder the offender focuses on the victim's breasts, abdomen, rectum or genitals (both male and female) in an expression of anger and frustration. Most of these offenders are categorised as 'disorganised'—their crimes appear to lack planning and organisation. They are more likely to masturbate and engage in postmortem mutilation than rape their victims. Offenders are obsessed with fantasies and act on 'a spur of the moment'. This type of offender usually lives or works in close proximity to the crime scene and uses a knife as a 'personal' weapon.

Is Derek Percy a serial killer? The term wasn't even invented when

Percy was apprehended washing blood from his clothes in 1969. Former FBI agent Robert Ressler is one of the foremost experts on serial killers. Ressler invented the term when he was investigating murderer Ted Bundy in the late 1970s. In his book *Whoever Fights Monsters* (Simon & Schuster, 1993) Ressler identified several key characteristics of what were formally known as 'repeat murderers'. These are:

- most serial killers are white and under the age of 35
- most serial killers are the products of dysfunctional families—typically an unloving mother and an absent father
- many serial killers are intelligent but are employed in menial jobs far below their intellect
- many serial killers suffer from physical ailments or disabilities
- the initial impulse to murder comes during a period of stress, such as the loss of a job or the break-up of a relationship.[24]

All five indicators can be applied to Derek Percy.

Considering the crime for which Percy was apprehended, three main characteristics stand out—child victims, a seaside crime scene and sexually-motivated sadism. Could this have been Percy's psychological 'calling card' for other possible murders? As shown on the chart, the victims of the other unsolved crimes were children under the age of 15. The Wanda Beach victims were slightly older than Percy's target group—boys between 4 and 10 and girls aged 9–14—and were pubescent young women. The ages of all the other children are consistent with Percy's writings and paraphilia.

As far as 'seaside' crime scenes are concerned, Christine Sharrock and Marianne Schmidt were murdered in the sandhills at Wanda Beach, the Beaumonts went missing from Glenelg Beach and Linda Stilwell was abducted on the waterfront at St Kilda. Simon Brook was abducted from the Sydney Harbour suburb of

Glebe but Allen Redston was murdered in suburban Canberra, and while some newspapers tried to continue the 'water' theme with the creek bed the body was found in, the AFP acknowledges this is drawing a long bow.

In regards to sexually-motivated sadism, Percy conducted a post mortem excision of his victim—from the sternum to the beginning of the vagina—and because this behaviour is relatively unique among sex offenders it provides an important insight into his character. The Wanda Beach victims were stabbed but they weren't sexually mutilated. However, Simon Brook was strangled and his genitals cut with a razor blade, and so this crime appears to have a direct correlation with the Tuohy murder. Victims at these three crime scenes (Wanda, Brook and Tuohy) had their throats cut and although rape may have been attempted, evidence of male spermatozoa was detected on the victim's bodies. Allen Redston was hog-tied and strangled, but there was no evidence of sexual activity. The bodies of the Beaumont children and Linda Stilwell, of course, have never been found.

Percy exhibited the following 'organised behaviour' at the Tuohy crime scene: he had ligatures in his vehicle to tie his victim; he used a vehicle to transport the victim to another area; he took the victim to a remote area to accomplish his purpose; and he brought the weapon to and removed it from the crime scene. The murderer associated with the other crimes scenes [with the exception of the Redston Case, where the murderer bound and wrapped the victim in materials found at the crime scene] also exhibited some degree of 'organisation'. But mercifully, Percy was no evil genius. Although he made preparations for the event, the abduction of Yvonne Tuohy was poorly thought out and resulted in his capture later that same afternoon.

Victims	Ages	Date	Place	Crime Scene	Injuries	Weapons	Postmortem Mutilation
Christine Sharrock & Marianne Schmidt	15 years	11 January 1965 (Monday)—school holidays	Wanda Beach (Sydney, NSW)	Murdered and buried in the sandhills at Wanda Beach	Blunt force trauma, stabbed (CS); stabbed, throat cut, attempted rape (MS)	Blunt object, serrated knife	No
Jane, Arnna & Grant Beaumont	9, 7 and 4 years	26 January 1966 (Wednesday)—school holidays	Glenelg (Adelaide, SA)	Unknown	Unknown	Unknown	Unknown
Allen Redston	6 years	27 September 1966 (Tuesday)	Curtin (Canberra, ACT)	Suburban, creek bed	Strangled	Ligatures, gag	No
Simon Brook	3 years	18 May 1968 (Saturday)	Glebe (Sydney, NSW)	Abducted from front yard, murdered in a vacant block	Strangled, throat cut, penis cut	Newspaper wads (gag), razor blade	Yes
Linda Stilwell	7 years	10 August 1968 (Saturday)	St Kilda (Melbourne, Victoria)	Unknown	Unknown	Unknown	Unknown
Yvonne Touhy	12 years	20 July 1969 (Sunday)	Warneet (Western Port Bay, Victoria)	Abducted from a beach track, murdered in a vacant paddock	Strangled, rape attempted, throat cut and disembowelled	Ligatures, face-washer (gag), knife	Yes

Experts believe that in regard to the Tuohy and Brook murders, 'the offender' is acting out of the same motivation.[25] Percy is extremely fantasy-motivated. In the writings seized by police, Percy wrote about the Tuohy murder before it actually occurred. He had fantasised (for about four years, he told police) about abducting children and subjecting them to various acts involving faeces. He also wrote about kidnapping a small boy and cutting off the penis.

The behaviour exhibited at the Tuohy crime scene, however, is very different than in the case of Allen Redston. The only 'fantasy' aspect to the Redston murder was the excessive use of ligatures. Percy was 18 years old in September 1966; slightly older than the Redston suspect (13–17 years) and although his fantasy life had already begun he does not appear to have any sexual interest in bondage. If Percy was involved in the binding of Allen Redston, it is unlikely that he would have been able to stop himself. Percy would also have written about the incident in the ensuing years—if only to relive the event—and there is no reference to the hog-tying murder of a child in his writings.

On 31 May 2005, Professor James Ogloff compiled a forensic psychological report on Derek Percy for the purpose of the Brook inquest.[26] Professor Ogloff wrote that it is exceedingly rare for a person to have such a serious sadistic sexual paraphilia, as in Percy's case. Many of the experienced forensic mental health professionals who have assessed him over the years have commented that his case is so unusual that it is the only one they have seen of that nature. Not only did Percy have the propensity for committing acts of torture, sexual assault and killing of young children from about 1965, he also committed his one known murder in that time.

It was Professor Ogloff's opinion that it is highly unusual as a first serious offence for an offender to carry out and complete a set of complex acts as those performed against Yvonne Tuohy. In his experience, most people who commit sexual homicide engage in other actions leading up to their first murder. After his arrest, Percy reported that his 'compulsion' to murder was so strong that he persisted with the acts even in the face of significant impediments: being threatened with a tomahawk by Shane Spiller; being disturbed by a family in another vehicle; and the increasing likelihood that he would be caught. Rather than ceasing the behaviour, Percy hid the girl in his car and drove her to another location. In Professor Ogloff's experience, such interruptions often lead the offender to cease the attack. But not Percy, which suggests that the murder of Yvonne Tuohy was not the first such attack that he had undertaken.

❋❋❋

Looking at all six crimes, it is my opinion that it is much more likely that Derek Percy was involved in the two crimes committed immediately before his capture in 1969—the murder of Simon Brook and the disappearance of Linda Stilwell in 1968—than the three crimes committed in the previous three years. I believe Percy started murdering once he broke away from his family and joined the RAN in 1967. If he had already started killing as early as 1965–66, his 'inactivity' during the year before he joined the navy is difficult to explain.

Percy's propensity to abduct Linda Stilwell in 1968 is beyond question: he wrote about a similar event; he regularly drove through the St Kilda area; he had access to a car and was on leave from the navy at the time. The frequency of these crimes suddenly increases once Percy obtains his car licence, and a modicum of independence from his family, in 1968. Simon Brook was murdered in May of that year; Linda Stilwell disappeared in August; a Mornington girl avoided abduction in early 1969;[27] Yvonne Tuohy was abducted and murdered in July 1969. Interestingly, all these crimes were committed on a Saturday or Sunday when Derek Percy was stationed in the area but was on weekend leave.

It is now apparent to investigators that Derek Percy was not involved in the death of Allen Redston in Canberra in 1966 and his potential involvement in the disappearance of the Beaumont children earlier that year—regardless of what he may have told school friend Ron Anderson—defies logic. But the Wanda Beach murders still create some controversy.

Despite the assertion by Melbourne detectives that Derek Percy is the Wanda Beach murderer New South Wales detectives believe that Christopher Wilder remains a legitimate 'person of interest' in the 1965 murders of Christine Sharrock and Marianne Schmidt.[28] While this could easily be dismissed as jurisdictional jealousy between competing state agencies, there is a compelling case for suspecting Wilder was the man responsible. Wilder was a 19-year-old apprentice carpenter in 1965—slightly older than the 16-year old 'surfie' suspect—but he had a young appearance and matches Wolfgang Schmidt's 'fat boy' description.

In writing my book *Wanda: The Untold Story of the Wanda Beach Murders* (New Holland, Sydney, 2003) I was given access to several volumes of original police files relating to the case. Going through my research notes, I found that Wolfgang's original description of the boy was of having an 'unshaven face'[29]—this was interpreted at the time as meaning the suspect was not yet shaving, but it could also have meant the exact opposite.

The fact that Wilder was able to lure two teenage girls away from a Sydney beach in the 1980s has always concerned New South Wales detectives—did he also lure the Wanda victims into the sandhills in 1965, overpower them and murder them in a frenzied sexual attack? Wilder was old enough to buy alcohol to give to one of the victims, charming enough to befriend the girls but also sexually deviant. He would also have been capable of bashing a Wollongong cleaning lady to death (Wilhelmina Kruger), murdering a prostitute (Anna Dowlingkoa) and transporting her body to a remote highway—two crimes that were readily linked to the Wanda Beach murders at the time.

Despite the circumstantial links to Derek Percy, Detective Sergeant (now Detective Inspector) Adam Barwick believes Christopher Wilder is a better physical, psychological and sexual 'fit' for the Wanda Beach murders—and on the available evidence, so do I. Half a century after Christine Sharrock and Marianne Schmidt lost their lives on windy Wanda Beach, the task remains for detectives to exclude either Wilder or Percy from the 'cold case' investigation.

In the official post mortem report of the Wanda case it states, 'the hymen of the girl SCHMIDT was found intact, but there was evidence of a recent abrasion indicating that intercourse had taken place and a number of male spermatozoa were present. A vaginal swab taken from the girl showed the blood grouping substances "A" and or "B" were not present, which indicates that the offender is probably a non secretor of the blood group "A" or "B" or belongs to the blood group "O".'[30]

Today, the sperm sample alone recovered from the crime scene would be enough to convict a 'known person' of the murder of Christine Sharrock and Marianne Schmidt but the New South Wales Government Records Repository in Western Sydney cannot confirm the status of the sample. New South Wales detectives can only assume that the number of different investigators handling the samples over the decades somehow led to them being misplaced—there is no other explanation. In 2000. the clothing that Christine and Marianne wore to Wanda Beach the day that they were murdered was DNA tested but New South Wales Police will neither confirm nor deny that a DNA profile was produced.[31]

The revelation that the Wanda murderer was most likely a 'non secretor of the blood group "A" or "B" or belongs to the blood group "O" may one day be enough to identify the person responsible but it still presents a problem in the case of Derek Ernest Percy. Because Percy was never convicted of a crime he is not recorded on the Victorian DNA database of almost 10,000 offenders. Police can only apply for the forcible taking of a DNA from a relevant suspect if 'they can convince a magistrate there are reasonable grounds for suspicion and material is available from a crime scene to enable DNA comparison'.[32] It is ironic that the one crime Derek Percy is least likely to have committed, the death of Allen Redston in Canberra in 1966, is the one case in which partial DNA from the crime scene is most likely to have been preserved. A simple check of Percy's medical records from his 40 years in prison to ascertain his blood type may exclude him from the Wanda investigation once and for all—or potentially complicate issues even further.

One of the suggestions from a law reform committee tabled in the Victorian parliament in March 2004 was that this legal loophole should be eliminated so that DNA samples could be forcibly taken from detainees such as Derek Percy who have not been convicted of a crime. Rob Hulls, the then Victorian Attorney-General, said that his government would consider making this change but, by April 2008, the new legislation had still not been passed.[33]

In June 2004, Derek Percy began a one-to-one sex offenders' program in Melbourne's Port Phillip Prison. According to a report that was leaked to the *Herald Sun*, 'Derek hopes that participation in the program might give him a chance at possible parole'.[34] In February 2005, the Leader of the Opposition in the Victorian Parliament, Robert Doyle, sought to make political capital out of Percy's case. If his party were elected to power, he said, it would introduce 'Hannibal Lecter' laws to ensure that Percy and people like him would never be released. He said: 'There should not be any chance at all that Percy can get out. And we will introduce laws which provide for "life lock-up" of special case prisoners who are beyond help or redemption.' In reply, Attorney-General Rob Hulls gave assurances that Percy would not be released while he was a danger to the community. 'This state has laws to imprison people for serious violent, sexual and drug crimes for an indefinite period of time.'[35] Percy, it appears, is going nowhere.

'Percy thinks he's smart,' Detective Sergeant Adam Barwick says. Having interviewed Percy twice, he then adds, 'He's not going to give you anything for free.'[36] Paedophiles and convicted criminals alike are master manipulators who spend a lifetime in denial of their crimes, so Percy is unlikely to make any admissions—and he hasn't for more than 40 years—while his mother is still alive and while he still holds out hope of being released.

The Percy family has obviously felt the impact of Derek Percy's crimes. Following their retirement to Queensland and the subsequent death of Ernie Percy in the late 1990s, Mrs Elaine Percy and her sons have been left to endure the subsequent investigation into Derek's movements before his capture. While Percy's younger brothers have remained silent over the years—understandably declining, perhaps, to be their brother's keeper—Mrs Percy continues to maintain that Derek has not committed any other offence against children. Now in her 80s, she has regularly been questioned during the past decade regarding her son's activities in the 1960s and continues to defend him.

By 2008, Derek Percy spent almost two-thirds of his life—39 years—in jail for the murder he committed when he was barely out of his teens. If Percy is not insane (if in fact, he ever was) why is he still in gaol? Percy has accumulated almost $200,000 from his naval pension over the past 40 years—a situation that has drawn much criticism of the Victorian government and the Federal Defence Department over the years. Critics believe that he should be stripped of the money and that it should be paid to his victims.[37] But Derek Percy has never been convicted of a crime and legally, there are no 'victims'—not even Yvonne Tuohy or her family. Justice, it seems, *is* blind.

'Percy's argument is that he should have been given a custodial sentence, which would have expired by now,' Adam Barwick says.[38] It is another strange irony of this particular case that if Percy had pleaded guilty to murder, he may now be out of gaol.[39] It is equally understandable that Percy would want to be transferred from prison to a mental hospital. Even compared to the minimum security Ararat Prison, hospital life would be like a 'retreat camp' Barwick admits. 'If Percy has to stay in jail for the time being or even the rest of his life, he obviously wants it to be as comfortable as possible.'[40]

Derek Percy has not known freedom since the day astronaut Neil

Armstrong walked on the moon. Psychiatrists who have assessed Percy believe he is effectively institutionalised inside the prison system and could not function in the outside world.[41] At age 60, Percy would still psychically pose a threat to children and so he is best left to his cell—with his chess, his model boat-building and any fantasies he still entertains—until he is old and infirm. One day soon, however, justice may knock on his cell door.

In 2008. Derek Ernest Percy's custodial supervision order once again came up for review.

Update

Derek Percy never received the release from prison he dreamt of for so long. Not even the long-awaited coronial inquest into the disappearance of Linda Stilwell in 2009 could compel Percy to provide any information that would link him to this and other unsolved crimes. Percy passed away in July 2013, aged 64, from lung cancer. Despite a visit from Victoria's Unsolved Homicide Squad just days before his death, he took his secrets of missing children to his grave.

Newspix

Derek Percy shows police where he hid knives under the front seat of his car following his capture in 1969 for the murder of 12-year-old Yvonne Tuohy.

Melbourne Records Depaertment

Twelve-year-old Yvonne Tuohy who was murdered in Warneet, Victoria, by Derek Percy in 1969.

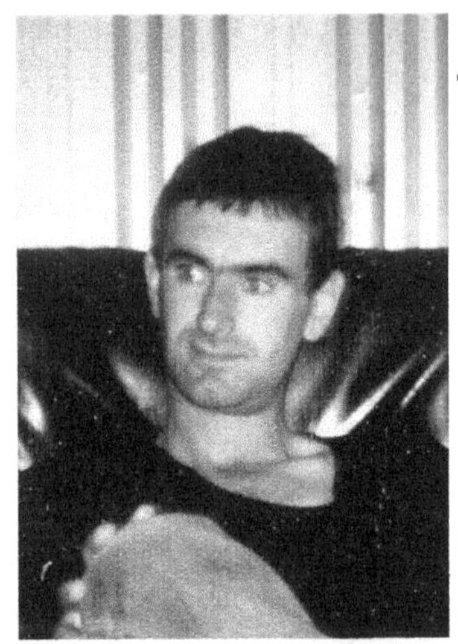

Newspix

Shane Spiller pictured in Wyndham, NSW, several years before his disappearance in 2002.

Newspix

Eleven-year-old Shane Spiller shows the tomahawk with which he fended off the attack by Derek Percy in July 1969.

Newspix

Police examine the partially exposed bodies of teenagers Christine Sharrock and Marianne Schmidt at the murder scene at Wanda Beach on 12 January 1965.

Newspix

Fifteen-year-old neighbours Christine Sharrock (left) and Marianne Schmidt, who were found murdered at Sydney's Wanda Beach on 12 January 1965.

Newspix

Six-year-old Canberra schoolboy Allen Redston was found murdered in the suburb of Curtin on 22 September 1966.

Newspix

The Beaumont children, (L-R) Arnna age 7, Grant age 4 and Jane age 9, who went missing from Adelaide's Glenelg beach on Australia Day in 1966.

MISSING
BEAUMONT CHILDREN

SOUTH AUSTRALIA

At 10.00 a.m. on Wednesday, 26th January, 1966 the undermentioned children left their home at 109 Harding Street, SOMERTON PARK to go to the beach at GLENELG (a distance of about two miles). They have not been heard of since despite extensive Police enquiries.

1. Jane Nartare BEAUMONT, 9 years – 4 ft. 6 in. tall. Hair: fair, ear length, sun bleached, pushed back with a fringe in front. Two front teeth prominent. Well spoken but stutters when excited.

2. Arnna Kathleen BEAUMONT, 7 years – 4 ft. tall, dark brown hair with a fringe, suntanned complexion. Dark brown eyes, plump build.

3. Grant Ellis BEAUMONT, 4 years – 3 ft. tall, brown hair with a fringe, brown eyes, olive complexion.

SUSPICION IS ATTACHED TO AN UNKNOWN MAN,

DESCRIPTION

Male, late 30's or early 40's, 6 ft. to 6 ft. 1 in., light brown hair long at the back with a part on the side, slim build and thinfaced, fair complexion.

Any person who can give any information relating to this matter is asked to contact their nearest Police Station

URGENTLY

A poster requesting information from the public in regard to the missing Beaumont children was circulated nationally and internationally.

South Australia Police

Newspix

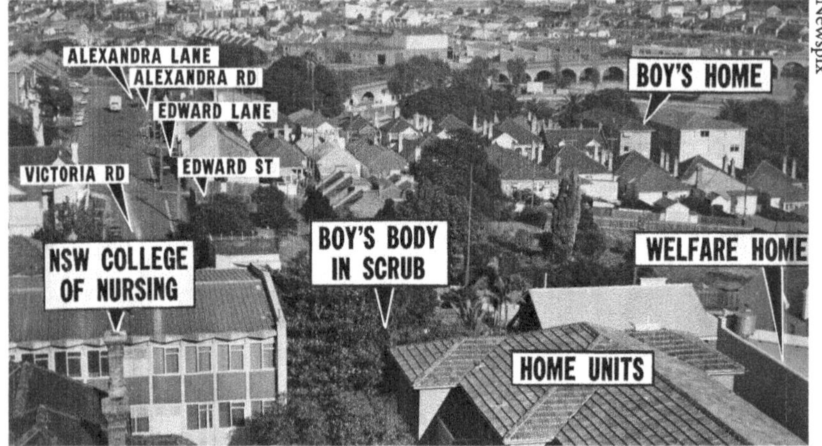

A photo illustration tracing the possible last steps of abducted toddler Simon Brook who was murdered in Glebe in Sydney in May 1968. The railway cutting at Jubilee Park that provided a possible link to Derek Percy's knowledge of the area can be seen in the top right-hand corner.

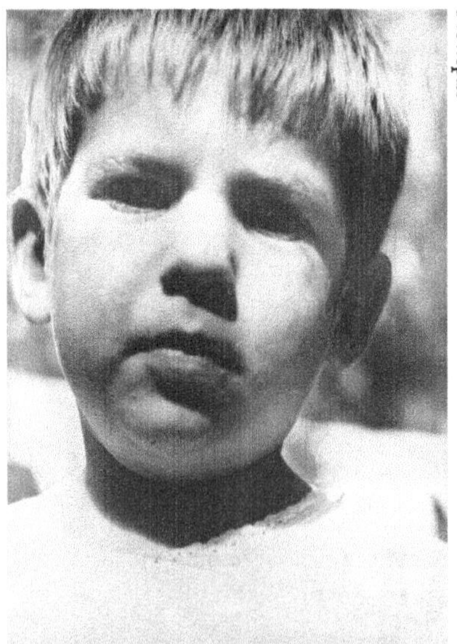
Newspix

Three-year-old Simon Brook who was lured from the front yard of his Glebe home and was found callously murdered 400 yards away.

Melbourne Records Department

The Stillwell children (L-R) Karen, Gary and Linda, when they arrived in Australia in the mid 1960s. Linda Stillwell went missing from St Kilda pier in Melbourne on 10 August 1968.

Kim White

Kim White (left) and Derek Percy as pictured in the Mt Beauty high school yearbook in 1965. Note the difference between White's tie and Percy's homemade tie, which was thought to be an important clue in one of the unsolved murders.

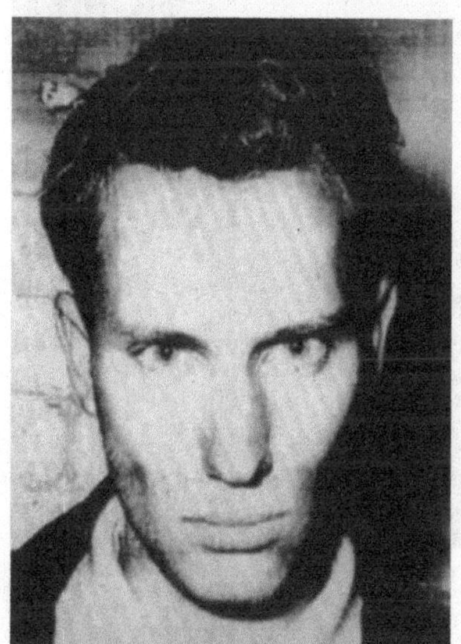

Melbourne Records Department

Derek Percy's mug shot after he was caught for the murder of Yvonne Tuohy in 1969.

South Australia Police

An artist's impression of the suspect in the disappearance of the Beaumont children in 1966. Is it Percy?

Newspix

Derek Ernest Percy, Victoria's longest serving inmate, in 2000.

Notes

Introduction

1. Silvester, J., 'I cannot recall: The refrain of a child killer', *Sydney Morning Herald*, 31 August 2007.
2. Silvester, J., 'Beaumonts: Killer quizzed', *The Age*, 3 February 2005.
3. Trial Transcript, *Regina v Derek Percy*, Supreme Court of Victoria, April 1970.
4. Appeal Transcript, *Herald & Weekly Times v Attorney General (Victoria)*, Supreme Court of Victoria, June–September 2001.
5. Review Transcript, *In the matter of major review of Derek Ernest Percy*, Supreme Court of Victoria, September 2003.
6. Review Transcript, *In the matter of major review of Derek Ernest Percy*, Supreme Court of Victoria, October 1998.

Chapter 1

1. Author interview with Detective Wayne Newman, February 2008.
2. Butcher, S., 'The Terry Floyd case', *The Age*, 30 November 2001.
3. Trial Transcript, *Regina v Derek Percy*, Supreme Court of Victoria, April 1970.
4. Review Transcript, *In the matter of major review of Derek Ernest Percy*, Supreme Court of Victoria, October 1998.
5. Author interview with Detective Wayne Newman, February 2008.
6. Author interview with Ron Anderson, March 2008.
7. Whiticker, A., *Wanda: The Untold Story of the Wanda Beach Murders*, New Holland, Sydney, 2003.
8. Whiticker, A., *Searching for the Beaumont Children*, John Wiley & Sons, Brisbane, 2006.
9. Hall, T., *Wanted: A Casebook of Unsolved Crimes*, Angus and Robertson, Sydney, 1982.
10. *ibid.*
11. *ibid.*
12. Author interview with Detective David Rae, February 2008.
13. Unlike previous police investigations, such as Operation Air, which was the name for the NSW Police investigation into the disappearance of several backpackers who had vanished into 'thin air' in the late 1980s and early 1990s, the codename Operation Heats has no special significance. After public criticism of the sensitivity of some codenames, they are now randomly selected by computer.
14. One of the more famous multi-agency police investigations concerned the murder of two Victoria police officers, Steven Tynan and Damian Eyre, in Walsh Street, South Yarra in October 1988. NSW Police questioned several 'persons of interest' living in NSW at the time. Four men were charged with the double murder but acquitted by the Supreme Court of Victoria.
15. Author interview with Detective Adam Barwick, October 2007.
16. Silvester, J., 'Our worst child killer', *The Age*, 22 April 2007.
17. Author interview with Detective Chris Sheehan, December 2007.
18. Tippet, G., 'What happened to Shane Spiller?' *The Age*, 17 June 2007.

Chapter 2

1. Author interview with the Casarotto family, February 2008.
2. Diphtheria in postwar Australia, see www.nrdgp.org.au
3. The township of Mt Beauty was created in 1949 to provide housing for the employees who worked on the scheme.
4. Silvester, J., 'One man, so many faces of evil', *The Age*, 22 April 2007.
5. *ibid.*
6. Author interview with Kim White, February 2008.
7. Silvester, J., 'One man, so many faces of evil', *The Age*, 22 April 2007.
8. Author interview with Bill Hutton, February 2008.
9. *ibid.*

10. The recounting of the incident at 'the gorge' at Mt Beauty is based on the author's interviews with Kim White and Bill Hutton, February 2008.
11. Mt Beauty Higher Elementary School Yearbook, 1965, courtesy of Kim White.
12. Trial Transcript, *Regina v Derek Percy*, Supreme Court of Victoria, April 1970.
13. *ibid.*
14. *ibid.*
15. Inguanzo, S., 'Former naval colleague breaks silence on killer', *Dandenong Star*, 6 September 2007.
16. Trial Transcript, *Regina v Derek Percy*, Supreme Court of Victoria, April 1970.
17. Silvester, J., 'Inside a web of evil', *The Age*, www.theage.com.au.

Chapter 3

1. This conversation is based on the author's interviews with Bill Hutton, Kim White and Ron Anderson in February–March 2008.
2. All quotes and events relating to the murder of Yvonne Tuohy are taken from the original trial transcript, *Regina v Derek Percy*, Supreme Court of Victoria, April 1970.
3. 'Dobby' is a Hindu word for a person who does the washing. 'Dobbing' in the armed services refers to the act of washing clothes. 'Dobbies' was the slang term some servicemen used to refer to their washing.
4. Tippet, G., 'What happened to Shane Spiller?' *The Age*, 17 June 2007.
5. Marshall, D., 'Please don't free my sister's killer', *Australian Women's Weekly*, March 2008.

Chapter 4

1. Author interview with Ron Anderson, March 2008.
2. All quotes referring to Derek Percy's trial are taken from *Regina v Derek Percy*, Supreme Court of Victoria, April 1970.
3. Doctors, the Judge clarified at one stage of Percy's trial, do not use the terms 'sane' and 'insane' to describe a patient—they use the term 'psychotic'. 'Sane' and 'insane' are only used in a court of law.
4. A 'karyotype' test identifies and evaluates the size, shape, and number of chromosomes in a sample of body cells. Extra, missing, or abnormal positions of chromosome pieces can cause problems with a person's growth, development and body functions, see www.webmd.com.
5. Online Medical Dictionary, see 'coprophilia' at www.cancerweb.ncl.ac.uk.
6. Silvester, J., 'Mind games', *The Age*, 15 August 1998.
7. Review Transcript, *In the matter of major review of Derek Ernest Percy*, Supreme Court of Victoria, October 1998.
8. Silvester, J., 'I cannot recall: The refrain of a child killer', *The Age*, 31 August 2007.
9. Percy's psychiatric reports as reported by Silvester, J., 'Mind games', *The Age*, 15 August 1998, unless otherwise stated.
10. *ibid.*
11. Review Transcript, *In the matter of major review of Derek Ernest Percy*, Supreme Court of Victoria, October 1998.
12. Silvester, J., 'Beaumonts: Killer quizzed', *The Age*, 3 February 2005.
13. Review Transcript, *In the matter of major review of Derek Ernest Percy*, Supreme Court of Victoria, October 1998.
14. *ibid.*

Chapter 5

1. Author interview with Detective Adam Barwick, October 2007.
2. Author interview with Wayne Gordes, February 2008.
3. All quotes relating to the Wanda Beach murders, unless otherwise stated, are taken from my book *Wanda: The Untold Story of the Wanda Beach Murders*, New Holland, Sydney, 2003.
4. Gibney, B., *The Beauty Queen Killer*, Pinnacle Books, New York, 1984.
5. Author interview with Detectives David Rae and Wayne Newman, February 2005.

Chapter 6

1. All quotes in this chapter are taken from my book, *Searching for the Beaumont Children*, John Wiley & Sons, Brisbane, 2006.
2. Author interview with Ron Anderson, March 2008.

3. Hunt, N., 'Von Einem suspect in Beaumonts' disappearance', *Adelaide Sunday Mail*, 22 September 2007.
4. Brown, R., 'The Beaumont Children', see www.beaumontchildren.com.au.
5. *ibid.*
6. *ibid.*

Chapter 7

1. In October 1979, the Australian Federal Police was formed under the Australian Federal Police Act 1979 following the merger of the former Commonwealth Police and the Australian Capital Territory Police.
2. Author interview with Detective Sergeant Chris Sheehan, December 2007.
3. All quotes regarding the murder of Allen Redston, unless otherwise stated, are from the transcript of proceedings of the coronial inquest held in Canberra on 9 June 1967.
4. Lendrum, R.E. and Paull, K.R., *Review of Police Inquiries into the Death of Allen Redston*, NSW Criminal Investigation Branch, 6 February 1967.
5. Hall, T., *Wanted: A Casebook of Unsolved Crimes*, Angus and Robertson, Sydney, 1982.
6. Silvester, J., 'One man, so many faces of evil', *The Age*, 22 April 2007.

Chapter 8

1. All quotes relating to the Brook case, unless otherwise stated, are from the summary of police statements, see 'Death of Simon Brook in 1968', 17 June 2005.
2. Brook, D., *Art Monthly Australia Magazine*, Issue 204, November 2007.
3. All quotes attributed to Dr Donald Brook are from the author's correspondence with Dr Brook, October 2007, unless otherwise stated.
4. Hindsight, 'The Hothouse: Art and Politics at the Tin Sheds', 12 June 2007, see www.abc.net.au.
5. Hall, T., *Wanted: A Casebook of Unsolved Crimes*, Angus and Robertson, Sydney, 1982.
6. *ibid.*
7. *ibid.*
8. Author interview with Detective Adam Barwick, October 2007.
9. 'Andy' is not the man's real name.
10. NSW Health Commission forensic biologist Mrs Joy Kuhl told a hearing into the 1980 disappearance of baby Azaria Chamberlain at Ayers Rock that she had found evidence of human foetal blood in the Chamberlain family car. This evidence helped convict Lindy Chamberlain of murder in 1982. The forensic evidence was later discredited and the Chamberlains were acquitted in 1988.
11. Hall, T., *Wanted: A Casebook of Unsolved Crimes*, Angus and Robertson, Sydney, 1982.
12. *ibid.*
13. *ibid.*
14. Brook, D., *Art Monthly Australia Magazine*, Issue 204, November 2007.
15. Marshall, D., 'Please don't free my sister's killer', *Australian Women's Weekly*, March 2008.
16. Lamont, L., 'Cold case murder: Jury "could convict"', *Sydney Morning Herald*, 14 December 2005.

Chapter 9

1. Silvester, J., 'Court accepts girl missing 40 years was murdered', *The Age*, 20 August 2007.
2. Stilwell, K., 'Remembering Linda', from a website in 2007 but now discontinued.
3. Hall, T., *Wanted: A Casebook of Unsolved Crimes*, Angus and Robertson, Sydney, 1982.
4. Stilwell, K., 'Remembering Linda', from website in 2007 but now discontinued.
5. Hall, T., *Wanted: A Casebook of Unsolved Crimes*, Angus and Robertson, Sydney, 1982.
6. Hickey, K., 'Search for missing girl, 7', *Herald Sun*, 12 August 1968.
7. Stilwell, K., 'Remembering Linda', from website in 2007 but now discontinued.
8. Hall, T., *Wanted: A Casebook of Unsolved Crimes*, Angus and Robertson, Sydney, 1982.
9. Hooper, K., 'Intense search for Linda fails', *Herald Sun*, 13 August 1968.
10. Hickey, K., 'Search for missing girl, 7', *Herald Sun*, 12 August 1968.
11. Hickey, K., 'Hitch-hike girl not lost Linda', *Herald Sun*, 15 August 1968.
12. Hooper, K., 'Intense search for Linda fails', *Herald Sun*, 13 August 1968.
13. Hall, T., *Wanted: A Casebook of Unsolved Crimes*, Angus and Robertson, Sydney, 1982.
14. *ibid.*

15. Hooper, K., 'Linda lost 6 days: Fears rise', *Herald Sun,* 17 August 1968.
16. *ibid.*
17. Hickey, K., 'Beaumont tie seen in Linda case', *Herald Sun,* 18 August 1968.
18. Hooper, K., 'Linda lost 6 days: Fears rise', *Herald Sun,* 17 August 1968.
19. Sharpe, D., 'A birthday Linda would have loved', *The Age,* 19 August 1968.
20. Hall, T., *Wanted: A Casebook of Unsolved Crimes,* Angus and Robertson, Sydney, 1982.
21. *ibid.*
22. Pollard, J.H., *Croiset the Clairvoyant: The Story of an Amazing Dutchman,* Doubleday, New York, 1964.
23. Stilwell, K., 'Remembering Linda', from website in 2007 but now discontinued.
24. Author interview with David Rae and Wayne Newman, February 2008.
25. Author interview with Ron Anderson, March 2008.
26. Silvester, J., 'Court accepts girl missing 40 years was murdered', *The Age,* 20 August 2007.

Chapter 10

1. Review Transcript, *In the matter of major review of Derek Ernest Percy,* Supreme Court of Victoria, October 1998.
2. *Herald & Weekly Times v Attorney General (Victoria),* Supreme Court of Victoria Appeal, June–September 2001.
3. 'Never Let Him Out', *Herald Sun News Pictorial,* 2 September 1998.
4. All quotes relating to Derek Percy's 1998 custodial review are taken from the review transcript, *In the matter of major review of Derek Ernest Percy,* Supreme Court of Victoria, October 1998, unless otherwise stated.
5. 'Paraphilia' refers to obtaining sexual satisfaction from non-procreative sexual acts and include recurrent, intense sexually arousing fantasies, sexual urges or behaviours involving non-human objects, suffering or humiliation of children, see www.webmd.com.
6. Silvester, J., 'Mind games', *The Age,* 15 August 1998.
7. Silvester, J., 'Our worst child killer', *The Age,* 22 April 2007.
8. All quotes and details relating to Derek Percy's 2003 custodial review are taken from the review transcript, *In the matter of major review of Derek Ernest Percy,* Supreme Court of Victoria, September 2003.
9. *ibid.*

Chapter 11

1. Trial Transcript, *Regina v Derek Percy,* Supreme Court of Victoria, April 1970.
2. Tippet, G., 'What happened to Shane Spiller?' *The Age,* 17 June 2007.
3. Silvester, J., 'Murder witness vanishes suspiciously', *The Age,* 4 February 2005.
4. Tippet, G., 'What happened to Shane Spiller?' *The Age,* 17 June 2007.
5. Silvester, J., 'Murder witness vanishes suspiciously', *The Age,* 4 February 2005.
6. Tippet, G., 'What happened to Shane Spiller?' *The Age,* 17 June 2007.
7. *ibid.*
8. *Herald & Weekly Times v Attorney General (Victoria),* Supreme Court of Victoria Appeal, June–September 2001.
9. Tippet, G., 'What happened to Shane Spiller?' *The Age,* 17 June 2007.
10. Silvester, J., 'Murder witness vanishes suspiciously, *The Age,* 4 February 2005.
11. Author interview with Detective Sergeant Mark Winterflood, March 2008.
12. Tippet, G., 'What happened to Shane Spiller?' *The Age,* 17 June 2007.
13. *ibid.*
14. *ibid.*
15. *ibid.*
16. Author interview with Detective Sergeant Mark Winterflood, March 2008.
17. Tippet, G., 'What happened to Shane Spiller?' *The Age,* 17 June 2007.
18. Crawford, C., 'Child killer pockets navy pension', *Sunday Herald Sun,* 8 May 2005.
19. Author interview with Detective Sergeant Mark Winterflood, March 2008.
20. Tippet, G., 'What happened to Shane Spiller?' *The Age,* 17 June 2007.
21. Author interview with Detective Sergeant Mark Winterflood, March 2008.
22. Tippet, G., 'What happened to Shane Spiller?' *The Age,* 17 June 2007.
23. *ibid.*

24. Author interview with Detective Sergeant Mark Winterflood, March 2008.
25. Tippet, G., 'What happened to Shane Spiller?' *The Age*, 17 June 2007.
26. Author interview with Detective Sergeant Mark Winterflood, March 2008.
27. Tippet, G., 'What happened to Shane Spiller?' *The Age*, 17 June 2007.
28. Author interview with Detective Sergeant Mark Winterflood, March 2008.
29. *ibid.*
30. *ibid.*
31. Tippet, G., 'What happened to Shane Spiller?' *The Age*, 17 June 2007.
32. *ibid.*
33. *ibid.*
34. Trial Transcript, *Regina v Derek Percy*, Supreme Court of Victoria, April 1970.
35. Author interview with Detective Sergeant Wayne Newman, February 2008.

Chapter 12

1. Author interview with Detective Adam Barwick, October 2007.
2. Author interview with Detective Wayne Newman, February 2008.
3. Brown, R., 'The Beaumont children', see www.beaumontchildren.com.au.
4. Silvester, J., 'One man, so many faces of evil', *The Age*, 22 April 2007.
5. Author interview with Detective Adam Barwick, October 2007.
6. All quotes relating to the Brook case, unless otherwise stated, are from the summary of police statements, 'Death of Simon Brook in 1968', 17 June 2005.
7. ABC Online, 'Prisoner quizzed over unsolved murder of Canberra boy', 4 February 2005.
8. The other cases reviewed by Professor David Barclay also included Operation Corium—the investigation into the disappearance and suspected murder of Megan Mulquiney in 1984; Operation Dunedin—the murder of Janelle Patton on Norfolk Island in March 2002; and Operation Manse—the murder of Susan Winburn in January 2004.
9. Operation Kobold, see ACT Policing *Annual Report 2004–2005* at www.afp.gov.au.
10. The case Professor Barclay assisted.
11. The codename Operation Kobold also holds no special significance. The name was randomly selected by computer.
12. Author interview with Detective Chris Sheehan, December 2007.
13. Murray, C., 'Use of low copy number (LCN) DNA in forensic inference', The Forensic Service, London, see www.promega.com.

Chapter 13

1. Silvester, J., 'I cannot recall: The refrain of a child killer', *The Age*, 31 August 2007.
2. Hoy, G., 'New information could solve murders', *The 7.30 Report*, 30 August 2007, see www.abc.net.au.
3. Author interview with Detective Sergeant Adam Barwick, October 2007.
4. Silvester, J., 'One man, so many faces of evil', *The Age*, 22 April 2007.
5. Silvester, J., 'I cannot recall: The refrain of a child killer', *The Age*, 31 August 2007.
6. 'The Psychology of Sexual Predation and Pedophilia', see *MegaLinks in Criminal Justice* at www.faculty.ncwc.edu, accessed 24 March 2006.
7. How perverse were Percy's fantasies? In one of the articles confiscated from his locker in 1969 Percy described the roasting of a baby on a spit on a barbeque and, over the course of a weekend, forcing abducted children to eat the flesh of the baby out and off each other's genitals.
8. Author interview with Detective Sergeant Adam Barwick, October 2007.
9. Silvester, J., 'Our worst child killer', *The Age*, 22 April 2007.
10. Author interview with Detective Sergeant Adam Barwick, October 2007.
11. 'Sydney toddler killed by "known person"', see AAP at www.ninemsn.com.au, accessed 13 December 2005.
12. Peter Zahra, QC, also worked on the brief that implicated NSW woman Kathleen Folbigg in the death of her four infant children from 1991–99. Folbigg's conviction also depended on circumstantial evidence with Zahra identifying four points of behavioural opportunity—

one of which was that she had been left alone with her three children. In 2003 Folbigg was convicted of three counts of murder and one of manslaughter and sentenced to 30 years (on appeal).

13. 'Sydney toddler killed by "known person"', see AAP at www.ninemsn.com.au, accessed 13 December 2005.
14. Author interview with Detective Sergeant Adam Barwick, October 2007.
15. Author's correspondence with Dr Donald Brook, October 2007.
16. Silvester, J., 'Court accepts girl missing 40 years was murdered', *The Age*, 20 August 2007.
17. Author interview with Detective Sergeant Wayne Newman, February 2008.
18. Author interview with Detective Sergeant Chris Sheehan, December 2007.
19. Author interview with Detective Inspector Brian Swan, July 2005.
20. As recently as the March 2008 issue of the *Australian Women's Weekly*, author Debi Marshall wrote a thoughtful article on the 'crimes' of Derek Percy from the perspective of the family of Yvonne Tuohy and the families of the victims of the other unsolved cases. Although Marshall refers to the Beaumont children (and Allen Redston) only fleetingly, the heading on the cover of the magazine reads 'True Crime: Australia's Worst Serial Killer Linked to Beaumont Kids'. It is clear that 42 years after the fact, the Beaumont children still sell magazines.
21. Author interview with Detective Sergeant Adam Barwick, October 2007.
22. Author interview with Detective Sergeant David Rae, February 2008.
23. Behavioural Science Unit of the Federal Bureau of Investigation, see www.fbi.gov.
24. Ressler, R.K., *Whoever Fights Monsters*, Simon & Schuster, New York, 1993.
25. Summary of police statements, 'Death of Simon Brook in 1968', 17 June 2005.
26. *ibid.*
27. Silvester, J., 'Inside a web of evil', *The Age*, see www.theage.com.au.
28. Author interview with Detective Sergeant Adam Barwick, October 2007.
29. Whiticker, A., *Wanda: The Untold Story of the Wanda Beach Murders*, New Holland, Sydney, 2003.
30. *ibid.*
31. *ibid.*
32. Brown, R., 'The Beaumont children', see www.beaumontchildren.com.au.
33. *ibid.*
34. Author interview with Detective Sergeant Adam Barwick, October 2007.
35. Crawford, C., 'Child killer pockets navy pension', *Sunday Herald Sun*, 8 May 2005.
36. Author interview with Detective Sergeant Adam Barwick, October 2007.
37. Brown, R., 'The Beaumont children', see www.beaumontchildren.com.au.
38. Author interview with Detective Sergeant Adam Barwick, October 2007.
39. In 1974, NSW teenager John Lewthwaite broke into a Greystanes home and murdered a 4-year-old girl. His intended victim was the girl's 9-year-old brother whom he intended to rape. Lewthwaite pleaded guilty and was gaoled for life but this was reduced to 20 years' parole on appeal. Despite public appeals, he was finally released from prison in 1999 after serving 25 years. Claiming to be one of the successes of the NSW prison rehabilitation system Lewthwaite breached his parole when he was arrested sunbaking nude with a male friend in the sandhills at Wanda in 2006 and was detained in custody for three months.
40. Author interview with Detective Sergeant Adam Barwick, October 2007.
41. Review Transcript, *In the matter of major review of Derek Ernest Percy*, Supreme Court of Victoria, October 1998.